W9-BQJ-094

RICHLAND PLACE
LIBRARY

ALSO BY JOHN KAAG

Thinking Through the Imagination:
Aesthetics in Human Cognition

Idealism, Pragmatism, and Feminism:
The Philosophy of Ella Lyman Cabot

AMERICAN
PHILOSOPHY

AMERICAN
PHILOSOPHY

A Love Story

JOHN KAAG

FARRAR, STRAUS AND GIROUX   NEW YORK

Farrar, Straus and Giroux
18 West 18th Street, New York 10011

Copyright © 2016 by John Kaag
All rights reserved
Printed in the United States of America
First edition, 2016

Excerpts from this book originally appeared, in slightly different form,
in *Harper's Magazine* and *The Chronicle Review*.

Library of Congress Cataloging-in-Publication Data
Names: Kaag, John J., 1979– author.
Title: American philosophy : a love story / John Kaag.
Description: First [edition]. | New York, NY : FSG, 2016. | Includes
  bibliographical references and index.
Identifiers: LCCN 2016001908 | ISBN 9780374154486 (cloth) |
  ISBN 9780374713119 (e-book)
Subjects: LCSH: Philosophy, American—Miscellanea.
Classification: LCC B851 .K33 2016 | DDC 191—dc23
LC record available at http://lccn.loc.gov/2016001908

Designed by Jonathan D. Lippincott

Our books may be purchased in bulk for promotional, educational, or business use.
Please contact your local bookseller or the Macmillan Corporate and
Premium Sales Department at 1-800-221-7945, extension 5442, or by e-mail at
MacmillanSpecialMarkets@macmillan.com.

www.fsgbooks.com
www.twitter.com/fsgbooks • www.facebook.com/fsgbooks

3 5 7 9 10 8 6 4

For Carol

The Library is a wilderness of books.

—Henry David Thoreau, Journal, March 16, 1852

CONTENTS

AMERICAN
PHILOSOPHY

PROLOGUE: MAYBE

Harvard University's Holden Chapel always struck me as an appropriate place to die. The forty-foot brick structure, which is the university's third-oldest building, has no front windows. Above its entrance are four stone *bucrania*, bas-relief ox-skull sculptures of the sort that pagans once placed on their temples to keep away evil spirits. On April 15, 1895, when William James was asked to address an audience of young men at the Georgian chapel, it was already more than 150 years old, a fitting setting for the fifty-three-year-old American philosopher to contemplate what he had come to believe was the profoundest of questions: "Is Life Worth Living?"

It was a place—and a question—I became intimate with in the spring of 2008. I'd spent months scouring Harvard for the origins of American philosophy. I was at Harvard on a postdoc at the American Academy of Arts and Sciences—a temporary reprieve from the permanent unemployment my loving but practical family was sure would follow after I finished my Ph.D. in philosophy—and I wasn't about to squander the unexpected opportunity to prove them wrong. The aisles at Widener Library, just steps from Holden, are altogether fifty miles long. In the autumn of that year, I'd walked their entire length. When I eventually came up empty, I trotted

across the Yard to Houghton Library, where rare books and manuscripts are kept, and combed through the personal papers of
Ralph Waldo Emerson and Charles Sanders Peirce. Still nothing.
It was only November, I told myself: early days. Research fellow-
ships are for searching—and searching and searching. I hunkered
down in my cubicle at Widener and tried to eke out the manuscript
I was supposed to be writing on the confluence of eighteenth-
century German idealism and American pragmatism. Things were
progressing, albeit very slowly.

But then, on an evening in the spring of 2008, I gave up.
Abandoning the research had nothing to do with the work itself
and everything to do with the sense that it, along with everything
else in my life, couldn't possibly matter. For the rest of my year at
Harvard I assiduously avoided its libraries. I avoided my wife, my
family, and friends. When I came to the university at all, I went
only to Holden Chapel. I walked past it, sat next to it, read against
it, lunched near it, sneaked into it when I could—became obsessed
with it. James had, as far as I was concerned, asked the only question that really mattered. *Is life worth living?* I couldn't shake it,
and I couldn't answer it.

For centuries, philosophers and religious thinkers, from the
twelfth-century rabbi Maimonides to the seventeenth-century
Englishman John Locke, had coolly articulated the belief that
life, for any number of unassailable reasons, was worth living. In
the thirteenth century the Dominican friar Thomas Aquinas argued that all things—be they amoebas or human beings—have a
natural life cycle put into place by an intelligent designer. Far be
it from any of God's creatures to disrupt it. Immanuel Kant's argument, five hundred years later, was less theologically speculative. Rational beings, he said, have a duty not to destroy our own
rational capacities. In Kant's words, "[S]uicide is not abominable
because God has forbidden it; on the contrary, God has forbidden
it because it is abominable."

William James had pondered the abominable since at least

his early twenties. By many accounts, he'd hit rock bottom in 1871, at the age of twenty-nine. As I sat on the still-frozen ground outside Holden in 2008, I had to agree—my twenty-ninth year was about as bad as it gets. One of the sketch pads I'd found in Houghton contained a self-portrait James drew in red crayon—a young man, seated, hunched over, with an inscription over the figure: HERE I AND SORROW SIT. Most of the reasons his philosophical predecessors offered to persevere in life bored James to death. To him, they were little more than clichéd maxims, out of touch with the particularities of depression and crisis. Still, he was well aware that such arguments had served as the existential anchor for an untold number of happy lives. Indeed, during his lecture in Holden Chapel he observed that his audience, a group from Harvard's Young Men's Christian Association, brimmed with what he often called "healthy-mindedness," a psychological and moral disposition that all but affirmed the conclusions of Aquinas and Kant.

The Harvard YMCA had been established in 1886 as an evangelical society. Most of the members of James's audience believed that the Bible is the Word of God and Jesus is Savior and Lord. The question of life's worth, for these devout men, was settled well in advance of any lecture. Denying the value of human life was blasphemy, and the ultimate form of this denial—suicide—an unspeakable sin. But James suspected that this affirmation of human life, as emphatic as it was universal, ignored the experience of a growing number of people who weren't so sure about the value of their own lives.

James, by then quite famous as the father of American psychology and philosophy, was one of these people—"sick-souled," as he put it. My own soul, from adolescence onward, had never been terribly robust, and that rainy spring it had taken a turn for the worse. James knew something the faithful often miss: that believing in life's worth, for many people, is a recurring struggle. He'd overdosed on chloral hydrate in the 1870s, just "for the fun of it," as he wrote to his brother Henry, to see how close he could come to the morgue without actually going there. James was not alone in his curiosity. A decade later his colleague Edmund Gurney, founder of the Society for Psychical Research, took the experiment with life and death too far, testing what turned out to be a fatal dose of chloroform. In response to Gurney's death, James wrote to his brother once again. "[This death] make[s] what remains here seem strangely insignificant and ephemeral, as if the weight of things, as well as the numbers, was all on the other side." *The other side.* As in: No. Life is not worth living.

No, as it turns out, is an answer that has much to recommend it in a place like Holden Chapel. Religious services were moved out of the building in the 1780s, and in the next century it served as a chemistry lab and classroom for the nascent Harvard Medical School, where cadavers were dissected. *The Gross Clinic*, painted by Thomas Eakins in 1875, gives some idea of the nature of surgery at the time. In it, several doctors perform an operation on a child, working without gloves as their patient's insides fester in the open air. The patient's mother sits nearby in horror, covering her face in a futile attempt to escape what James understood all too well: At the end of the existential day, we are all a bunch of smelly carcasses. James would have been aware of the chapel's gory medical history as he pondered life's worth with the YMCA.

•

On March 11, 2008, I watched my father die. His liver was in bad shape. His esophagus was shot to hell. Saying you have esophageal squamous cell carcinoma is often a very long way of saying you drank too much, which my father did. At the end, tragically, ironically, he couldn't even swallow. The same thing that beat up his liver and throat also destroyed his family. I didn't much like him. So I surprised myself when I accepted my stepmother's invitation to watch him die on a snowy evening at a hospital in Buffalo, New York. But there he was, swollen hands, puffy face, no breath—something out of Dr. Gross's clinic. It all seemed like a cruel joke. Maybe life *was* worth living. But maybe you would live only to die surrounded by a distraught second wife and your estranged and dry-eyed sons.

The truth is, I'd often imagined—and occasionally fantasized about—my father's demise. In my dreams, at the brink of death, he'd finally realize how short life actually was, how one could mess it up, squander the opportunity to be deeply and irrevocably responsible. The shadow of death, I imagined, had that sort of power. And so, at the end, he'd talk to me like a loving father would to his son. He would convince me that our brief time together hadn't been a hollow, painful waste. He'd tell me how not to become a drunk, or a deadbeat husband, or a runaway father.

Of course, none of this happened. When I got to the hospital, he was already largely gone, as silent and unconscious as he'd been for most of my life. There was no great sense of closure, no teachable moment. Just the painful confirmation of all my suspicions, that life was pretty much meaningless.

James entertained this grim possibility rather seriously. When faced with unshrinking hardships, he told the audience at Holden, we're inclined to believe not in "the old warm notion of a man-loving Deity, [but] that of an awful Power that neither hates nor loves, but rolls all things together meaninglessly to a common doom." Not even the protective *bucrania* can save us. "This," he continued, "is an uncanny, a sinister, a nightmare view of life, and its peculiar *unheimlichkeit*, or poisonousness, lies expressly in our holding two things together which cannot possibly agree." On the one hand, we cling to the hope that our world is both rational and meaningful; on the other, we may eventually come to see that it is neither. We have great expectations for our lives, but we die in the wintry hellhole of Buffalo or get hacked up on tables in Holden Chapel.

James could have told his audience at Holden that life was planned out in advance and that lasting existential meaning was ensured by a benevolent and all-knowing God; that, as Leibniz argued in the seventeenth century, we live in the best of all possible worlds; or that we have a moral duty to go on even if it turns out that this world is, at root, evil. He could have tried to sugarcoat my trip to Buffalo, to tell me that despite all appearances, life was *necessarily* meaningful. In other words, he could have lied. But he didn't. Instead, he answered life's most difficult question in the most honest way possible: "Maybe," James said.

"It all depends," James explains, "on the liver." The liver, three pounds of reddish-brown flesh wedged below the diaphragm, was once considered the source of blood and therefore the seat of life itself. Back in the time of the *bucrania*, people would gut an animal just to get a good look at one. The liver was the sine qua non of many ancient forms of divination. Seers from Babylon to Rome examined the organ—much as phrenologists would later study the shape of the skull—to divine a future that was just barely within one's control. The liver, according to the ancients, was a way to negotiate the vagaries of chance. Had I looked at my father's liver when I was young, it might've told me all sorts of things: that he would attempt to help me get over my fear of the dark by turning off the lights in the garage and locking me in, that my mother would never fall in love again, that becoming him would be the single greatest fear of my life.

In the years that have followed my father's death, I've slowly come to think that perhaps things aren't quite as dark and inevitable as this. I've come to see how empowering James's "maybe" can be. It took writing a book about it—this book—for it to really sink in. For American philosophers like James, determining life's worth is, in a very real sense, up to us. Our wills remain the decisive factor in making meaning in a world that continually threatens it. Our past does not have to control us. The risk that life is wholly meaningless is real, but so too is the reward: the ever-present chance to be largely responsible for its worth. The appropriate response to our existential situation is not, at least for James, utter despair or suicide, but rather the repeated, ardent, yearning attempt to make good on life's tenuous possibilities. And the possibilities are out there, often in the most unlikely places.

PART I

HELL

IN A DARK WOOD,
A LIBRARY

I spent my spring at Holden with James. Then the tourists descended on Harvard Yard—gawking, photo oping, jabbering, ridiculous tourists. In hindsight I know they're no more ridiculous than an angst-ridden philosopher camped out on a blanket in the quad, contemplating the sorry state of his father's liver. But at the time, my urge to kill them all was competing with my urge to kill myself. So on a warm afternoon in June I fled Cambridge, setting out on a final, desperate mission to recover the fathers of American philosophy and to answer James's question once and for all. My day of philosophical pilgrimage started with a drive out to the white clapboard house in Concord that Ralph Waldo Emerson once called home, then spending the afternoon wandering the two-mile loop around Walden Pond. I returned to the Yard only as dusk was approaching and my tourist nemeses were dispersing. In the twilight, I read Emerson's "American Scholar" address in what I figured was likely the precise location where he'd given the lecture in 1837. Oliver Wendell Holmes had called it "America's Intellectual Declaration of Independence," a call for American thinkers to take control of their intellectual destiny. After finishing the piece, I made a quick stop at Kirkland Place, just down the street, the house where Charles Sanders Peirce had grown up. Peirce had taken Emerson's challenge seriously and had created the first genuinely American philosophy, amassing a body of work that was simultaneously scientifically rigorous and unexpectedly spiritual. Then I dropped my car off in a garage in downtown Boston before walking the rest of the way to the Durgin-Park Oyster Bar in the North End. That's where the Harvard idealist Josiah Royce met his students in the 1890s to discuss salvation and immortality before he shuffled back along the Charles River to his Cambridge home. I thought nothing of salvation and immortality at Durgin-Park, opting instead to drink myself senseless. At the end of the night I stumbled home and tried to convince my wife I wasn't drunk.

I was looking for help in all the usual places, all the wrong places. According to Thoreau, we spend no small effort "denying the possibility of change. This is the only way, we say; but there are," he assures us, "as many ways as there can be drawn radii from one centre." Is life worth living? James had found his answer at Holden Chapel, but I had to leave Harvard and Boston entirely. The road was all but forgotten. I am so grateful that I eventually found it.

When you travel north from Boston, after you leave 495 and hit Interstate 95, everything passes rather quickly and you're in New Hampshire before you know it. But then things slow down. Route 16 into the White Mountains is an odd little stretch, the sort of road that can't decide whether it wants to accommodate cars, trains, or buggies. It's stuck, like the small towns it bisects, between two eras. It was built at a time when the Boston Brahmins, who included many Cambridge intellectuals, migrated north to escape the summer heat. The signs of their migration can still be seen: Victorian mansions atop idyllic bluffs, impressive stretches of railroad—now inoperative—hitching posts next to boarded-up 7-Elevens. The 7-Elevens are another type of sign—indicating that the migration is over.

When you reach Route 113 and turn right, you're getting close. If you go through the tiny New Hampshire town of Chocorua and pass William James's summer home, you know you've gone too far. James bought the house in 1886, when he'd finally made enough money as a Harvard philosopher to afford a retreat. But it's not what you are looking for. Backtrack and travel 113 toward the village of Madison. You'll pass a number of places selling antiques, sad little shops dedicated to helping people stay afloat in the present by selling off their pasts, entrusting their memories to strangers.

Route 113 jogs left after a time and passes the borough hall. At this point fir and spruce trees grow right up to the shoulder of the road, making it impossible to see more than a hundred yards ahead or behind. This protected forest is a welcome reminder that not all old things go to waste. Turn left onto Mooney Hill Road and start up the hill. This is the road less traveled in American philosophy. In fact, it doesn't look like it's been traveled at all, at least not by anyone without four-wheel drive. Keep going. You think you might be lost. You are, in a sense—the terrain of philosophy you're approaching has been largely unexplored for more than a century.

At every fork in the road, take a left. A few miles on a deserted dirt road seems like forever, so you'll be relieved to see the one-room schoolhouse ahead. Now turn right onto Janus Road and make the final ascent. If you look to your right, you'll have a clear view of the Sandwich Range of the White Mountains, with Mount Washington off your right-hand shoulder. If you look to your left, at first you won't see anything except white pine, but then you'll catch sight of two stone buildings of Georgian architecture. One is a very large house. The other is set back in the woods, a short walk from the mansion. Covered with windows, it looks nothing like Holden Chapel. That's the Hocking library. You've arrived at West Wind.

"Traveling is a fool's paradise," Emerson once said, "[since] my giant goes with me wherever I go." That's generally true, but when I travel to certain places, my giant leaves me alone long enough for me to think. William Ernest Hocking found—or rather made—one of these rare places at West Wind.

Like many American philosophers, Hocking didn't initially intend to become one. Born in Cleveland in 1873, he spent his teenage years in Joliet, Illinois. His mother came from the Pratt family of Southbridge, Massachusetts, previously from Plymouth Colony and, prior to that, from the *Mayflower*. His father, a Canadian, studied medicine in New York and Maryland before moving his family west in the early 1870s. Hocking, the first of five children, grew up in a staunch Methodist family and underwent what he would later call a "conversion experience" that cemented his teenage faith in the Almighty. After finishing high school in 1889, he worked for four years as a surveyor and mapmaker in an attempt to save enough money to enter the University of Chicago, but the financial panic of 1893 dashed these plans, and he settled for Iowa State College of Agriculture and Mechanic Arts (now Iowa State University) instead.

Hocking wanted to be an architect or an engineer—at least that was the plan, until he read Herbert Spencer's *First Principles* in his third year of high school, at the tender age of fourteen. Spencer spent most of his career disseminating Darwin's theory of evolution, a theory that would radically affect American philosophy in the coming century and, to this day, fundamentally challenge religious faith. When Hocking's father discovered his son immersed in *First Principles*, he did what any reasonable Methodist would do: He insisted that his son return it to the public library. But Hocking's father hadn't said he couldn't check it out again. So that is what he did the next week. And this time he hid Spencer in the haymow of the barn and promptly lost his religion. This crisis of faith was Hocking's first foray into metaphysical thought. His reading of William James's *The Principles of Psychology* in the early 1890s was his second.

By the time the teenage Hocking read the *Psychology*, James was well on his way to founding a school of thought known as American pragmatism. Pragmatism holds that truth is to be judged on the basis of its practical consequences, on its ability to negotiate and enrich human experience. James's pragmatism was just grounded and practical enough to convince a would-be civil engineer that philosophy wasn't a complete waste of time.

On the way to philosophy Hocking toyed with the idea of studying religion exclusively. He was one of the youngest attendees of Chicago's 1893 World's Parliament of Religions, held in conjunction with the World's Columbian Exposition. No one is sure, but he might have met his future teachers Josiah Royce and George Herbert Palmer at this event, as they both gave talks there. What we do know is that Hocking came to Cambridge to study philosophy at Harvard in 1899, finishing his undergraduate studies two years later.

He was one of the last students to work under the "Philosophical Four": James, Royce, Palmer, and George Santayana. Hocking, twenty-six at the time, didn't waste the opportunity. Looking back on his student years, Hocking wrote, "I believed and believe it the strongest Department of Philosophy on the planet . . . it was strong because the individual men were strong, and sufficiently varied so that most students could see in some one or other of the central group one who spoke directly to his problems."

Hocking's reading of Spencer had disabused him of the notion of a benevolent and all-powerful God, and he desperately wanted to find some intellectually reputable replacement. He had come to work with James, but the famous psychologist-philosopher was in Europe when Hocking initially arrived. While he waited for James to return, Hocking mastered German and French, continued his study of mathematics and the physical sciences, and took classes on metaphysics and aesthetics with Royce and Santayana. "I worked greedily and happily," he later wrote, "suffering only because I was limited to six classes at a time."

Hocking, however, was not your average bookworm. In the spring of 1900 he planned his first trip to Europe, to see the International Exposition in Paris. He was broke—"impecunious," to use his word—so he and seven other Harvard students sought the help of a Mr. Buffum. Buffum was, according to Hocking, "a not too reputable cattleman's Agent . . . of the waterfront of Boston" who hired the students as cattlemen on the SS *Anglican*. They shipped out of Charlestown, the primary port of Boston, on June 14. "We were interlarded," Hocking wrote, "with eight experienced cattlemen to make four squads of four men each, to each squad being assigned 125 Texan steers." The journey took twelve days, and they landed in Victoria Docks, London. The students were then set free for seven weeks to experience the best of European culture. The fusion of real life and high culture embodied an important strain of American philosophy that Hocking sought to preserve for the remainder of his life.

Shortly after Hocking's return to Harvard in the fall of 1900, William James also came back. James had been working on the manuscript of *The Varieties of Religious Experience*, a book that attempted to preserve a space for religious experience in a world increasingly dominated by science. As an undergraduate, Hocking attended the seminars James held as he refined *Varieties*. One evening, after reading a section of the manuscript to his students, James, who was edging toward sixty, turned to Hocking: "Hock-

ing, why did you sit there with a perpetual frown on your face?"
Hocking later admitted being unaware of the frown—he had simply been focused or, better yet, "enthralled." After graduating
with his doctorate from Harvard in 1904 and spending two years
teaching at Andover Theological Seminary, Hocking moved to
California to join the faculty at Berkeley. Instead of dedicating
himself to philosophy, however, he spent most of his time in San
Francisco helping to rebuild after the great earthquake of 1906,
honing what would become the architectural skills necessary to
design and build an estate in the White Mountains. In 1908 he
was called to Yale to teach, and when his mentor Josiah Royce
died, in 1916, he assumed Royce's chair in philosophy at Harvard,
which was widely recognized as the most prominent position in the
field. By the end of his forty-year career at Harvard, Hocking had
become one of the icons of American philosophy. By 1944 he was
only the sixth American to deliver the famed Gifford Lectures in
Scotland (the other American Gifford lecturers being Josiah Royce,
William James, John Dewey, Alfred North Whitehead, and Rein-
hold Niebuhr).

On my first trip to the Hocking estate, I knew much more about
his teachers than about Hocking himself. I'd driven to Chocorua
to help organize a conference on the life and work of William
James. Today, most philosophy conferences are held in enormous
nondescript hotels in enormous nondescript cities, so this little
gathering of philosophers at the Chocorua Public Library had
piqued my interest. I knew the conference would be good, but not
quite good enough to assuage my abiding fears that philosophy
really didn't matter. So once again I found myself elsewhere—this
time considering the delectable virtues of *Schnecken* at a German
pastry shop at the junction of Routes 16 and 113. The place didn't
even have a name, just a sign outside that read COFFEE FOR SALE.

This is where I found Bunn Nickerson. Bunn was one of those fellows you hope you'll become when you turn ninety-three. He was sharp and wiry and nothing like most of the philosophers I meet. He walked slowly, like most old philosophers do, although his hobble wasn't a function of long-standing inactivity, but of farming and skiing.

I'm not sure why I talked to Bunn (in my profession one learns to be circumspect). I do remember being embarrassed when he asked me what I did for a living.

"I teach philosophy," I said, bracing myself for the awkward silence that usually follows this admission.

It turned out that Bunn had grown up with philosophers, or, more accurately, grown up in a little house on a corner of one philosopher's—"Dr. Hocking's"—land. Today, philosophers have arguments and the occasional student. Most of them don't have "land." Bunn made it sound like the realm of a philosopher king, and this wasn't too far from the truth: The Hocking estate, as I would find out, comprised one stone manor house, six small summer cottages, two large barns, and one fishing pond with three beaver hutches, all situated on four hundred acres of field and forest. And a *library*. Bunn must have seen me light up when he said the word. In an act of generosity I've never been able to understand, he offered to take me there. Getting to see it struck me as a very good reason to skip out on the rest of the conference planning, so I piled into the old man's blue Dodge pickup and we bumped up the hill toward "Dr. Hocking's land"—or, as Bunn called it, "West Wind."

FINDING WEST WIND

Today, most academics don't have personal libraries worth talking about, so they avoid a problem many nineteenth-century intellectuals had to face in the twilight of their lives—what to do with an intellectual home after it's permanently vacated. Of course, the books can be donated to a large institutional library. Widener is full of volumes once owned by Harvard's famous alumni. When this happens, however, the books are lost among the millions of others in the stacks, reorganized in a homogenized Library of Congress categorization. The books are put in rigid order, and the unique integrity of the original collection is lost. To avoid this fate, writers in Hocking's day would often give their libraries to like-minded friends and students.

When Bunn and I got to West Wind, the Hocking library looked abandoned. On the trees surrounding the buildings were NO TRESPASSING signs, but Bunn didn't seem to care. He explained that the members of the Hocking family still spent time on the land, particularly in the summer months, but no one was around on that brisk fall day. Bunn climbed out of his truck, trotted down the hill away from me to explore his old haunts, and, waving at the library, invited me to "look around." The building was constructed of rough-hewn, multihued granite, as solid (and almost as large) as a house. From the outside, I couldn't tell whether it had two full stories, but I was able to make out the skylights in the roof, which probably filled the space with glorious reading light. It was definitely grand enough to suggest that its owner had never intended it to be abandoned. The front bore large arched windows and three sets of French doors. I peered in and was reminded of William James's love of Goethe's *Faust*. Surrounded by well-read books in the opening scene, Faust laments the fragility of human knowledge:

> I've studied now Philosophy
> And Jurisprudence, Medicine,—
> And even, alas! Theology,—
> From end to end, with labor keen;
> And here, poor fool! with all my lore
> I stand, no wiser than before . . .

James had pored over Goethe in his youth; he possessed Faust's polymathic abilities—he could have been a painter, a biologist, a surveyor, a novelist, a theologian—but James also shared Faust's sense that human capacities, even seemingly impressive ones, were pitifully limited. "All natural goods perish," James wrote. "Riches take wings; fame is a breath; love is a cheat; youth and health and pleasure vanish." As I peeked into the Hocking library for the first time, I thought this was probably a place where goods come to perish. Of course, I yearned to go inside. I assumed I should wait for one of the family members to let me in, but I began to wonder if the family would ever come back. Maybe they just weren't interested in old books. I couldn't wait until the summer to look through the books. Maybe this was my only chance. "He who refuses to embrace a unique opportunity," James wrote, "loses the prize as surely as if he had tried and failed."

Then, through the window, I spotted the *Century Dictionary* on a shelf. First published between 1889 and 1891, it was a masterpiece of lexicographical detail, running more than seven thousand large quarto pages, with ten thousand wood-engraved illustrations. When the *American Anthropologist* reviewed this dictionary a year later, the reviewer agreed with the growing sentiment of the time—saying that it was "the most conspicuous literary monument of the 19th century." Some of the best minds in America had worked for years on this first edition, including one of the founders of American philosophy, C. S. Peirce. I'd always had a certain strange fascination with Peirce—the kind of fascination that makes you write a doctoral dissertation.

After the dissertation was finished, I decided to write a book on him. Peirce was compulsive, brilliant, and just a little mad. Son of the Harvard mathematician Benjamin Peirce, he picked up his brother's copy of Whately's *Elements of Logic* at the age of fourteen and breezed through it. Despite being trained as a chemist and geodesist, Peirce considered logic and metaphysics his lifelong calling. He was always an outsider to mainstream philosophy, a strange place to be for arguably the most original philosopher of the nineteenth century. His work in logic and mathematics anticipates that of Gödel and Russell. His writing on the philosophy of science easily rivals that of Popper and Kuhn. And his papers in *The Journal of Speculative Philosophy* in the late 1860s would set the terms for the first three decades of American pragmatism. James and Royce looked to him for inspiration and guidance.

In February 1903 James tried to convince Charles Eliot, Harvard's president, that Peirce would flourish if he had a stable position in the philosophy department: "He is one of our 3 or 4 first American philosophers," James argued, "and it seems to me that his genius is deserving of some official recognition." Eliot was unconvinced—Peirce's reputation as a troublemaker preceded him. Despite his achievements, Peirce never fit in—he was always meddling, often quite effectively, in other people's research. He dissected his colleagues' carefully crafted arguments with the unnerving ease of young brilliance. Over the course of his life, Peirce perfected the art of self-sabotage and foiled his friends' ongoing attempts to secure him a permanent position and source of income. So he found part-time employment better suited to a genius, writing entries for the *Century Dictionary* in a few fields of study: logic, metaphysics, mathematics, mechanics, astronomy, weights and measures. Once I spotted this dusty edition, I had to page through it, even though I felt a little like a trespasser. But this wasn't breaking and entering, I thought. When doors are unlocked, it is just entering. I'd take a quick peek and leave things as I'd found them.

On reflection, I know these are excuses for pretty bad behavior. But it could've been much worse. The year before, a Hocking relation had explored the empty library without the family's permission. Except this guy was high on heroin. And he proceeded to steal four hundred rare books—among them a first edition of Thomas Hobbes's *Leviathan*, published in 1651—and ship them to his home in Berkeley, California. At the library's entrance, next to the dictionary, was a manila envelope labeled INVENTORY. I scanned it quickly to find a list of extremely expensive books:

Rene Descartes. *Discourse on the Method* (First English Edition 1649).—(FBI Returned)

John Locke. *Two Treatises of Government* (1690).—(FBI Returned)

Immanuel Kant. *Kritik der reinen Vernunft* (Riga: 1781).—(FBI Returned)

These were first editions—hundreds of them—written by the European philosophers who had inspired and then frustrated such American intellectuals as James. Hocking collected them for one reason: He was in search of the origins of American philosophy. At the time, I didn't know what the FBI had to do with philosophical classics, but it turns out that the federal government is surprisingly good at tracking stolen books across state lines. Apparently the Hockings went to the Madison police, who went to the FBI, who retrieved a good number of the expensive volumes. Some, however, are still missing. When the thief was apprehended and brought to trial a year later, the court record notes, he "reported that he had made several attempts to convince the Hocking family to take better care of the books, but the family refused to comply . . . The defendant claim[ed] he took the books to protect them and had no plans to sell the books for money." That said, he took more than a quarter of a million dollars' worth of books and did sell some of them. I carefully set the inventory list back in its place and turned to the dictionary. Its cover was original, tan leather that had taken on a dark patina over more than a century of use. The pages were surprisingly brittle for a book of its relatively young age, a fragility born of mold and of enduring many seasons of freezing temperatures followed by warmer spells.

I looked at a few random entries—"maid-pale," "maid-servant," "maieutic"—just enough to realize that what went into dictionaries, and into philosophy, had changed radically since the time of Peirce and James. At one point, philosophers like Peirce could determine the very language we use. They had the power to define reality. But no longer, and this was, at least for me, no small tragedy. Over the last century, mainstream philosophy had retreated into the upper reaches of the ivory tower, and as it specialized and professionalized, it largely lost touch with the existential questions that drove James and Peirce. Above the dictionary, on an unfinished oak shelf, was a set of leather-bound volumes: *The Journal of Speculative Philosophy*, where Peirce had made his mark. It was the first run of the complete set, from 1867 to 1893, all twenty-five volumes. I'd just take a look, and then I really would leave. I wanted to see Hocking's signature, so I gingerly pulled the first volume from the shelf.

Hocking's name was not inscribed in the front of the book. Instead, "Charles S. Peirce" was written in tight, neurotic script. The volume slipped out of my hands. As a professional philosopher, I very rarely hyperventilate while doing research, but Peirce was a notorious recluse. Most of his books had been sold or carried off to Harvard at the end of his life, but somehow this little treasure—Peirce's own copy of his first and most famous publication—had ended up here.

The last decades of the nineteenth century are often regarded as the Golden Age of American Philosophy. This era coincided with an equally exciting transition in European philosophy, marked by the birth of phenomenology, a school of thought that, not unlike American philosophy, held that philosophical questions must emerge from experience and that their answers must be judged on their ability to enrich lives. Phenomenology would eventually grow into existentialism and postmodern philosophy. All golden ages, however, eventually fade—in this case, with the passing of a number of great American thinkers. William James died in 1910; Charles Sanders Peirce in 1914; Josiah Royce in 1916; George Herbert Palmer in 1933; Edmund Husserl, the German father of phenomenology, in 1938. So William Ernest Hocking, who had studied with them and outlived them all, apparently took care of their books.

Many of the volumes in this library were from the seventeenth and eighteenth centuries and extremely precious, but many more contained their original owners' marginalia, and these were absolutely priceless. When Hocking died, in 1966, his son Richard— also a philosopher—became steward of the collection. He'd tried repeatedly to donate the entire collection to Harvard, but with little luck. Harvard—like the relative from Berkeley—would have cherry-picked the selections, but had no intention of preserving the library in one piece. Its unity, however, according to Richard, is what made the collection so special. When Richard died, in 2001, the books simply remained in the dark wood at the end of Janus Road, in New Hampshire. Richard's three daughters tried valiantly to look after the collection, but they lived all over North America and had the entire estate to worry about, not to mention their own lives.

Books are just paper, wood pulp smashed and dried. In the realm of rodents and termites, they're quite valuable: They're tasty, and when torn into small bits, their pages make for cozy little nests. For a decade the Hocking library had been actively used— just not by humans. The porcupines and bugs had set up house, making sure that this great mass of paper didn't go wholly to waste. "WHOEVER looks at the insect world," wrote Emerson in "Quotation and Originality," "at flies, aphides, gnats, and innumerable parasites . . . must have remarked the extreme content they take in suction, which constitutes the main business of their life. If we go into a library or news-room, we see the same function on a higher plane, performed with like ardor, with equal impatience of interruption, indicating the sweetness of the act." I looked hungrily at the inventory one last time and then back at *The Journal of Speculative Philosophy.* The 1651 *Leviathan* was rare. The 1690 *Two Treatises of Government*, an anonymously written first edition that had served as the basis for American political liberty, was rarer still. In the last year, first editions of both had gone to auction. Hobbes's masterpiece had brought $32,000; Locke's tract was sold by a book dealer in Dallas for $41,000. As a student, I'd watched these auctions from a distance, snooping around the Internet to see what philosophy could actually be worth. The books on the inventory at West Wind, the classics of modern philosophy, could have been under glass at the British Library or at Yale or at the Huntington Library in San Marino, California. But there was, I imagined, only one copy of *The Journal of Speculative Philosophy* with C. S. Peirce's name in it. It was irreplaceable. And it was under a thin film of dust in the Hocking library. The termites would get to it soon.

As a kid, I buried things in the backyard just so I could dig them up many years later. The Hocking library turned out to be the largest time capsule I'd ever opened. It was one large room, partitioned into different working nooks by walnut built-ins. In truth, there were no real walls. Just bookshelves and windows. I estimated about ten thousand books in total. To my right and left, at opposite ends of the building, were two large marble fireplaces, tall enough that I could have stood in them without stooping too much, substantial enough that they could've kept the whole building warm until October or November at least. Oriental rugs, mismatched and nearly worn through, covered the library's wide oak floorboards. The first-generation Stickley rocking chairs— with their solid walnut slats and musty horsehair seats—looked as if they hadn't held visitors for many years. A cramped winding staircase—more of a ladder, really—led to a loft above.

Hanging from opposing walls were two enormous portraits— one of Hocking, his square Cornish jaw set just firmly enough that you knew he meant business, intellectual and otherwise; the other of his wife, Agnes. They looked down on me with what I could only imagine was quiet disapproval. Hocking had married Agnes O'Reilly in 1905. She was the daughter of the celebrated poet and journalist John Boyle O'Reilly, who in the late nineteenth century was the editor of Boston's Irish paper, *The Pilot*. Before that he'd been a convict. O'Reilly was a central player in the Irish nationalist movement in the 1860s and had been sentenced by the English to twenty years of penal detention in Western Australia. He escaped in 1869 and eventually made it back to Ireland and then to New England.

I was used to square-jawed philosophers, but Agnes's beauty truly scared me. She reminded me of someone, though I couldn't, at the time, place her. Her portrait wasn't complete; the sleeves of her dress were just a few scribbles of underpainting. I was later reminded of Hocking's comment in *The Meaning of God in Human Experience*, published in 1912, that "idealism fails to work . . . chiefly because it is unfinished." But then I remembered the next line: "Unfinishedness is not in itself a blemish . . . there are tolerable and intolerable kinds of unfinishedness." This portrait was the tolerable kind. Agnes's face was finished in careful detail. Especially her eyes—calm, gray, and omniscient. I wonder if the man from Berkeley had caught her eye on that February evening as he packed up the books. If he had, he probably wouldn't have had the gall to complete the heist.

I couldn't imagine stealing books from Agnes. Or even that blue-and-white Qing vase sitting on the desk across from me, flanked on one side by books of English common law and on the other by early translations of Buddhist and Hindu texts. The vase looked old and valuable, as if it had found its proper place between these shelves, between Eastern traditions and Western institutions.

Turning away from English common law, I was finally convinced of something I'd often suspected—that classical American philosophy was actually an amalgam of European thought, Asian philosophy, and that of the New World. The task of classical American philosophy was to declare its intellectual independence while remaining firmly rooted in the distant past. "Where do we find ourselves?" Emerson asks in his essay "Experience." Always on a staircase, he answers: "[T]here are stairs below us, which we seem to have ascended; there are stairs above us, many a one, which go upward and out of sight." The task of life is to transcend the past, to never remain where one starts, to find a place of one's own.

This was the predicament Emerson faced as a writer in Concord, Massachusetts, in the 1840s: how to reclaim the foreign, often hostile, intellectual tradition in a way that made it new; how to proceed with and without its guidance. Worshipping the past was obviously unacceptable to Emerson, as it resulted in a world without growth or originality, but ignoring history was equally dangerous. In the much-repeated words of George Santayana, "[T]hose who refuse to learn from history are [also] bound to repeat it." Hocking had clearly taken this point to heart. It meant learning from any wisdom tradition that might provide insight into the chances for human salvation. A pragmatist, Hocking remained dedicated to the idea that philosophy could affect human experience, but he was also an idealist who hoped that experience was a gateway to another, more lasting, more meaningful reality. I would later find out that this hope had led him to initiate an active discourse between Eastern and Western thinkers: In 1939, 1949, and 1959, he organized the East-West Philosophers' Conferences at the University of Hawaii, where he was joined by D. T. Suzuki and Hu Shih, two of the first thinkers to popularize the study of Chinese Buddhism in the West. I discovered that the bookshelves at West Wind were filled with inscribed first editions. Some of the older commentaries of Hinduism and Buddhism, however, were from the late nineteenth century—too old for Hocking to have been the original owner. I wondered who these books had belonged to.

Surveying the shelves, I was reminded that American thinkers had not been uncritical admirers of Eastern philosophical traditions. "Thank God," Thoreau once wrote, "no Hindoo tyranny prevailed at the framing of the world, but we are freemen of the universe, and not sentenced to any caste." Thoreau was not about to endorse any metaphysical system that compromised his ability to choose his own path. At the same time, he was attracted, almost against his will, to the Eastern idea that freedom—the really meaningful variety—depended on one's ability to move with, rather than against, the world at large. Thoreau was repeatedly drawn to Buddhism for this reason. I knew that he'd owned a copy of Burnout's French translation of *The Lotus Sutra*, and I secretly hoped that this translation had made its way to New Hampshire. The *Sutra* suggests, in a nutshell, that all human beings, no matter their lot in life, have an innate Buddha nature, their own inherent capacity for wisdom and, more important, for compassion. This means that each of us, in his or her own way, can pursue a life of freedom—freedom from suffering and fear. This sounded pretty good to Thoreau, and to Hocking too, if the preponderance of Buddhist and Taoist commentaries in the library was any indication. To my disappointment, however, Thoreau's *Lotus Sutra* was nowhere to be found. But eventually I came across, quite by accident, what I desperately needed to find.

🐦

They were side by side on the shelf closest to the desk, as if someone—perhaps Hocking himself—had just spent the afternoon working through them: Henry Clarke Warren's *Buddhism in Translations* and Paul Carus's *Buddhism and Its Christian Critics*. These works, published in the late 1890s, were after Thoreau's time, but they became mainstays for the next generation of American intellectuals who wanted to use Buddhism to think through the concepts of freedom and salvation. Warren was a recluse, but Carus, an American philosopher in his own right and a close friend of Hocking and James, was truly a rare bird: a philosopher who actually *liked* people. He, independently of Josiah Royce and a very young Hocking, also attended the World's Parliament of Religions in 1893, one of the first events in history to promote interfaith dialogue. After the parliament, Carus renewed his study of non-Western religions and in 1897 published *Buddhism and Its Christian Critics*, an evenhanded treatment of two world religions to which Carus professed no allegiance. He was a self-described "atheist who loved God," happy to join the ranks of American thinkers, such as Emerson, Thoreau, and Dewey, who thought that an exclusive commitment to a particular institutionalized religion could have the unintended consequence of thinning out what James would call the "varieties of religious experience."

"Wm. James." The scrawl on the flyleaf of the Carus book was unmistakable. I'm now so relieved that the man from Berkeley had snatched only the conspicuously expensive books and generally overlooked the volumes that would've been simply impossible to replace. These were the books James read in the 1890s as he formulated *The Varieties of Religious Experience*, in which he was on the trail of "experiences of individual men in their solitude, so far as they apprehend themselves to stand in relation to whatever they may consider the divine." In other words, he was searching for some indication that each of us was not, despite evidence to the contrary, inconsolably alone in an uncaring universe. I hadn't given *The Varieties* a great deal of thought since my father's death. All I could think about was Buffalo and the dissected bodies in Holden Chapel; the God talk in *The Varieties* made my stomach churn. But that was about to change.

Alone in an empty library, in a deserted wood, in a nearly forgotten field of American philosophy, I felt momentarily at home. Often secure and well-ordered homes are also tight and repressive. I knew all about these sorts of homes. I had one myself back in Boston. My sense of the Hocking library, however, was something different—spacious but intensely intimate. By some strange twist of fate I was on the verge of experiencing something more enduring, more meaningful than my minor scholarly life. West Wind was not, despite appearances, a place where things came to perish. In the years after his 1895 lecture at Holden Chapel, James came to suspect that there might be ways to escape the specter of life's meaninglessness. Social organization, professional affiliation, athletic camaraderie, physical exertion, experimental drug use—James found that all of these worked to broaden a person's otherwise narrow conception of selfhood. But they didn't work well enough, which is why he remained fascinated by religious experience and spiritualism. In preparing *The Varieties*, he was, like Carus, completely uninterested in advocating for any one religious doctrine; rather he was obsessively interested in the way certain mystics (from Saint John to Meister Eckhart to Eckhart's student, Heinrich Seuse) had come to know the reality of the unseen. James's interest in mysticism also led him to Carus's book on Buddhism.

As I looked through the spotty marginalia James had left in the book, I thought about his recurring obsession with religious experience, about how bound up it was with the hope for salvation. Salvation as a theme can be found in all world religions, but James wasn't primarily interested in its place in any particular theological framework. He understood it more generally, more experientially: Salvation is a singular, deep-seated response to an individual's feeling utterly lost. James often felt himself so, and he was attracted to the Buddhist sense that existential alienation is not the inevitable outgrowth of being human. He wanted, quite desperately, to be saved from himself. I ran my fingers over a passage he had underlined in Carus's book: "He who has attained *arúpam*, the formless [or the spiritual], surrenders with it all the petulancy of self, for jealousy, spite, hatred, pride, envy, concupiscence, vainglory—all these and kindred ambitions—have lost their sense. He is energetic, but without passion; he aspires, but does not cling; he administers, but does not regard himself an owner; he acquires, but does not covet."

Philosophers are generally unimpressed with "spiritual" explanations, and some of us spend our careers cultivating petulancy, pride, and vainglory. But the Hocking library was no place for "all these and kindred ambitions." Its shadowy nooks and crannies, filled with half-eaten treasures, provided just enough space for a visitor to lose himself, or at least the last vestiges of his self-importance. It was possible, surrounded by the moldy remains of great books and porcupine scat, to come to terms with the existential fragility that most of us, most of the time, try to ignore.

As a graduate student, I'd learned about James's investigations of the spiritual realm, which I'd viewed with suspicion as a weird by-product of his Victorian upbringing. But on this rapidly dwindling fall afternoon I was about to have a change of heart. I peered across the alcove to another volume that just had to be James's: a

well-worn original copy of *The Year-book of Spiritualism for 1871*.
Sure enough, it was, purchased when James was thirty. Years before he wrote *The Varieties*, in the midst of what might have been
his most serious bout of depression, he had become fascinated by
the reality of the unseen. Being a good pragmatist, however, he
wanted proof of this reality. For more than two decades he attended
regular meetings with spiritualists living in Cambridge and was
one of the founding members of the American Society for Psychical Research, an organization whose members were either convinced of or at least deeply interested in the existence of the
spiritual world. James's fascination with ghosts wasn't a fetish or a
novelty. It was more serious, more philosophically grounded.
Along with friends of his such as Henry Bowditch, James wanted
proof that when we die, we aren't fully gone.

The American Society for Psychical Research was founded in
Boston in 1884. Its mission was to investigate all things supernatural. This was not some nut-job organization, but it was not
altogether normal either. One of its founders, G. Stanley Hall, had
come to Harvard to do doctoral work with James in the late 1870s
and was awarded the first psychology degree in the United States.
With James's support, Hall organized a group of researchers to
explore the possibility of spirit contact, divining rods, multiple
personality, and telepathy. By 1890 Hall had resigned from the
organization, concluding that parapsychology amounted to vicious
pseudoscience. But others, such as James and Bowditch, mar-
shaled on into the turn of the century. In 1909 James reflected on
twenty-five years of ghost busting:

At times I have been tempted to believe that the creator
has eternally intended this department of nature to remain
baffling, to prompt our curiosities and hopes and suspicions
all in equal measure, so that although ghosts and clair-
voyances, and raps and messages from spirits, are always

seeming to exist and can never be fully explained away, they also can never be susceptible of full corroboration.

Despite the bafflement—or perhaps because of it—James and his fellow researchers attended the séances and mind experiments that were conducted regularly through the 1880s and 1890s. Unlike most psychics, however, the members of the society documented and published their findings. None of these findings were anywhere near conclusive, but they did their part to push the boundaries of science, to explore an area that science couldn't quite explain.

James was hired to teach anatomy at Harvard in 1872, the same year he acquired *The Year-book of Spiritualism*. He was not satisfied as a physiologist. He complained that the factual, objective approach of the anatomist missed something crucial in its understanding of human nature. "[A] fact," he wrote, "too often plays the part of a *sop* for the mind in studying these sciences. A man may take very short views, registering one fact after another, as one walks on stepping-stones, and never lose the conceit of his 'scientific' function." But for James something important was lost: the sense that a human being was more than a series of disparate material realities. A person is more than just a bundle of perceptions and nervous reactions. More than just a body that can be dissected and discarded. James hoped that there was something ethereal, transcendent—something even ghostly—that was free from the constraints of our physical lives. This led him to play with nitrous oxide in the early 1880s, in the belief that psychotropics might open portals to other realms of experience. It also led him back, repeatedly, to religious experience.

Later, James would come to have a very personal and more serious stake in the spiritualism of the late-Victorian era. In July 1885 his eighteen-month-old son, Herman, contracted whooping cough and died. The whole family was devastated. James wanted to believe that the boy was not fully gone. In September, James visited Leonora Piper, a medium who had become a Boston sensation for supposedly channeling spirits. James found Piper's "spirit control" sorely lacking, but he concluded that the woman might very well have what he called "supernormal powers." At the end of his life, he begrudgingly admitted that evidence was "yet lacking to prove 'spirit-return.'" He therefore "[left] the matter open" with the hope that science would one day have more than just an inkling of the supernatural, would understand what James called the "dramatic possibilities of nature," the possibility that the deceased are never irretrievably gone. Under the watchful eyes of Agnes Hocking, as I read James's scribblings about ghosts and ancient Asian traditions, I wondered whether, for me, that day had finally come. Because William James was right in front of me exactly a century after his death.

Bunn took me home that evening in his blue Dodge pickup, though I have no recollection of what we discussed. The main thing I remember about the ninety-three-year-old is mistaking him for a ghost when he peeked his head into the front door of the library. In fact, he almost was. He died the next spring, before I could see him again.

As Bunn waited in the truck, as darkness crept in at the end of my first visit to West Wind, I scanned the shelves and with a growing sense of panic pulled only the books that simply had to be rescued: James's copies of Kant, Hegel, Schopenhauer, Nietzsche, Berkeley, Condillac, Clarke, and Wolff. Some of them, like the first editions of Clarke and Wolff, were more than three hundred years old and were unlike anything I had ever put my hands on. "Vellum" is another name for skin—at one point, philosophy was bound up in the stuff. I reached down to pick up James's first edition of Samuel Clarke's *A Demonstration of the Being and Attributes of God*, published in 1705, and gently fingered its cold white surface as if it were a sacred relic. The term "philosophical corpus" had never made sense until now. I turned the book over. Tenderly. It was a little body: skin wrapped around something beautiful and inexplicable. Putting it under my arm, I turned to the back corners of the library. Tucked away on one of the back shelves was Josiah Royce's library: Descartes, Spinoza, Fichte, Mill, Dilthey, Lotze, Tarde, Boole. These books were filled with marginalia. I took a quick look at one of Royce's jottings—something written in Greek about God and strife—but then grabbed the books that I could carry. I would think about marginalia later. This wasn't just any set of books. It was the bridge between European and American philosophy. That afternoon at dusk I had the unshakable sense that I was missing the most important part of West Wind, and over the course of three years I saw that this premonition was more correct than I could have known.

Instead of stealing them, I piled the books next to the *Century Dictionary* in the front entryway. That way they'd all be in one place when I came back for them. Then I remembered how easy trespassing was. They'd be in one place for me—or for anyone else who stumbled across the library. I moved them out of the front entrance and hid them in three rusty gray filing cabinets behind Hocking's enormous oak desk. Only I would find them there. By this point I'd wholly forgotten whom these books actually belonged to. The man from Berkeley responded to this convenient sense of oblivion by stealing them. I just hid them so that no one else could take them. An hour later, as Bunn and I bumped down the hill into the darkness below, I realized how foolish this was. There was absolutely no guarantee that I'd ever return to the library. Maybe the Hocking family would finally clean it out and send the file cabinets to the junkyard. Maybe they would never forgive my trespass. Maybe they'd put a gate at the bottom of Janus

Road to deter snoops like me. Maybe another well-meaning American philosopher would find the library, but not the books. Maybe, on the drive back to my unhappy marriage, I'd get in the fatal crash I often imagined. Maybe I wouldn't be able to find my way back.

"PESTILENCE-STRICKEN MULTITUDES"

"Consciousness," according to William James, "is in constant change." Consciousness is not a unitary thing, but a process—a "stream," as he calls it—that flows despite our best efforts to dam it up. I would have loved to stay in New Hampshire, to stop time on an afternoon in a forgotten library, but according to James, "no state once gone can recur and be identical with what it was before." Things pass away, and you're often left casting about to recover them, even when you can't remember exactly what it is you're looking for.

Months had passed since my first visit to West Wind, and I wanted desperately to return, even if only in my head. "[W]e make search in our memory for a forgotten idea," James instructs, "just as we rummage our house for a lost object . . . we visit what seems to us the probable neighborhood." We look not for the memory itself, but for its known "associates." One chilly March afternoon on my way home from Harvard Yard, I popped into a pastry shop called The Biscuit and waited for the bakers to bring out the *Schnecken*. As I waited, I found myself thinking about the words of the French Renaissance philosopher and essayist Michel Montaigne when he wrote of marriage: "Marriage is like a cage; one sees the birds outside desperate to get in, and those inside equally desperate to get out." Montaigne's birdcage made painful sense. Marriage was something entered into expectantly and then suffered begrudgingly, at least in my case. I was trapped—my only hope that some moment of transcendence or perfect recall might whisk me away. At last the *Schnecken* arrived—just like the ones at the nameless coffee shop in New Hampshire—perfect morsels of golden brown coated with a mix of pecans and syrup. Their buttery aroma and that of my not-so-fresh coffee wafted into my expectant nose. And then—nothing. The *Schnecken* didn't transport me back to the Hocking library. It didn't open some portal to escape the ennui of my urban academic life. As I left the shop, I tossed my half-eaten *Schnecken* into the trash, stopped at a bar, and took the most indirect route possible back to our apartment on Commercial Street.

The nineteenth-century German philosopher Arthur Schopenhauer argued that human beings, even when they fall in love, are a bit like porcupines. We crave intimacy, the kind of familiarity that temporarily quells our fears about being completely alone in the universe, but this closeness means that we invariably stab the ones we love. My marriage was a bit like that. From the beginning, when I met my wife in our first year at college, we both wanted, sometimes desperately, to be close. But we bungled it rather badly. We were tender, perhaps too tender, meaning that we were often moved to sympathy or compassion, to a state of vulnerability, like a brush burn that won't heal. We picked at each other for more than a decade. William Thackeray once claimed that "early love affairs ought to be strangled or drowned, like so many blind kittens." Since *all* cats are born blind, the implication is pretty clear—young love rarely grows into something mature and healthy. I'd been a good son and a decent brother, but these experiences of love did pitifully little to prepare me for romance. After classes ended on Friday afternoons, she and I would go to the same family-style Chinese restaurant. We went so often that the owners got to know our names, our birthdays, our orders—moo goo gai pan, with chicken; mu shu vegetables, no oil. One evening, in a rare moment bordering on passion, we stopped on the sidewalk on our way out and had a non-perfunctory kiss. The owners rushed out the door after us. They were horrified to see a couple they'd long assumed were siblings kissing like that. We weren't siblings, we just acted the part—sniping, teasing, cutting each other down to size. I, at least, didn't have a clue how to be in erotic love. I often wished that someone would put us out of our misery. But no one did, so we groped through the next decade like two blind kittens.

Three weeks later, in the midst of yet another marital squabble brought on by my botched attempt to be romantic, Royce's marginalia from the library came back to me all at once:

συμβαίνει δ' Ἐμπεδοκλεῖ γε καὶ ἀφρονέστατον εἶναι τὸν θεόν· μόνος γὰρ τῶν στοιχείων ἓν οὐ γνωριεῖ, τὸ νεῖκος, τὰ δὲ θνητὰ πάντα· ἐκ πάντων γὰρ ἕκαστον.

Something strange, I remembered, that Aristotle had said in *De Anima* about Empedocles's view of God and strife: "God is most foolish: for He is completely alone in not knowing the one thing that every mortal being knows, namely Strife." Strife and doubt—they were what I felt my life had been all about for a long time. I had what Peirce called a "pillow-sharing acquaintance" with both of them; they were nightly companions. As I stretched out that evening and peered wide-eyed into the darkness—with the customary eighteen inches that separated me from my Strife on our king-size mattress—I couldn't help thinking that God was definitely not in bed with us. He had no idea about the mess our marriage had become. A life I wanted desperately to escape. The next morning I woke up, got into the car, and drove back to New

Hampshire. I took no one. I told no one. I just left. It was the first free action—save for entering the library—I'd ventured in years.

The drive took much less time than it should have, and I tracked down Ken Schneider, the reverend at a local church, who took me back to West Wind. Schneider introduced me to the Hocking family—William's granddaughters, Jennifer, Jill, and Penny—and in the days that followed, they generously began to include me in their hopes and plans to save the library. The Hocking sisters had much in common: their graying hair, their lack of makeup and other pretenses, their modesty, their frugality, their respect for all things artistic, their fear of change, and their obviously complex love of one another. But each of them was obsessed with a different aspect of West Wind.

Jennifer was most worried about its ecosystem, so worried that I sometimes felt strange talking to her about the books. She was adamant that the wild acreage should remain untouched. I imagined that she secretly considered the books to be a burial ground for an untold number of trees. Jill, by my estimation the most bookish of the three, was concerned about the intellectual legacy of West Wind. Somehow she'd cultivated the false belief that she wasn't smart enough to be a philosopher, which she must have picked up as a result of being surrounded by her grandfather and father and a bunch of other male philosophers when she was growing up. But she had dreams of opening the estate as an artists' retreat modeled after the Bread Loaf Writers' Conferences at Middlebury College. Penny had more modest goals: She wanted to sort the family heirlooms and fix the roofs that might protect them. She was the keeper of the Hocking-O'Reilly family history, a history so complex it would boggle my mind for years to come. Over a lunch of tea cakes and mini-sandwiches, overlooking the Presidential Range, we struck upon a rescue plan for West Wind. I would work at the library on weekends through the coming fall. The cataloging and transcription of the marginalia would take months, even years, and I wanted to make sure we didn't miss anything. Jennifer, the de facto groundskeeper, would let me into the building (or, as it turned out, give me the key). I'd reach out to a number of university libraries to see if they might agree to house the collection—the University of Southern Maine was right down the road and seemed like a natural spot.

The sisters told me that they were surprised and relieved that someone, a philosopher no less, was interested in caring for the books. Proximity sometimes precludes perspective: They'd lived at West Wind for so long that the place had become ordinary to them, and they were genuinely shocked that anyone would be excited about the library. I, on the other hand, was shocked that no scholar had gotten there first; the archived correspondence of William Ernest Hocking looks like one grand index of twentieth-century intellectual life, with more than seven thousand correspondents in total. He was good friends with James, Royce, Palmer, Husserl, Robert Frost, Alfred North Whitehead, Richard Feynman, Dean Acheson, and Bertrand Russell (maybe "friend" isn't the right way to describe the notoriously abrasive Russell, but they were close). And he was better than good friends with the Nobel Prize–winning author Pearl S. Buck. So, yes, I was interested in West Wind.

In the following months I started cheating on my wife with a roomful of books. I made the trip to New Hampshire repeatedly. My wife and mother—in a unison that always infuriated me—demanded to know where I was going. I could have told the truth. Instead, I chose to lie, making up conferences that needed to be attended and friends I wanted to visit. Up until that point my life had been so routine, so scripted, so normal, so *good*—but my brief encounter with my dead father the previous year had brought that life to an unceremonious end. Nothing about life is normal. And nothing about life has to be good. It's completely up to the liver. The question—Is life worth living?—doesn't have a scripted, public answer. Each answer is excruciatingly personal and therefore, I thought, necessarily private. Ella Lyman Cabot, a close friend of Hocking's and one of the few women who took graduate courses in philosophy at Harvard under James and Royce, once wrote, "We live alone, thoughts that are deepest drawn / and purest in our inner consciousness / Abide undreamed by the common throng." The thoughts I had at West Wind were mine, and mine alone. So I lied.

West Wind became my escape, but also my place of penance. Guilt and anxiety—the deep-seated Calvinist variety that have no particular object—kept me from eating and sleeping. Jennifer, who is one of the kindest women I've ever met, watched my steady decline into poor health and assured me that when I came to work on the books, I could have dinner with her and sleep in the warm farmhouse or in the less warm but still dry manor house. Instead, I skipped meals, hiked up to the grassy field behind the library, and pitched my tent. On the occasions I intentionally forgot the tent, I stretched out on the ground. I could say that this reflected my love of American philosophy, my desire to create a little bit of Thoreau's experience at Walden, to go "to the woods to live deliberately," and all that. But the truth is that I wanted nothing more than to escape, to experience something well outside the ken of my anesthetic life. And a bit of self-destruction did the job nicely, at least for a time.

I got sick up in those hills in the cold spring dampness, and when summer rolled around, I picked up Lyme disease in the forests behind the Hocking house. Lyme is not unlike a failed marriage: Its onset is almost indiscernibly slow, so gradual that by the time you're diagnosed, you can hardly remember a time when you weren't terribly ill. In truth, many patients with Lyme can't remember a damn thing. Lyme encephalopathy is characterized by a dysfunction of the cerebral cortex, resulting in the "brain fog" of short- and long-term memory loss. I do remember my knees throbbing like hell. Most of my appendages tingled and eventually went numb. By the time I went for treatment, I was so dizzy and disoriented I had to do the unthinkable—ask my wife for help. She silently drove me to the Mass General ER, where a team of doctors diagnosed me with "a mild case of meningitis" and, after a few days in the hospital, sent me home with a massive dose of antibiotics. The cure for the disease, like the cure for most dying relationships, is even worse than the symptoms themselves. Twelve weeks of doxycycline—three months of diarrhea, nausea, blistering mouth, sun sensitivity, and more dizziness. Not that any of this stopped me from going up to the library. Eventually my wife discovered a credit card statement with a series of purchases from gas stations in New Hampshire, reamed me out for lying to her, and then offered to accompany me on any future trip. But I always found a way to politely keep her away from my escape.

One evening in late September, alone on a hill at West Wind, I began to think about Charlotte Perkins Gilman. The nineteenth-century feminist and author of "The Yellow Wallpaper," an autobiographical tale of stifled and forgotten genius, Gilman routinely got cut out of the American philosophical canon. She was a serious writer at a time when serious writers were still not meant to be women. She abandoned her husband and a conventional New England life in 1888 and fled, with her daughter in tow, to Pasadena, California, where she began to make her name as a lecturer. At some point in the spring of 1891 she fell in what she would later call "really passionate love" with Adeline Knapp. This was not the sort of friendship you talked about in public. "I now," Gilman wrote, "have some one to love me, and whom I love." A year later Gilman did what few other women of her time dared—she got a divorce and sent her daughter back to be raised by her ex-husband. This sort of freedom looked, at least from the outside, like sheer madness. But to Gilman it made perfect sense—she'd fallen in love and wasn't about to talk herself out of it. And this seemed as good a reason as any to terminate formally a marriage that had probably already died. It was, by my estimation, the best decision of her rather difficult life.

At some point during that September night at West Wind I too decided to leave my spouse and finally admit that I was in love with another woman I hardly knew. The love was unrequited, but that scarcely mattered. My decision, free but apparently insane, made me feel even more guilty. But it also, at least for the time being, relieved the anxiety that had plagued me for more than a year. My father had walked out on us when I was four, and I was brought up by my truly exceptional mother, who gave me many things, among them a profound fear of divorce. In hindsight I know that this aversion was one of the few things holding my silently dismal marriage together. But when my father died, this semi-neurotic fear had died with him. From the outside, the marriage didn't look that bad, but as Thoreau once said, "lives of quiet desperation" rarely do. High in the New Hampshire mountains, the decision seemed reasonable enough, but as I headed for home at the end of the weekend, I began to doubt my resolve, so I made a Ulysses contract with myself that I couldn't break. At a pawnshop outside of Derry, I sold my wedding ring for $278, just enough money to buy the case of mediocre pinot noir that I needed to temporarily forget the whole ordeal. I never made it home that night, instead hightailing it back to the Hocking estate. The wind had picked up, so I decided, for the first time, to sleep in the library.

The night was objectively terrifying: pitch-black (despite my father's misguided efforts when I was a child, I've only recently mastered my fear of the dark), the sounds of scampering paws in the walls, Dorian Gray–style portraits looming above. The rodents and ghosts could have me, I thought. I couldn't see how they could make my life any worse than it already was. I listened to the growing storm outside and, oddly, for the first time, pondered the meaning of "West Wind." It might have something to do with

Pearl S. Buck, who had called her first novel *East Wind: West Wind*. I imagined Buck owning a similar manor house closer to the coast and naming it East Wind as a subtle testament to her unspeakably close friendship with Hocking. But the timing didn't make sense, given that Hocking and Buck became lovers only in the twilight of their lives. Plus, I couldn't imagine the Hocking family house being named for another woman. So I decided that West Wind probably referred to the famous poem by Percy Shelley, "Ode to the West Wind."

O wild West Wind, thou breath of Autumn's being,
Thou, from whose unseen presence the leaves dead
Are driven, like ghosts from an enchanter fleeing,

Yellow, and black, and pale, and hectic red,
Pestilence-stricken multitudes: O thou,
Who chariotest to their dark wintry bed

The leaves whispered across the roof. There were even more inside—"pestilence-stricken multitudes" bound with brittle spines and thin covers. The library would get cold again that winter, and most of the books—the ones we hadn't already saved in dry storage—would freeze. What a hopeless poem. What a hopeless place.

On Monday, back at work, a colleague, a gray-eyed woman named Carol Hay, whose office was directly across the hall, asked how my trip had been. She was the one and only person I actually wanted to tell. But I lied and told her it had been terrific.

FRAUD AND
SELF-RELIANCE

On a dreary morning in October I stood in the rain on the muddy shoulder of Route 16, reciting lines from Emerson's "Self-Reliance," which struck me as more than a little self-righteous. My Subaru was jacked up on a flimsy-looking mechanism I'd just used for the first time. Anyone could change a tire—except me.

"Trust thyself: every heart vibrates to that iron string."

Emerson could go fuck himself.

My tire iron was stuck in the mud about a dozen yards from the car—exactly where I'd thrown it. The bolts on the flat tire had been screwed on by a pneumatic wrench. How was a mere mortal like me supposed to get them off? I'd always fancied myself as having the type of wiry strength Emerson would have respected. I'd spent my time at school swimming, rowing, running, and generally trying to prove that I was someone worthy of the fathers of American philosophy—I'd taken its underlying story of rugged individualism to heart. But now a few tight bolts had forced me to question my role in this story. I looked down at my wet hands. They were red and blistered from my failed attempts to loosen the bolts. The pain in my hands told me to use my foot. Of course the goddamned tire iron just bent. And then broke. And then was thrown as far as possible.

The thing about Emerson is that you tend to remember him at the least opportune times: "A man is to carry himself in the presence of all opposition as if every thing were titular and ephemeral but he." My flat tire wasn't ephemeral and titular. I was. The self upon whom I was supposed to rely couldn't even fix its own car. I called AAA, a service my mother had wisely purchased for me. AAA called a local mechanic, who called his assistant, who slowly made his way to the breakdown lane of Route 16.

I shook hands with my savior in some feeble attempt to make us equals. His hand was tough and thick and told me he'd saved many, many people before. My hand probably told him that I was a philosopher suffering from Lyme.

"You can't force it. You just need to apply some steady pressure," he said, loosening the last bolt with an effortless twist.

"What do I owe you?" I asked.

"No worries, man. It's covered."

I dug through my pockets and came up with a handful of waterlogged bills, which I insisted on giving to him—my salvation had to be worth something—and then I slowly drove the rest of the way to West Wind. Emerson was quite emphatic on this point: "I say to you, you must save yourself . . ." Yet that did not seem to be in my power.

By then I'd been visiting New Hampshire regularly for more than a year. Things were going much better with the cataloging than they were at home in Boston. When I finally hit Route 113 and turned for the library, I'd cooled off a little. I didn't actually hate Emerson: I admired him to the point of envy. He, like James, was well acquainted with personal loss. He had married his first and most ardent love, Ellen Louisa Tucker, but she died just five years into their relationship. Emerson was crushed, and he pined after her for the rest of his life, preserving the memory of a twenty-something girl who'd contracted tuberculosis. "The mourner reads his loss in every utensil of his house, in every garment, in the face of every friend," Emerson wrote. "The dead do not return."

But they also never fully leave. Emerson went to Ellen's tomb daily for months. On March 29, 1832, he wrote exactly one sentence in his journal: "I visited Ellen's tomb and opened the coffin." But after a time, Emerson pulled himself together and got on with life. By 1835 he was happily remarried, and in the next decade he was able to deliver "The American Scholar" and "Self-Reliance"—forward-looking, often ebullient lectures that set the tone for classical American philosophy.

Emerson instructs his reader to be actively, freely engaged in life when faced with hardship—unencumbered by the past that threatens to haunt it. I'd begun to read Emerson when my older brother, Matt—whom I idolized—brought home a collection of his essays from university. My stubborn fourteen-year-old self found the essays both cool by association and inaccessible enough that I just had to crack them. I never did "crack them" in the sense of fully figuring them out, but I ended up opening them again and again for the glimmers of clarity they would occasionally yield. Over time, I came to realize that this was the point of reading Emerson and, for that matter, Thoreau and Margaret Fuller and all the rest of them. The reason to read the American Transcendentalists wasn't to hang on to their every word, but to be inspired by them. This early American philosophy was about inspiration, about moving beyond the inert and deadening ways of the past.

When I got to the library that day, it was already late afternoon, and as it was fall in New Hampshire, it was almost dark. There were now working lights on most of the first floor—an odd mix of original Tiffany lamps and bare lightbulbs hanging from rafters. With the Hockings' blessing, I'd spent many evenings on the first floor, cataloging such treasures as the volume that now sat on the reading table next to the fireplace. I'd plucked it from the shelves the previous week but hadn't had a chance to take a close look. It was bound in what's known in the antiquarian business as "three-quarter calf," a slick-looking leather binding that's still used to restore valuable books. It looked so new and shiny that I'd almost missed it the first time around. The archive-worthy materials at West Wind could usually be evaluated by the amount of weathering they showed, but this time that filtering method had led me astray.

I sat down on one of the Stickleys, opened the marbled board to the first page, and looked at the inscription: "Henry Lee, Esq. With the author's regards. December 1875." The handwriting was shaky but easily recognizable. In Emerson's later life his mind slowly left him, but he'd managed to hold on to his handwriting for the most part. I flipped to the next page: *Letters and Social Aims*. 1875. First edition. This was a neat little book, though far from Emerson's best. In fact, many people claimed it was his worst. Some even thought that he wasn't the primary author, suggesting that his literary executor, James Elliot Cabot, had created a sort of "Frankenbook," revising and piecing together Emerson's unpublished essays for the volume. For me, what was intriguing about this particular book wasn't so much its content, but the path it might have taken to West Wind. There were a number of possible scenarios I could conjure, all of which underscored the interesting and generally forgotten fact that American philosophy often emerged from the most pivotal moments of American history.

The Emersons and Lees went way back—so far back that their long-standing relationship was forged during the American Revolution. It's impossible to understand American philosophy without grasping how it sprang from this conflict. Emerson's grandfather, William, had built the Old Manse in Concord in 1769, a building that now commemorates the first battle of the Revolution. He'd been the chaplain of the Provincial Congress when it met in Concord in 1774, and then he took up the post of chaplain for the Continental Army when the war began. When he died from camp fever while on campaign, Emerson's father, also a William, was a boy of only seven.

Lee's revolutionary roots were even more distinguished. He could trace his family back to Anne Hutchinson and John Cotton. Hutchinson was the Puritan woman who dared to contradict the Puritan ministers of the Massachusetts Bay Colony in 1636. Cotton was the minister who inspired her to do so. The freethinking Hutchinson was fed up with her Puritan leaders' draconian work ethic. The settlers no longer had to be strictly obedient to the British crown, but in those early years the Puritans demanded ever-greater obedience from their followers. Hutchinson was tired of taking orders. Inspired by Cotton's sermons, she argued publicly that salvation could not be achieved through good works alone but turned on the acceptance of grace, a personal conversion that had absolutely nothing to do with the church hierarchy of the Puritans. She was exiled for her belief—truly radical in her day—that religious salvation came hand in hand with political and personal freedom. Her ideas percolated through the next five generations of American thinkers. Many years after Hutchinson's death, one of her descendants gave birth to Henry Lee's grandfather, Joseph. By this point the Lee family was no longer terribly interested in ideological or theological matters. Their revolution was to be fought not over the Bible, but over economics and politics. Joseph Lee's family was one of the most powerful shipping clans in America at a time when the British colonial taxes were particularly onerous. On December 16, 1773, Joseph and several hundred of his most zealous buddies decided to dump English tea into Boston Harbor. When the Boston Tea Party led to the Revolution, Lee allowed his merchant ships to be recommissioned as privateering vessels, and the Beverly Privateers of the American Revolution were born.

What must it have been like to have ancestors like this? More than a little intimidating, I imagined. The unspoken goal for nineteenth-century American thinkers was to live up to their families' revolutionary spirit. No small trick, considering the relative peace and stability that existed in the early 1800s. In the 1830s

Emerson and Lee, each in his own way, decided to rebel against the one American institution that hadn't undergone radical transformation in the previous century—Harvard. Harvard hadn't changed with the Revolution; it was dominated first by a bunch of old-school Calvinists and then by a surprisingly conservative group of Unitarians. Both groups staunchly disapproved of the liberal Unitarianism that had begun to gather momentum. Echoing his ancestors' rejection of institutionalized religion, Emerson argued that salvation could be achieved through intuition of the divine in nature. He was a proper adult when this debate began, and he made a well-respected career of his iconoclasm. Lee was an improper teenager at the time and resorted to other methods of protest.

Lee entered Harvard at the age of sixteen in 1834. Back then, the college wasn't an altogether reputable place. The students terrorized unsuspecting tutors and partied hard, and Lee was no exception. In his first year, his class of freshmen initiated what has come to be known as the Harvard Rebellion of 1834. One day, a Greek tutor by the name of Dunkin asked a freshman, John Bayard Maxwell, to recite his lesson. The pupil refused and was suspended for insubordination. In response, his classmates set Dunkin's room on fire. Things escalated from there. The president of Harvard was burned in effigy, guards were badly beaten, and tutors, all of them, were physically intimidated. Amid the chaos, Lee bolted one of his tutors into his bedroom—screwing the door closed from the outside, making it impossible for the tutor to escape. For this relatively harmless prank Lee was suspended and exiled to the manor house of Ezra Ripley, the minister in the nearby town of Waltham.

This is where Emerson and Lee first met, at the home of Ezra Ripley. An odd fellow, Ripley was respected by the traditional members of the Harvard community, but unlike most of them, he welcomed debate between conservative and liberal thinkers. Emerson was thirty-four when the young Lee was "sentenced" to Waltham, and they met during one of Emerson's visits. Their interaction was fleeting at the time, but Emerson came to see Lee as more than an average hooligan. In the next three years Emerson would write and then deliver two of the most critical lectures on the failures of Harvard and, by extension, the failures of the American educational system: "The American Scholar" and the "Divinity School Address." In these lectures he poetically gave voice to the general sentiment of Lee's class of 1834: American education and religion needed to leave the dogmatism of the past behind and tailor their lessons to the promise and innovation of young minds.

"The American Scholar," delivered in 1837, was at first widely admired. "We will walk on our own feet," Emerson promised, "we will work with our own hands; we will speak our own minds . . . A nation of men will for the first time exist, because each believes himself inspired by the Divine Soul which also inspires all men." Anne Hutchinson would have been proud. Equal parts egalitarian and progressive, "The American Scholar" was just reverent enough to keep from alienating the stuffy Harvardites. But the "Divinity School Address" was another matter. Given in the summer of 1838, the lecture pulled no punches regarding the role of church hierarchy in pursuing salvation—saying it had none. At the outset, Emerson said, "Let me admonish you, first of all, to go alone; to refuse the good models, even those most sacred in the imagination of men, and dare to love God without mediator or veil." For the Harvard overseers, this was blasphemy, and they proclaimed that Emerson would never again give a lecture on college grounds. The proclamation almost held: He wasn't invited back for thirty-two years. Only in 1870 was he asked to give the University Lectures that initiated graduate studies at Harvard. And who welcomed him back? The onetime hooligan Henry Lee.

Lee remained a troublemaker, but he had become famous during the Civil War for organizing Union troops in Boston when President Lincoln called for the defense of Washington in 1861. With this reputation and ample family funds, he was invited to serve on the Harvard Board of Overseers in 1867; he accepted and held the post until 1879. He oversaw the construction of Memorial Hall, the massive High Victorian Gothic building at the center of campus, and supported the organization of the University Lectures, which included a very grateful Emerson and a young philosophical upstart named Peirce. Just days before the elderly Emerson returned to lecture at Harvard, he was invited to James Elliot Cabot's Brookline home, where Henry Lee's children were putting on a play of *Alice in Wonderland.*

How had Lee's copy of *Letters and Social Aims* gotten to West Wind? Emerson probably gave Lee the book in 1875, and when Lee died, in 1905, his family probably gave the book to Richard Cabot (James Cabot's son). Richard Cabot and William Ernest Hocking had taken Royce's classes together in the 1890s and become best friends. In fact, Richard Cabot introduced William to Agnes O'Reilly, whom he would later marry. Cabot was the namesake and godfather of Hocking's son, Richard—Jill, Penny, and Jennifer's father and the most recent owner of West Wind. So when Richard Cabot died in the 1930s, the book became part of Hocking's time capsule. Looking back, I had the realization that at one point in the not-so-distant past, philosophy wasn't the sort of thing that was discussed only at formal conferences and in arcane journals. It was exchanged over dinner, between families. It was the stuff of everyday life.

The more time I spent on the Hocking estate, the more it seemed that all roads in American philosophy converged at West Wind. Yet looking around the library, it was impossible not to feel utterly alone. Nobody cared about this circuitous history. Nobody cared anymore about self-reliance or about the possibility that philosophers could also be political or existential heroes. Philosophy was no longer intensely personal.

Emerson and the rest of his cohort encouraged their readers to face the unavoidable tragedies of life with Promethean fortitude. After my disaster with the tire iron, to say nothing of the seeming tragedy of the rest of my life, I thought all of this was a pipe dream. Life was tragic—they'd gotten that much right—and on a few rare evenings, ensconced in a first-floor nook with Hocking's notebooks on idealism, bathed in the warm glow of the Tiffanies, I'd almost bought into their just-so story about self-reliance and salvation. This wouldn't be one of those evenings. Instead, I pulled myself up from the rocker, slunked across the library, looked up to pay my respects to the portrait of Agnes, and went directly upstairs.

In the attic, I pulled the cord on the one overhead bulb, which turned out to be wholly insufficient for snooping. So I fished out my headlamp from my pocket and worked my way back into the eaves, where Penny Hocking had spent many a summer day. There, her mother, Katherine, had assiduously stored box after box of family correspondence, many of the letters written in the early nineteenth century from such places as Chicago, Albuquerque, and San Francisco—parts of the country that were, at the time, frontiers. I had some vague idea that these rivaled the books for being the most valuable part of the library, at least monetarily speaking, but I wasn't an antique collector or that sort of history buff, and these letters were deeply personal for the current generation of Hockings. So I avoided them. I didn't want to trespass any more than I already had.

But on my last visit, the shelf next to the boxes had bothered me, so I flipped on the high beams and went digging. Headlamps are uniquely modern devices. I was, for the first time all day, the master of my own brightly lit, if pitifully small, dominion. I got to determine, with pinpoint accuracy, what I saw and what I didn't. The visible world was mine and mine alone. The unseen world didn't matter, because I said so. My dominion in the attic felt secure and protected, like a private island in the middle of the ocean. I cast my beam around a few corners, and then the "O'Reilly books" entered my spotlight.

When Agnes's father, John Boyle O'Reilly, the Irish revolutionary and—as far as the English were concerned—terrorist, was condemned to a sunbaked penal colony in Australia, he had risked everything to escape. I'd overlooked this shelf for many months, thinking that it had nothing to do with the history of Transcendentalism and American pragmatism. My angle of vision had kept me from seeing what was now patently obvious: Most of the books weren't written by O'Reilly. They were written by one of his closest American friends: Walt Whitman.

Lined up like sentinels were early editions of *Leaves of Grass*; I recognized the brown leather cover of the 1860 edition. This was the third printing. In the years that followed its initial 1855 publication, Whitman had decided that his work was too short. He'd been right about the massive volume that came out a few years later: "I am large, I contain multitudes." I paged through quickly: "I am larger, better than I thought, / I did not know I held so much goodness." I had finally come to terms with James's dark meditation at Holden Chapel, and perhaps I could even accept Emerson's suggestion that I should be self-reliant, but Whitman's buoyancy—that I could not abide. William James would, with equal parts admiration and bafflement, call the famous poet one of the temperamentally optimistic. Whitman even wrote anonymous reviews of his own writing—sparklingly reverent reviews. He sought out an endorsement of *Leaves of Grass* from Emerson and emblazoned the praise from his "master" on the spine of later volumes: "I greet you at the beginning of a great career." Emerson was nonplussed but could hardly criticize Whitman's ingenuity—after all, Whitman had probably just taken Emerson at his word: "genius borrows nobly." Once his reputation was solidified, Whitman sat for dozens of daguerreotype portraits and gave them away like business cards. Many of these photos—now framed and under glass—became heirlooms, passed from one generation to the next as evidence that the family had once cared about poetry and ideas. Even the Hockings were not immune from this sort of display.

The frame was oblong and larger than I'd expected—it was on the floor, propped haphazardly against the shelf. I pulled it out of the shadows and wiped the grime from the glass. There was Whitman, peering out like Rip Van Winkle. Beneath the portrait was a note:

> *Camden, New Jersey*
> *March 26, 1885.*
>
> *Dear Boyle,*
> *I send you some mail with this little roll of pictures— take your choice, what you like for yourself. Send one to Bagenal, as I have not got his address . . . I am well as usual—but am very lame—Have not been anywhere outside for over a year . . .*
> *Walt Whitman*

The discoveries at West Wind were no longer shocking, but the idea that things so precious could go to waste so easily was deeply unsettling. Then again, sometimes West Wind could be exasperating: "I am well *as usual*," Whitman wrote. How could one be at once "very lame" and "well as usual"? You'd have to be either a superhero or a liar.

A mature and healthy Whitman met John Boyle O'Reilly four years earlier, in February 1881, at the inaugural meeting of the St. Botolph Club, a literary society that was modeled after the Century Association in New York. Its membership list read like a Who's Who of Boston: Henry Cabot Lodge, John Singer Sargent, and Henry Houghton and George Mifflin of the eponymous publishing house were all in the club. St. Botolph's was a swanky Brahmin affair that convinced Whitman—if he still needed convincing—that he'd finally made it into the New England literati. He was in the process of finishing what many scholars consider the last true edition of *Leaves of Grass*. The little volume had started as twelve poems but three decades later was edging toward four hundred. When Emerson died, in 1882, Whitman sought other champions, and O'Reilly, who was quickly becoming a cultural icon in Boston, fit the bill.

In the Hocking attic, someone had tucked news clippings between the Whitman volumes, and they documented, with surprising clarity, the relationship between their acclaimed relative and his still more famous friend. O'Reilly had made daily visits to the poet's Boston study as Whitman finished his final edits. Whitman welcomed his guest and admired—nay, envied—the Irishman's brave escape and flight to the New World. To Whitman, it sounded romantic.

I picked up a book from a pile next to the O'Reilly shelf—a volume from Horace Traubel's *With Walt Whitman in Camden*. Traubel had been Whitman's literary executor, a professional role that was equal parts respectful and parasitic. After Whitman died, Traubel documented in excruciating detail the conversations they'd had in the poet's final years. This had immortalized Whitman and earned Traubel a modicum of notoriety. I flipped to his account of a conversation he had with Whitman in the late 1880s. Traubel explained that "something or other induced me to mention John Boyle O'Reilly. This started W. [Whitman] right off":

"Oh! He is not the typical Irishman: rather Spanish: poetic, ardent . . . You know his life in outline: he has given me glimpses into it: short, sharp, pathetic look-ins . . . They were like this: it was in his prison days: the prisoners suffered from bad food or too little food or something: O'Reilly is deputed to present a complaint: he does it: the overseer does not answer—pays no attention whatever: raises his hand, this way"—W. indicates it—"hits Boyle— slaps him in the mouth—violently—staggers him or knocks

him over . . . What must that have meant to O'Reilly?
he was a mere boy . . . O'Reilly has had a memorable life:
this is but a sample item: he is full of similar dramatic
introspections."

Dramatic introspections? The American poet made oppression
and incarceration sound like a campfire story. Whitman, along
with Emerson and Thoreau, is often praised for his simple, even
harsh language, for the way he entreats his readers to return to
the hard core of human experience, for his insistence, in the words
of Thoreau, on "sucking the very marrow out of life." But maybe
Whitman couldn't stomach O'Reilly's story without sugarcoating it,
without making it more uplifting than it actually must have been.
It is possible that O'Reilly liked being idealized in this way—
maybe it was easier than recalling his previous life's reality—
but maybe he secretly hated it. I hadn't read much of O'Reilly's
poetry, but something of "The Dreamer" had stuck with me.
I searched through the shelf to find it:

I am sick of the showy seeming
Of a life that is half a lie;
Of the faces lined with scheming
In the throng that hurries by.
From the sleepless thought's endeavour
I would go where the children play;
For a dreamer lives forever
And a thinker dies in a day.

I had no real idea when he wrote this, but I now imagined it
was right after recounting one of his "dramatic introspections."
O'Reilly had given Whitman a theatrical story that the poet could
embellish to his heart's content, but the Irishman alone was left
with the memory of its brutality.

The distance from Boston to Bunbury, Australia, was 11,566

miles. In 1867, after his sentencing by the British courts, a young O'Reilly had boarded the *Hougoumont*, an English prison ship bound for Western Australia, and slowly made his way to Bunbury. When he escaped two years later, it was largely under his own power—from Bunbury to a little town called Dardanup, to Java, to Mauritius, to the British colony of Saint Helena, to Liverpool, to Philadelphia, and finally to Boston. This is the stuff of Transcendentalist glory: a perfect case of self-reliance. At every turn, authorities attempted to recapture O'Reilly, to return him to a life of servitude, to punish him for his participation in the Fenian uprising against British rule. This Irishman knew concretely what Emerson only conjectured in theory, that "for nonconformity the world whips you with its displeasure."

Many philosophers and writers admire this sort of individualism but want no part of it. One of the great myths of American philosophy tells us that when Thoreau was thrown into prison for protesting the Mexican-American War, Emerson came to visit him, shocked that his young friend was behind bars. "Henry," Emerson asked, "what are you doing in there?" According to legend, Thoreau replied, "Waldo, the question is, what are you doing out there?" Emerson held that protesting an isolated event or trend was pointless without a full-scale spiritual reform of society, but this seemed an obvious philosophical cop-out to Thoreau, who, like O'Reilly, was loath to let the perfect become the enemy of the good. This conversation probably never occurred, but it is emblematic of the dynamic between Whitman and O'Reilly: Whitman admired the convict's daring escape but failed to fully grasp the political realities that might cause one to be imprisoned. In response to O'Reilly's support of Irish political rule in the 1880s, Whitman chided him for being "too concerned about the Irish vote," failing to realize that the mere act of voting was associated with a personal and national ordeal that most white nineteenth-century American thinkers could scarcely imagine. O'Reilly was painfully aware of the censure and physical punishment used to suppress insurrection, a pain made all the more acute by the intellectuals who failed to understand his most intimate commitments.

I flipped to Traubel's account of the early 1890s to see if Whitman had any wisdom to share about O'Reilly's death. Here was Whitman at his romantic best—or, as the case may be, worst: "I have not got over it yet—it was a startling story! And such a fellow! What the handsome light and shadow of the man! He had the fine port, the dark hair and eyes—of the Irish-Spanish mixture he was. When I looked at him I never wondered again why it was said to the credit of Ireland that it had come of Spain, or a thick Spanish mixture. Insomnia 'a strange freak.'"

"Strange freak" indeed. The very things one wants to escape in sleep are the very things that keep the insomniac awake. Sleeplessness had always been my most dependable nightly companion—a bedfellow intent on replaying my day's failures into the wee hours of the morning. But I'd never come out and asked for a sleeping pill, which would have been abhorrent in my family. O'Reilly was the head of a similar family. His wife suffered from what was called "nervous prostration," a common diagnosis for morbidly unhappy women of the nineteenth century. Chloral hydrate was prescribed to calm her nerves and make sure she slept reasonably well. Her husband hated that she had to take this sort of palliative for a mind that was supposed to be clear and constant.

I continued to sift through the clippings and eventually found an obituary from August 10, 1890: "John Boyle O'Reilly, editor of the *Pilot*, died at an early hour this morning at his summer cottage, at Hall, from an overdose of chloral. He was suffering from insomnia and took the dose to produce sleep." This put an end to my snooping for the evening; I was done. But I'd read enough to ensure that I wouldn't sleep a wink. The reporter had done his homework carefully, describing the way O'Reilly's wife, Mary, had found her husband sleeping soundly at the living room window, his head in his hands, looking out to sea. When she wasn't able to rouse him, she called the doctors, who managed to coax out his last words: "wife's medicine." Then he died. I wished the reporter had overlooked some of the details. It would've been easier to think that John Boyle O'Reilly had died of heart failure (which is what many Boston papers reported in the days following his death).

I scrambled out of the eaves, my headlamp-dominion bobbing wildly out of control. As I pulled the cord, the attic fell into darkness. On my way down the ladder I twisted my ankle, pitching headlong onto the large chesterfield at the bottom, clipping my elbow on its arm. This is when I decided it was time to forget the day. There was a bottle of bourbon in the trunk of my car. I never drank in the library (it seemed sacrilegious), so I sat on the lip of my hatchback and finished the bottle. Then I grabbed an armful of dirty laundry that had accumulated in my backseat and returned to the library. Dumping these clothes on the floor in front of one of the enormous fireplaces, I pulled the cleanest shirt from the heap, stuffed everything else inside the shirt, and tied the arms together. I stretched out on the chesterfield with my makeshift pillow. At some point during the night I managed to sleep, despite dreams of self-reliance and chloral hydrate.

WALDEN AND
FROZEN LAKES

I opened my eyes. Slowly they focused in on the white lettering next to my head: AMERICAN ACADEMY OF ARTS AND SCIENCES. It was a shirt I'd been given during my year as a postdoctoral fellow at Harvard. The American Academy sits on a small wooded corner of Cambridge next to the Divinity School, called Norton Woods, and for many years has been the temporary residence of a few lucky academics called the "Visiting Scholars"—recently minted Ph.D.s from across the country who are paid what seemed to me at the time an exorbitant sum to spend the year reading and writing. The academy was originally set up to create a space for academic scholarship in the New World, as an institution to rival the Royal Society in London. This was the place where American intellectual life was to take root.

My eyes shifted beyond the white lettering and caught sight of what looked like little clumps of dirt on my makeshift pillow. Then I realized it was rodent droppings, and I remembered that mouse shit carries hantavirus. Just what I needed: respiratory disease and kidney failure. Grabbing a bar of soap from my duffel, I sprinted off across the back meadow behind the library. By the time I got to the pond, my shirt and pants were already off. I'd totally forgotten that this was someone else's property and that it was October in New Hampshire. The water quickly reminded me of the latter. The word "bracing" isn't quite right. I was a good swimmer, but not in this weather. Still, I dove in deeper and let the frozen lake do its work. As a kid, I'd fallen through the ice on my neighborhood skating pond. It wasn't fatally deep, but I remembered being stuck waist-deep and trying to claw my way out, only to break more of the ice. It was the closest thing to hell I'd ever experienced. Interestingly, the deepest pits of Dante's *Inferno* are not hot, but unearthly cold. Evil incarnate is trapped hip-deep in the frozen lake of Cocytus, which was only slightly colder than a pond in New Hampshire on the brink of winter. Soon the water began to feel almost comfortable, which was my cue to get out. I looked across the pond and finished washing out my mouth. On some level, I knew my behavior was absurd. The pond water I was swallowing would give me giardia before it inoculated me against the hantavirus I might have inhaled the night before.

Thoreau had similar moments of crisis in his self-made hut on the banks of Walden Pond. He had the good sense not to write them all down, but a few made their way to me in my studies of American philosophy: "What am I at present? A diseased bundle of nerves standing between time and eternity like a withered leaf that still hangs shivering on its stem. A more miserable object one could not well imagine." This was from January 1843, two years before he made his three-mile relocation from Concord to Walden. There were undoubtedly high-minded reasons why he went to the woods, but there were also some simple ones that I had an easier time identifying with. Thoreau was widely reported to be physically repulsive. Louisa May Alcott joked to Emerson that Thoreau's demeanor "will most assuredly deflect amorous advances and preserve the man's virtue in perpetuity." Nathaniel Hawthorne was even more straightforward: Thoreau "is ugly as sin, long-nosed, queer-mouthed." Maybe Thoreau went to Walden to escape, to grow his neck beard in peace.

I pulled my shriveled body out of the water and, looking down, ardently hoped that Jennifer and her daughter, Joanna, hadn't decided to go for a midmorning walk close by. I pulled on pants (just in case), hobbled back up the hill, and got into my car to enjoy the heated seats.

As I thawed, I puzzled over Thoreau's self-loathing. Surely he had the imagination and the perspective to know that an untold number of people led much more miserable lives than he. Thoreau never had to face starvation and beatings on a prison ship. His were the problems of privilege, the neurotic difficulties one faces when absolutely nothing is really wrong, the abiding anguish that afflicts those even in a world of heated seats. Thoreau lived at the beginning of such a world and embodied the strange dissatisfaction that would quietly, secretly come to define it. The problem wasn't that life was hard, but that it had become too easy. People, and not just royalty, at long last had free time and therefore had to figure out the best way to use it. This freedom of choice caused them no end of anxiety. One could choose so many things! Just that week I'd walked thirty reluctant undergrads through Viktor Frankl's *Man's Search for Meaning* and tried to explain what Frankl meant by the "existential vacuum"—the infinite array of possibilities that we first worlders have the chance to explore. At first the students thought the vacuum sounded pretty cool.

"John," asked one excited fellow, "you mean I can do whatever I want?"

"Yes, that's right. Anything."

He grinned.

"But that also means you are solely responsible for your choices. Totally, utterly, inconsolably alone in deciding what to choose."

The grin faded. Modernity has no shortage of things designed to distract us from our own angst: small talk and Facebook and college classes and dates and holiday get-togethers and jobs and money and marriage and *stuff*. This is just the way civilized life hums along. For many people, it works with such seamless precision that its machinations seem not only convenient but completely necessary. Of course, very little is necessary, and Thoreau knew this. He had a hunch that frenetic busyness should not be the business of human life, that chatter makes one feel horribly alone, that well-paid jobs are different from "callings." And that long relationships are not necessarily synonymous with meaningful ones. (He never married.)

Sitting in my car that morning, I decided I never wanted to go back to the city. I'd follow Thoreau's lead and stay at West Wind. My life would become an experiment in Thoreauvian self-cultivation, a project that had always struck me as more manageable and realistic than trying to embody Emerson's "self-reliance." I didn't need to be heroic, but could I become at least a slightly better person by avoiding the pettiness of everyday life? "Simplicity, simplicity, simplicity!" Thoreau instructed. "I say, let your affairs be as two or three, and not a hundred or a thousand; instead of a million count half a dozen, and keep your accounts on your thumb-nail." What exactly do people "make," Thoreau asked, when they "make a living"? They make money; they spend money; they buy stuff; they waste stuff. Thoreau thought that they generally fritter away life.

American philosophy—from Jonathan Edwards in the eighteenth century straight through to Cornel West in this one—is about the possibilities of rebirth and renewal. "We must," Thoreau insists, "learn to reawaken and keep ourselves awake, not by mechanical aids, but by an infinite expectation of the dawn, which does not forsake us even in our soundest sleep." Thoreau's charge in *Walden* has been recast by so many American thinkers in so many different ways that I'd come to regard it as a type of wishful thinking, a reminder of how close to impossible it is to remain meaningfully awake to our lives. Living this way requires a kind of attentive optimism that I wasn't sure many of us were capable of anymore.

I pulled myself off the heated seats just as Jennifer appeared from behind the library. I must've been quite a sight. Unshaven, barefoot, still slightly blue from the cold. Jennifer didn't seem to notice, and she smiled broadly. I was grateful and did my best to return the gesture. She responded by giving me a hug. As a rule, philosophers don't hug. Most of us do this meaningless cheek kiss thing that is supposed to make us look sophisticated and European, or we just ignore each other altogether. Jennifer Wiley, the fifty-year-old granddaughter of Agnes Hocking, hugs. This was the best I'd felt in months.

"Let's have dinner at the lower farmhouse in a little while. I have something cooking down there."

I nodded and said something that I hoped sounded vaguely impressive about what I planned to accomplish in the library meanwhile.

"Okay. Sounds good," she said, turning to leave. "I'm going to scythe this afternoon."

Suddenly the idea of helping Jennifer scythe felt vastly more important than working in the library, so I asked if she could use a hand.

Of course she didn't need one. Saviors like Jennifer and the man with the tire iron don't need assistance with the tasks of everyday life. They are self-sufficient all by themselves. But Jennifer heard the underlying plea and said, "Sure, that'd be great."

This time I felt myself make a better show at smiling. Turning to the car, I must have gestured for her to get in.

"It's easier to walk," she said matter-of-factly.

Thoreau wrote "Walking" in 1851. Over the next decade, he would lecture on this essay a dozen times, more than on any other.

It was, by many accounts, his favorite. "Let me live where I will," Thoreau writes, "on this side is the city, on that the wilderness, and ever I am leaving the city more and more, and withdrawing into the wilderness." Once my shirt was back on and buttoned, Jennifer and I started off down the dirt road and I was struck by my sadly narrow understanding of West Wind. Fixated on worm-ridden books and obsessed with the prospect of finding dusty artifacts, I hadn't really taken the time to appreciate the landscape supporting the library.

Walking gives one many things, according to Thoreau, but one of its greatest gifts is time. In my pursuit of self-perfection, I'd taken up running in high school—long, fast, gut-wrenching sessions that left me nauseated for the rest of the day. Often I would run to the gym, tear my body apart with weights, and race home. On these outings there was never enough time; I was always behind the clock and racing to catch up. Thoreau's walking, an activity that seemed perfectly suited to Jennifer, served a very different purpose:

> [T]he walking of which I speak has nothing in it akin to taking exercise, as it is called, as the sick take medicine at stated hours—as the swinging of dumb-bells or chairs; but is itself the enterprise and adventure of the day. If you would get exercise, go in search of the springs of life. Think of a man's swinging dumb-bells for his health, when those springs are bubbling up in far-off pastures unsought by him!

For Thoreau, walking is not something one has to do. It isn't a great test of will, but walking with care requires an attention to the present that is extremely difficult to maintain. Thoreau thought there was something sacred in walking, and he said that the best way to do it was to "saunter," from the French *sainte terre*. The point of walking was to move in such a way as to make, or keep, the land holy. The destination was pointedly unimportant. Of course you had to decide where to go—or, better, how to go—but the point of walking was not to get anywhere in particular. The point, if one could call it that, was to experience the sublime in the mundane. And this experience, so common yet so rare, had intrinsic value, the sort of value that made a life worth living.

I looked across the valley to a distant hillside I'd never seen. Jennifer surveyed the hill carefully, as if each clearing had a role to play in some divine plan. "The deer sleep up there," she explained. "You can see where they bed down when you walk around in the morning." Jennifer was the one granddaughter who wasn't at all bookish. She deferred to her two sisters on matters of philosophy and never missed an opportunity to downplay her skill with words. She was quiet. I wondered what she thought about when she went walking. "Where do you walk, Jennifer?" I asked. She laughed. "Oh, all over. It doesn't matter." She probably had her favorite jaunts, but she seemed like the type of person who could be at home anywhere, even—and perhaps most especially— mid-step. She knew what Thoreau called "the secret of successful sauntering. He who sits still in a house all the time may be the greatest vagrant of all; but the saunterer, in the good sense, is no more vagrant than the meandering river, which is all the while sedulously seeking the shortest course to the sea."

The dirt road took a hairpin turn around a stand of bare apple trees and opened out into a grassy field in the middle of nowhere. Nowhere was pretty damned beautiful. This, I thought, was why Robert Frost—who'd visited West Wind often—instructed us to take the road less traveled. I remembered Frost writing that he and William Ernest Hocking had been "thoughtful friends of long standing," and I hoped I could one day say the same of Hocking's granddaughter.

The field stretched down the hill toward the tree line, framing an old white farmhouse with a pale green roof. Jennifer lived in this house all by herself. This year, she'd stay through the winter instead of moving back to Tamworth, a little town across the valley. She didn't mind the solitude. She ducked back into the barn that was connected to the house. I assumed she would emerge with heroic implements fitted to the epic task of scything that awaited us. The pile of firewood neatly stacked next to the front porch was shoulder height—more evidence of Jennifer's Thoreauvian husbandry. Thoreau never became a husband, in the usual sense of the word, but he maintained that husbandry—the simple act of tending one's own garden—was the proper alternative to a life of modern alienation. When he went to Walden, he knew that his retreat stood in marked contrast to the cultured existence that occupied so many other Harvard graduates: "Those summer days which some of my contemporaries devoted to the fine arts in Boston or Rome . . . and others to trade in London or New York, I thus, with other farmers of New England, devoted to husbandry." Husbandry. This term for farming comes from the Old Norse verb *búa*, which means "to dwell," to be in one place, to make a home for oneself. "Ancient poetry and mythology," Thoreau writes, "suggest, at least, that husbandry was once a sacred art; but it is pursued with irreverent haste . . . by us, our object being to have large farms and large crops merely." Our present age understands husbandry much as it does walking: something that has to be done as quickly and efficiently as possible, as a means to get somewhere or something.

Looking around at the remains of a garden at the edge of the house, I was struck by the careful expertise that must have gone into it. I'd spent my first summer at West Wind glued to rare books, trying in vain to understand something essential that I'd missed in American philosophy. All the while, Jennifer had been down here chopping wood and gardening, enacting scenes from *Walden*. Sophistication was frequently overrated. What did I know about husbandry? For a second I thought about the woman who used to be my wife. We had finalized the divorce earlier that year, and at that very minute she and her new fiancé were on their way to a new home in a midwestern farming state in the heartland. She'd chosen a fighter pilot, which was, by my estimation, about as far as you could possibly get from a philosopher.

Once again, Jennifer saved me from my thoughts. "Are you ready?" she asked.

The scythe wasn't exactly what I was expecting. It looked a bit like a rake with a flimsy ax head—a dull and rickety thing with a loose, rusty blade. The pine handle, or "snath," as it is known in scything circles, was about three feet long—far too short for me—and felt as if it would fall to pieces in my hands. I'd imagined something fearsome, or at least sturdy, something fit for Winslow Homer's *Veteran in a New Field*, a painting of a Civil War veteran mowing his way effortlessly through an endless stretch of golden wheat. Jennifer, however, was pretty pleased with the tool, and her scything tutorial made the work look easy. Relax, feet wide, knees bent, arms straight, pivot on the balls of the feet, and twist at the waist. Ideally, the blade just skims the ground, slicing through grass and soft plants without getting stuck in the dirt. I'd thrown discus in high school, and it seemed a little like that. But I was really bad at throwing discus and, it turned out, worse at scything. I couldn't seem to let go, to get my whole body into it. I muscled through using only my arms, which wore out in a matter of minutes. When I noticed how slowly I was going, I tightened my death grip, redoubled my efforts—again, only with my arms— and buried the blade two inches into the ground. Rocks were my greatest adversaries, and they were everywhere. The sound of steel striking granite rang through the hills at West Wind that afternoon. Jennifer just smiled and silently made her way through the meadow. As I hacked my way through the dirt, I took some comfort in knowing that Thoreau had faced his own troubles in tending the fields around Walden: "My auxiliaries are the dews and rains which water this dry soil, and what fertility is in the soil itself, which for the most part is lean and effete. My enemies are worms, cool days, and most of all woodchucks. The last have nibbled for me a quarter of an acre clean." Thoreau hated the nibbling beasts (making an exception to his vegetarianism to devour one). I gave my scythe a mighty Homeric sweep, and the blade fell off.

"You can't force it, John. Just work slowly."

I bent over to pick up the blade. Jennifer was right, of course. Forcing things wasn't working out. I turned around to watch her carefully pivot through the grass. Nothing was rushed or hurried. She had nowhere else to be. But somehow she was still making good time. I turned back to my work. One "cannot be happy and strong," Emerson informs his reader, "until he too lives with nature in the present, above time." That woman was happy and strong. I'd always assumed that self-reliance was a matter of radical self-*assertion*—that it amounted to leaving one's current self behind in favor of some future, more compelling form, that it depended on one's ability to resist and deviate from one's sur-roundings. But Jennifer's movements suggested something quite different. Minutes later, hours later, I looked up again. She was still gliding and pivoting through the pasture, avoiding the thick patches that gave her trouble, revisiting them again from a new angle. And then she stopped.

"I need a break," she confessed.

For the first time in my life I considered the possibility that the paragons of self-reliance might be those who know when they need a break. Doug Anderson, my first and most beloved philoso-phy teacher, had suggested something similar when I was still a student, but I'd not taken him seriously at the time. He'd been worried about my sanity and compulsiveness, and I'd assumed he was offering paternalistic advice veiled as a philosophical lesson. He told me that "Self-Reliance" was never to be read by itself, that Emerson had written a sister essay called "Compensation." He suggested that I read the two in tandem. I did, but it didn't make sense to me. The two seemed diametrically opposed. In short, "Compensation" argues that no matter how hard you work, no matter how desperately you strive to free yourself from natural or societal constraints, you'll inevitably fail. Or at least eventually need a break. For the Emerson of "Compensation," brazen self-assertion was, at best, counterproductive because it failed to recognize something basic about human nature—namely, that it was part of, rather than apart from, the workings of nature. Self-reliance, properly understood, was always situated, ever so carefully, in a wider cosmic order. "Human labor, through all its forms, from the sharpening of a stake to the construction of a city or an epic, is one immense illustration of the perfect compensation of the universe. The absolute balance of Give and Take."

Jennifer and I settled on the front porch to survey our work. She explained that I'd just taken part in a Hocking family ritual. Every year the relatives—most of them academics from around the country—would make the pilgrimage to West Wind to do the season's haying. They no more had to come to West Wind than Thoreau had to go to Walden. They could've stayed in their offices at the University of Chicago or Harvard or wherever. But they came anyway. The adults would scythe, the teenagers would pitchfork the grass into piles, and the smaller kids would follow behind picking up the remains. I was taken back to Shelley's "West Wind," the wind that blew the leaves as pestilence-stricken multitudes all over God's creation. The hay probably looked a little like that. Occasionally a child on the edge of her teenage years would try her hand at the pitchfork and someone would end up at the hospital, but for the most part everything went smoothly. Even to the untrained eye, this wasn't fertile land. Definitely not the sort one would seek out for the purpose of farming. It was rocky, arid stuff that was good for pine trees and not much else. The Hockings kept returning out of principle, or something even deeper than principle: desire for the experience.

I looked at our little piles of grass. "They used to be bigger," Jennifer said, reading my mind. "We used to put the hay on the floor of the barn and the kids would jump from the second floor."

I grinned until she told me how her cousin Waud had landed on one of the thinner piles and broken his arm. More trips to the hospital. Unnecessary trips. I didn't have to be playing with blades and hay piles. There were people, like Jennifer, who didn't just play at husbandry, I thought. They lived out in the Midwest, in remote regions of North Dakota and Montana. Carol, my gray-eyed colleague, was one of these people—or at least she'd grown up with people like that. Not many philosophers grow up in Saskatchewan, four hundred miles north of the Montana border, but she had. I cringed to think what she would say about my scything. At one point, over too many beers, I'd asked her if it was the cold that kept her native land so clear of trees. "Um, no." She'd blinked. "People farm it. Grassland turns to forest unless it's farmed. Or you can burn it—apparently that's what the aboriginal people did. But prairie never stays prairie by itself." Farming was an ongoing attempt to insert oneself into the workings of nature. Jennifer explained that when they were kids, you could see all the way to Mount Chocorua. There'd been no trees to obstruct the view, because so much more of the land, now forest, had been devoted to farming. This, I guessed, was one reason why the Hockings came for the haying at West Wind: In an age of heated car seats, they were trying to remind themselves of the simple work of cultivating the earth, of the ongoing effort that goes into making a home.

Jennifer went inside to get an early dinner ready, and I went to check out the strange black box, about the size of a large toaster, sitting several yards from the porch. It had silver wings—four of them—attached to its top, and it smelled a bit like chicken. I'd never seen a solar oven before, and I cracked it open; inside was a chicken—one of those real, live animals you see when you go to a farm show, but dead. My ex-wife had spent years trying to convince me to give up meat, but I'd dug in my heels and kept eating flesh, mostly out of childish spite. It took my friend Carol exactly one night to convince me. She'd gone on about how animals have the same capacity for suffering that we do, and how anything capable of suffering has an interest in not suffering, and how this interest in not suffering is surely more important than our interest in eating cheap factory-farmed meat, at least when we have so many other options. We'd argued for a while, but I realized after about twenty minutes that my position was untenable. So I had stopped arguing and stopped eating meat.

"Are you ready for dinner?" Jennifer called from the kitchen.

She joined me outside with a knife and cutting board. For a split second I thought of the dissection tables at Holden Chapel, then swallowed hard and tried my best not to be sick. Meticulously, she deboned and carved the body. This, like scything, was sacred work. The chicken had come from a barn down the road where they still raised fowl in relatively humane ways. Though I was not convinced to partake of its flesh, I didn't judge the woman with the knife either. In the ebb and flow of compensation, little animals sometimes had to be roasted in sun-drenched boxes, and small pastures of grass eventually withered and died. Destruction was the inevitable by-product of survival. Thinking about my personal crisis of the last year, about the wreckage of my emotional life, I really hoped that was the case. Remembering the rest of the first canto of "Ode to the West Wind," I realized that Shelley's poem wasn't actually that dismal.

> The wingèd seeds, where they lie cold and low,
> Each like a corpse within its grave, until
> Thine azure sister of the Spring shall blow
>
> Her clarion o'er the dreaming earth, and fill
> (Driving sweet buds like flocks to feed in air)
> With living hues and odours plain and hill:
>
> Wild Spirit, which art moving everywhere;
> Destroyer and Preserver; hear, O hear!

The first stars peeked out from behind low-hanging clouds. I thanked Jennifer for my dinner of cheese, bread, and locally grown apples (she'd graciously changed the menu when she noticed I wasn't touching the flesh) and then returned to the library to spend another night on the chesterfield. Inspecting the sofa for mouse scat, I stretched out. Hay, everywhere. Spring would come. Hay, all around. West Wind: destroyer *and* preserver.

PART II

PURGATORY

THE TASK OF SALVATION

It was nearly daybreak, and a light rain played on the roof above me. Boxes of books surrounded my makeshift bed. I'd promised myself that I would finish packing them and tote them off to dry storage, but after a day in the fields with Jennifer, the prospect of spending another hour inside with a cast of dead white men seemed suddenly unappealing. Through the shadows I could just make out a photograph on the mantel: two of Hocking's beloved teachers, Royce and James, sitting on a split-rail fence on the crest of a pasture outside Chocorua, which was no more than five or six miles from the Hocking library. Royce, who rarely took a break from philosophical speculation, had come to visit James's summer house in 1903 and had made yet another attempt to convince him of the existence of God. James was bored, which made him mischievous. He already believed in God, but Royce's God was too constrictive and meddling for James's religious tastes. According to legend, when James's daughter snapped this picture, her father cried, "Royce, you're being photographed! Look, out! I say *Damn the Absolute!*" For James, beautiful afternoons were for walking and breathing—not for abstract systematizing. We are free for such a short time, according to James, that there are often better things to do than philosophy. I roused myself and realized that if I got busy boxing and cataloging the Descartes and Hobbes, I might still have plenty of time for a hike.

"Trivial." That was James's word to describe most of the rare books I was to spend my morning organizing. In 1895, just three months after delivering "Is Life Worth Living?" at Holden Chapel, James explained to George Howison, the founder of the philosophy department at Berkeley, that this belief about the value of the history of philosophy "came out of one who is unfit to be a philosopher because at bottom he hates philosophy, especially at the beginning of a vacation, with the fragrance of the spruces and sweet ferns all soaking him through with the conviction that it is better to *be* than to define your being." At its best, according to James, philosophy helps us make sense of life—to understand it, yes, but also to awaken us to its nuances and potentialities. The love of wisdom is supposed to guide us in living more fully, more meaningfully. But in the modern era, which reached its height in the writings of Descartes and Hobbes, philosophy had begun to lose its existential bearing. James didn't have much time for it, particularly at the beginning of a camping trip in the Adirondacks, a vacation he routinely took to restore his mental health. Large swaths of European thought didn't make *sense* of life, but rather rationally deconstructed it, overintellectualizing everyday practices and reducing the richness of human experience to a small number of discrete aspects. In the process, James thought, philosophy, which had the potential to be the most significant of intellectual pursuits, became "trivial."

I reached into my first box of the day for a book that was largely responsible for James's disgust: the first Latin edition of Descartes's most famous work, *Dissertatio de Methodo*, published in Amsterdam in 1644. There was one passage from Descartes that I wanted to read before getting down to the business of cataloging. It was the heart and soul of rationalism, arguably the most important claim of modern philosophy—"*Cogito ergo sum*" (I think, therefore I am). American philosophers working in the nineteenth century were a diverse group of thinkers, but they found common ground in their critique of this seemingly innocuous statement. The *Cogito* is the concluding argument of a very intense investigation. American philosophers such as James appreciated Descartes's inquiring spirit and the skepticism that drove his philosophical argument, but they also thought that the Frenchman had ultimately reached the wrong conclusion.

Descartes wrote *Discourse on the Method* as a response to a growing crisis in Europe. In the first half of the sixteenth century the Catholic Church had begun to come undone. In 1517 Martin Luther had tacked his 95 Theses, which outlined the sins of the Catholic Church, to the door of All Saints' Church in Wittenberg, Germany. This act initiated a dramatic break from the hierarchy and dogmatism of Catholicism that had structured much of everyday life for centuries. The theological crisis intersected with the scientific revolution: The findings of Galileo, Newton, and Kepler began to challenge long-standing assumptions about human nature and its relationship to the wider natural world. According to Galileo, we were not the unquestionable center of the universe. We were, at best, spinning around something much larger than ourselves and, at worst, simply spinning out of control. Unlike the dogmatic certainties that had held sway since the Middle Ages, the truths that science struck upon were flexible or, more frighteningly, provisional, ready to be overturned at any moment. At the same time, the discovery of the New World presented not only a social and political crisis but also a metaphysical one. For most Europeans, this discovery was tantamount to making contact with life from another planet. Modern skepticism was born at this historical moment and served as the backdrop for Descartes's philosophical system.

I flipped through a second edition of Descartes's *Meditations*—once owned by Royce—which I'd found wedged beneath the chesterfield: "The Meditation of yesterday has filled my mind with so many doubts, that it is no longer in my power to forget them . . . and, just as if I had fallen all of a sudden into very deep water, I am so greatly disconcerted as to be made unable either to plant my feet firmly on the bottom or sustain myself by swimming on the surface." Drowning. Hyperbolic doubt is a little like that. Descartes understood that your own body weight pulls you down against your will, and you eventually suck in water instead of air. When set on the high seas of doubt, it is tempting to cling to a small handful of things about which one is fully, absolutely certain. In the absence of certainty, some of us manufacture it from scratch and then defend it as if life depends on it. This is what Descartes did with the *Cogito* argument. In response to the existential crisis of his day—and the skepticism it begat—he produced one truth that could underpin human knowledge. Many things, according to Descartes, can be doubted: Perhaps institutions of authority are deeply flawed; perhaps our senses mislead us; perhaps the material world is just the grand hoax of God; perhaps God isn't even in charge, and the Devil, the real master of the universe, rejoices in deceiving us. But there was one thing he could not doubt—that he was a thinking thing. What is most essential—or, in his words, "clear and distinct"—about an individual is the existence of his or her mental capacities.

Turning back to the *Discourse*, I looked down at the short Latin sentence. Just three words. Most American thinkers agreed: The *Cogito* was brilliant and rock solid—but more than a little strange. The essential truth that Descartes eventually uncovered is merely this: that to the extent that he is thinking, he exists as a *"res cogitans,"* a thinking thing. This was the sort of truth rationalists could believe in, one that did not require empirical evidence. It became what Descartes called his "Archimedean point," an axiom upon which he could rebuild the human sciences and prove the existence of God. He'd struck upon the something that would keep his world from going to pieces.

Despite the argument's logical consistency and originality, thinkers working in the wake of Descartes slowly came to a rather disturbing opinion—namely, that many brilliant discoveries are deeply misguided. Something can be a certainty yet also be absolutely meaningless. Thinkers such as James suggested that defending brilliant but meaningless certainties is quite foolish. Descartes was so determined to secure human knowledge—to maintain order and rationality—that he would sacrifice almost anything to complete his task. American intellectuals of the late nineteenth century tended to believe that he'd sacrificed the very thing good philosophers were meant to address: the uncertainties and deep existential questions of life itself. They pointed out that in its search for order, the *Cogito* argument had relinquished a question that was supposed to remain central: What makes life significant? According to James and Dewey, Descartes's fixation on being a "thinking thing" ended up prioritizing mental powers over all other aspects of sentient life and ignored the basic bodily processes of organisms, the social contexts that ground our lives, and the emotions that touch us deeply. James, Royce, and Hocking were also quick to point out that Descartes's argument worked well to prove his own existence as a thinking thing, but it said absolutely nothing about the value of the world outside his immediate subjective life. This is what most philosophers of this century called "the problem of other minds." Cartesian rationalism was a type of island mentality, solipsistic to a fault. In James's words, "Descartes's life was absolutely egotistic."

American pragmatists had a problem with Descartes's conclusions but also with his philosophical method. They suggested that searching for a single absolute truth was not the appropriate, much less the only, response to personal or intellectual insecurity. Sometimes insecurity was a good thing. In many cases, it meant that you had the chance to be free.

I'd spent the better part of a decade defending something that wasn't really worth defending, something allegedly certain but largely meaningless: a supposedly well-ordered marriage. At least ostensibly, it would have lasted well into old age if I hadn't realized that defending it, working on it, arguing about it was wasting the life it was meant to secure. Long after my marriage had fallen apart in the concrete, I spent many years defending the solidity of marriage in the abstract, but the abstraction ultimately did little to assuage my most personal feelings of insecurity and isolation.

I turned Descartes over in my hands and laid him to rest in the box. James had concluded his note to George Howison in 1895 with a stark admission: "I am a victim of neurasthenia, and the sense of hollowness and unreality that goes with it. And philosophical literature will often seem to me the hollowest thing." Neurasthenia was the nineteenth-century term for depression and the irritability, headaches, and lassitude that went with it. Today, it is usually attributed to biological causes, to the fate of our physiology; and James the medical student knew there was something to this. But James the humanist was unwilling to believe that a life's efficacy was determined by material factors beyond our control. He would spend much of his later life arguing that the meaning of human existence turned on freedom. Many of the most celebrated figures from the history of philosophy, however, overlooked this empowering idea.

Who was the original owner of these first editions of Descartes? It was not, I was almost sure, a lover of Jamesian freedom. I'd begun to stack the remaining seventeenth-century books on Hocking's desk: a good-size pile edging a hundred, with the two most valuable on top. I picked up the smaller of the two and opened it to the cover page. It wasn't likely, but it wasn't impossible either: Maybe the Descartes volumes had once been owned by this author—Thomas Hobbes. It was *De Cive: Philosophical Rudiments Concerning Government and Society*, 1651. This was the first English version of the work, which, along with *Leviathan*, secured Hobbes's place in the pantheon of philosophical greats.

Hobbes met Descartes in Paris in 1648. According to most accounts, the meeting between them was respectful, if lukewarm. Respectful because Hobbes recognized that Descartes was a genius when it came to logic and geometry, lukewarm because Hobbes was a materialist and Descartes was decidedly not when it came to the human soul. But as American thinkers such as Royce observed, there were deep and abiding similarities between the two thinkers. Like the *Discourse on the Method*, Hobbes's *De Cive* had been written in a time of crisis. The Reformation, which had so pointedly challenged notions of truth and authority for Descartes, spilled over into the political strife of the Anglo-Spanish War. In 1588 Hobbes's mother heard the news of the impending invasion of England by the Spanish Armada; terrified by the prospect, she went into labor prematurely, giving birth to Thomas. Looking back on the circumstances of his birth, Hobbes writes that "fear and I were born twins together." The religious wars of Europe got under way in 1618 with the Thirty Years' War, and Britain itself fractured along religious lines in the English Civil War about a quarter of a century later. So Hobbes was not crazy or pessimistic when he imagined—for the first time in *De Cive*—that life in the state of nature, in the absence of civil society, was best described as a *"bellum omnium contra omnes"*—a war of all against all. In this tumultuous historical setting, Hobbes's objective was not wholly different from that of Descartes: Both men were in search of security.

As the Chicago pragmatist John Dewey, a friend of James's, argued in 1918, Hobbes wanted desperately to find a solid basis on which to rebuild political authority. Hobbes was a Royalist, which meant that he fled England when the Civil War broke out in 1642, and he wrote this first edition in response to the beheading of Charles I. For Royalists everywhere, the execution of the king was a tragedy of unprecedented proportions. Not only did it signal the continuation of the political crisis in Britain, it also put a point on a belief that had gained currency in the previous century— namely, that kings and queens were not divinely appointed. The execution, for many, amounted to the death of God. Under these dramatic circumstances, Hobbes undertook the difficult task of *rationally* justifying the power of the monarchy. He realized that the foundational principle for grounding modern politics could not be derived from the hitherto unquestionable divine right of kings. Instead, it had to emerge from the rational self-interest of individuals who faced real social and political problems. Hobbes argued that when confronted with chaos, all rational individuals should prefer lockstep order over the risks of freedom. They should agree to institute an absolute monarch, what Hobbes termed the "Leviathan," to maintain some semblance of peace and security. The modern social contract was born. Dewey conceded that this was a brilliant philosophical move, but one that stood to jeopardize personal freedom for centuries to come.

I cracked open the brittle cover of the first-edition *Leviathan*. Today, the first page of a book is often its most boring part—a bunch of copyright information or some banal, platitudinous dedication. But in the seventeenth century it was often the most informative. If you understand the etching on the frontispiece of Hobbes's *Leviathan*, you don't really have to read the rest.

Even before finishing the manuscript, Hobbes began to consult Abraham Bosse, a French artist who would be commissioned for the etching for the frontispiece. Hobbes's intention was to depict an argument that was three hundred pages in the making. After dozens of false starts and failed attempts—revisions that drove Hobbes to distraction—Bosse pulled it off.

Hobbes's Leviathan is represented by a giant king, arms raised Rocky-style, looming over a landscape that is dwarfed by comparison. This is no simpering aristocrat of the seventeenth century. In his right hand the king holds a sword. In his left, a crosier. He is covered in chain mail from the neck down. Above him are inscribed the words from the book of Job to describe God: *"Non est potestas Super Terram quae Comparetur"* (No power on earth can compare to him). His chain mail is a thing of artistic beauty. If you look closely, though, you see that it isn't chain mail at all. What looks like metal links are, in fact, the profiles of tiny men and women—the subjects of the Leviathan. Hobbes argued that legitimate and absolute authority came from the rational self-interest of each and every person. Each subject gives up his or her (yes, there are women in the chain mail too) personal liberty in return for the security that the Leviathan provides. This quid pro quo became the basis of the social contract that underpinned the modern nation-state for the next three hundred years. And it was the hard core of Hobbes's philosophical project, which established rational principles for a political state that was less susceptible to civil war.

I squinted at the chain mail. All those frightened little people. They weren't forced to obey the king, but their fear of insecurity compelled them to take orders. The subjects of the Leviathan couldn't have cared less about one another; they weren't standing arm in arm out of some deep sense of fellow feeling. Hobbes's "non-tuism" (literally, "non-you-regarding") suggested that people were pointedly indifferent to the interests of their neighbors; fear and self-interest are what brought them together. For most of my life, despite my on-again, off-again love for American philosophy, Hobbes and Descartes had been my go-to men when it came to explaining human behavior. People were generally scared sense-less and would do just about anything to quell their fears. They cooperated, became friends, and fell in love, but at the end of the day they loved exactly one person—themselves. Relationships were, at best, functional: ingenious ways of coping with individual frailties and neuroses. Non-tuism made sense too. It wasn't that I had malevolent intentions when it came to others; I'd just never cared much about them.

Looking up from my boxes of philosophy, I caught sight of a small marble bust on the corner of the mantel behind the picture of James and Royce. It wasn't Hobbes or Descartes: It was Dante. A five-inch monument to humanistic genius. The contrast between the *Divine Comedy*, published in 1320, and the tracts of modern philosophy was not lost on American thinkers of the nineteenth century. Hocking—along with every other thinker from the Golden Age of American Philosophy—loved Dante as much as he disliked Hobbes and Descartes. In 1843 Emerson produced the first English translation of Dante's *La Vita Nuova*, or *The New Life*, a work the Transcendentalist called "the Bible of Love." The poet James Russell Lowell, who was a frequent visitor at the James and Peirce households and who, with the help of Charles Eliot Norton, installed the *Divine Comedy* as a centerpiece of educational life at Harvard in the 1860s, explained the poem's appeal. It was, in Lowell's words, "a diary of the human soul in its journey upwards from error through repentance to atonement with God." It was to be read personally, tenderly, as a how-to manual for living a meaningful life. Personal salvation wasn't just a single triumphant moment of beatific insight, as some of the Transcendentalists had suggested. Moments of insight do occasionally happen, but Dante's point is that the real trick to salvation is that there's no trick to salvation. It's just work, plain and not at all simple. Salvation is revealed in the long road of freedom and love. Pragmatists like Peirce and James—who assumed the mantle of philosophy from Emerson after the Civil War—knew that this journey was an arduous one and that it almost always began in hell. It was a journey filled with Lyme disease and mouse droppings and frigid water, but one in which you could still possibly make a bit of progress toward the light.

I was, once again, getting offtrack, but I didn't care. I went to Hocking's desk, sat down, and went rooting through one of its side drawers. The book I found was thickly bound and "diced"—

scored with a diamond pattern on the cover. The leather was still soft, and it had been read so often, so ardently, that the raised sections of the binding had developed a high patina. It was Hocking's copy of the *Divine Comedy*. I grabbed the bust from the mantel and placed it with the book in the box with Hobbes and Descartes. If I had to slog my way through "trivial" philosophical research, Dante could join me. Over the last month, I'd begun some arcane cataloging system for the books, the rubric of which I'd wholly forgotten by that point. I just needed to pack up the rest of the seventeenth-century books—the ones the thief had missed—and move them to the dry storage container the Hockings were renting a few miles away. There I could separate them by date—or was it by topic?—and type out all the annotations and bibliographical information. This would be tedious. But maybe I'd learn something along the way.

When I finished packing the books, it was almost noon. Eleven boxes in total: 151 books, 110 first editions. I wondered why Hocking had been intent on rescuing so many of the books that American thinkers had roundly criticized. His collection proved that despite their attempt to twist free of the European tradition, American thinkers still pored over the writings of Descartes, Spinoza, Leibniz, Hobbes, Wolfe, Locke, Kant, Mill, and Hegel. Hocking's teachers thought that you had to understand an entire tradition in order to criticize it. Today, philosophers aren't supposed to care about the past. They're supposed to construct sound philosophical arguments that are timeless, divorced from the cultural and historical context from which they first emerged. This ahistorical approach, however, often has the strange consequence of producing theories that have no bearing on any time or place. Dante was timeless, but only because every single character of the *Comedy* was a figure from the past. Most of the figures in the *Inferno* and *Purgatory* had screwed up in any number of infamous ways, but their screwups were worth talking about. American philosophers felt this way about Descartes and the rest of their European interlocutors: misguided but instructive—even, and perhaps especially, in their mistakes.

I shoved the last of the books into the trunk of the Outback and headed for their new home.

North Conway Dry Storage is situated on a largely deserted road at the base of Mount Washington and looks like a cross between a mausoleum and a meth lab. But, at least on that fall day, it would be relatively warm and dry. I punched in the code for the giant maroon gate, which opened slowly and closed behind me as I rolled through with a trunkful of philosophical corpuses. Box F, Crate 73: The Hockings had yet to discuss any final plans for permanent donation of the books, so I could only hope that this would not be the library's final resting place. Box F was a long, echoey, fluorescent-lit hallway lined with locked doors. On my first visit, nearly a year earlier, the room had seemed like something out of a dystopian nightmare. By this point, however, it had become another home away from home. Crate 73, at the end, was the size of a large outhouse. I pulled the key to its padlock, which Jennifer had given me, from my pocket. She was, among other things, profoundly trusting despite the fact that books had been stolen from the family. The padlock came off, and the door creaked open. The books already filled three dozen neatly stacked packing boxes. The hallway was climate-controlled, but fall in New England meant that the cement floor was still pretty chilly. Over the course of a year of work, I'd learned to come prepared. I pulled two large insulated sleeping pads from the container and spread them out in the hallway. My desire to go for a hike was quickly fading, and I decided to read for the rest of the afternoon. But I refused to waste it on Descartes or Hobbes; I dug around in the boxes until I found the well-worn treasure from Hocking's desk and reacquainted myself with Dante.

In his younger years, William James was obsessed with the *Inferno*, the first movement of the *Comedy*, terror and despair perfectly suiting his melancholy. He recognized something familiar in the torture of its hell-bound souls: They were unwilling or unable to free themselves from their past. James grew up in a controlling household, with a father he both worshipped and feared. Henry James Sr. had inherited a sizable family fortune in midlife, which freed him from traditional occupational duties and allowed him to obsess over his children's upbringing, which drove most of the James children to one form of mild insanity or another.

Most of William's decisions as a young man reflected his father's desires (Alice Gibbens, whom James married in 1878, was explicitly Henry Sr.'s choice). Admittedly, the days in James's Inferno passed, but they did so in accord with someone else's plan. There was no such thing as a future, at least not in the sense of being able to transcend the present moment on one's own terms. It was this fixity that James and Dante found truly unbearable. According to Dante, the damned

> Cursed God and their own parents
> And humankind and then the place and time
> Of their conception's seed and of their birth.

As a teenager, James played with the idea of becoming a painter. He fixated on Delacroix's *La Barque de Dante*, a massive work that depicts an early moment from Canto XIII of the *Comedy*. As Virgil ferries Dante across the river Styx, the damned writhe in the water below. Virgil stands straight and resolute; Dante just cowers. James wrote to his brother Henry that Delacroix was "always and everywhere interesting," in no small part because the existential situation he depicts—that one can, at any point, go overboard and irreparably lose his bearings—is at once so universal and so pointedly personal.

As James grew older, he began to work his way out of hell through a philosophical purgatory of trial and error—the result of which became an important aspect of his pragmatism. Although he was interested in mystical transcendence, pragmatism is usually geared toward more modest, earthly goals. It has a perfectionist streak, but its idealism is in the process, always on the way. In James's words, "ever not quite." This mountain of Purgatory has its appeal. It is realistic but hopeful—the one place in the *Comedy* where individuals make progress on their own terms. At the beginning of *Purgatory*, at the base of the hill, Dante asks his guide, Virgil, how long it will take to summit the mount. Virgil informs him that there isn't a concrete answer: The duration of the ascent depends on the pilgrim, on his virtue, and, more important, on his self-knowledge. Volition, personality, insight— these actually matter in Purgatory. The mountain, at least the way Dante describes it, is the place where lives are won or lost— "Wherein the human spirit doth purge itself / And to ascend to heaven becometh worthy." The souls in Purgatory retain many of their human attributes, and their acts of repentance are meant to be frighteningly familiar. The souls in Purgatory look a hell of a lot like us, working out the problems of being human. And these problems, for Dante, were the problems of freedom and love.

To what extent are we free? And if we are free, what should we do with our freedom? Dante's questions were central to American philosophy. As I sat there at the base of Mount Washington reading about Purgatory, I still wasn't exactly sure what love had to do with salvation, but Dante had given a clue. At the beginning of the *Divine Comedy*, Dante meets Beatrice. She's no ordinary woman. She's a vision of a woman, a symbol of beatific love. Of course she vanishes immediately, and Dante spends the next hundred cantos trying to catch another glimpse of her. That she doesn't love him back immediately is what makes the story so tantalizing, and so realistic. He follows her, dreams about her, writes about her, secretly lusts after her. Her vision is what propels him through the underworld and up the mountain. The story of the *Comedy* is the story of Dante's attempt—his bungling, faltering, laborious attempt—to love in the right way.

I made a halfhearted effort to comb through the other boxes, but after inspecting the remains, I only ended up imagining how Dante might have evaluated these long-dead thinkers. Most of them wouldn't have fared particularly well. Many titans of modern philosophy weren't particularly worried about freedom and love, and were happy to sacrifice them on the altar of order and rationality. Dante would not have approved. James developed an entire philosophy in protest. At least since Emerson's day, American philosophy has made its name by deviating from such modern European thinkers as Descartes, attempting to resuscitate the concepts of free will and genuine communion that Dante held so dear. Transcendentalists and pragmatists alike made this departure in their insistence that philosophy should not be exclusively concerned with abstract concepts and "pure reason," but was meant to help individuals work through the trials of experience in their New World.

Under the fluorescent lights, I lost all sense of time. I read Dante for hours, hunched over on my insulated mat. I was making progress, although not the sort I'd planned on, and I stopped only when I realized how light-headed I was. I'd skipped lunch (and dinner), but perhaps there was something in the car. I stepped out into the New Hampshire darkness. Another day had passed me by. The backseat was empty except for a six-pack of Rolling Rock. I thought about drinking it in the car, but that seemed too cold and lonely, so I took it inside and drank it where I could keep reading. I'd have to bring a real, live companion the next time I came up, I thought, and I really would go for that hike. I clearly needed my own Beatrice. By midnight my six-pack was gone. Three hours later I stopped reading. I woke up on the concrete floor in the wee hours of the morning, just in time to head south toward UMass Lowell to teach a group of undergrads about American intellectual history. After class, Carol pulled me aside to inform me that I looked like hell, which wasn't too far from the truth.

I should have hated Carol.

In the academic world, permanent teaching jobs are hard to come by. In the discipline of philosophy, they are bloody scarce. Each fall, thousands of newly minted Ph.D.s are released into the job market, most of them hoping to secure an underpaid junior teaching job at a college that might eventually lead to a safe, cushy tenured position in which they can ride out the rest of their career. The whole thing resembles Hobbes's nasty, brutish state of nature, where life is a "perpetuall warre of every man against his neighbor."

In this war, Carol and I had been enemies. We had both interviewed for the exact same job, a coveted tenure-track position that would allow the victor to live in Boston and enjoy a reverse commute to Lowell, and out of hundreds of candidates we had been selected as finalists for the post. The search committee voted on which of us to hire and came out evenly split—half of the committee wanted me, a specialist in American philosophy; the other half wanted her, with her strengths in feminist ethics and Kant. This situation could have resulted in a failed search, meaning that neither of us would have gotten the job, but instead, the provost, in a moment of Solomon-like wisdom, managed to make two tenure-track positions available, and we were offered identical positions. The fight was not over, however—we both assumed that only one of us could get tenure six years down the line. She was, in other words, the competition. And Hobbes would have encouraged me to hate her.

A hundred years ago, men began to compete with women in the field of philosophy. Before then, men stole ideas from them, were inspired by them, and relied on them for domestic and material support but rarely considered them peers. Even women as brilliant as Carol rarely became philosophy professors—they became Charlotte Perkins Gilman or Agnes Hocking, influencing the field from the sidelines. When they did manage to sneak their way into the discipline, they usually fled to an intellectual no-man's-land—colleges in St. Louis or California—where the Ivy League patriarchy had yet to be fully entrenched. Marietta Kies, one of the first women to teach philosophy in North America, had to go to Michigan for her doctorate in the 1880s, and then had to move even farther west to get a permanent post at a tiny liberal arts college in Oakland, California. Women in philosophy nowadays have only a slightly easier time of it. Those who make it through their doctorate and land a tenure-track position remain a rare and especially sharp breed of intellectual.

Carol had the uncanny knack for argumentation that defines what is known as "analytic philosophy." Today, there are two schools of philosophy: the analytic school and everything else. Analytic philosophers tend to understand philosophy as the task of parsing arguments, breaking down complex and confusing phenomena by analyzing their constituent parts. Like scientists at a laboratory bench, these thinkers dissect human experience in order to see how it ticks. Of course, this dissection often results in the distortion or destruction of the experience itself, but many analytic philosophers don't seem to care. They scrutinize for a living. Scrutinize. It's a strange word. Literally, it means to sort through the *scruta*, the shit. Carol scrutinized me just for the fun of it and came to the conclusion that American philosophy was full of it—a mess of such ill-defined concepts as "freedom" and "experience." I consoled myself by insisting that she didn't understand it. The point of American philosophy isn't to be "right" in any definitive sense of the word; such Cartesian certainty struck most American pragmatists as overly simplistic or just plain arrogant. The point of American philosophy is not to have a specific, rock-solid point, but rather to outline a problem, explore its context, get a sense of the whole experiential situation in which the problem arises, and give a tentative yet practical answer. Carol, perhaps rightly, figured that anyone could tackle problems at this vague level of specificity. The role of a philosopher, she thought, was to be much more specialized.

Beginning in the 1950s, analytic philosophers began to make their definitive departure from the rest of the humanities. They were intent on making philosophical reflection rigorous, which meant aligning the discipline, which has been historically coupled with literature and the arts, with mathematics and logic. Writing twenty-five hundred years ago, Thucydides anticipated what would happen to scholars who refused to support the analytic domination of the field: They suffered the fate of the neutral Melians in the Peloponnesian War and were simply wiped out. American philosophers were, in fact, a bit like that. From its inception, classical American philosophy represented a philosophical middle ground, aiming to mediate between competing theoretical schools, between the thinkers who focused on the trees and those who saw only the forest. American philosophers such as Peirce and James wanted to see forest *and* trees. In this they were not unlike the German philosopher Immanuel Kant, who'd spent the last decades of the eighteenth century bridging the gap between empiricism and rationalism, the two dominant strains of modern philosophy. According to Kant—and the pragmatists—the gap needed to be bridged so that the disparate parts of human experience (which the empiricists analyzed) could be unified in some objectively valid form of knowledge (the sort of knowledge that rationalists cherished).

American philosophers picked up where Kant left off, suggesting that careful scrutiny, the kind Carol was so good at, was indeed valuable, but could go only so far in making sense of human experience. There was also a holistic, qualitative dimension to experience that couldn't be dissected in order to be understood. To get a sense of this unity, American pragmatists drew heavily from such post-Kantian thinkers as Schiller, Coleridge, Schelling, and Goethe: Romantics who wanted to revive the idealism of Dante and even Plato. These Romantics were also the thinkers, in the European tradition, who began to think through a notion of freedom that would be more amenable to an American ethos. In the twentieth-century battle for academic philosophy, pragmatists remained too committed to this idealism to be good analytic philosophers and too committed to science to join the rest of the humanities. So American philosophy died off or headed for the hills of northern New Hampshire. And that's where Carol and I were headed on one beautiful day in late November.

My previous trip to West Wind had sparked a hope to find a Beatrice to lead me through Purgatory, but I now realized how misguided that hope had been. Carol was a friend, and Beatrice and Dante weren't friends, and they certainly weren't equals. Carol wasn't a figment of my imagination, either, or some chaste vision of godly perfection—she could swear a blue streak, think circles around me, and drink me under the table. She and her husband had been in a long-distance relationship for most of her adult life, a circumstance that seemed to suit her quite nicely. She was, in a word, independent. As we drove up to West Wind that first time, we chatted nonstop as we usually did at the office or over beers. This time I told her about my divorce—about which she had absolutely nothing to say—and we chatted about pragmatism and how it intersected with Dante's vision of beatific love.

Carol reminded me of something I'd conveniently overlooked on my last trip to visit the books: Beatrice had been a real person. Her name was Beatrice Portinari, and Dante had seen her one morning in Florence, walking arm in arm with her "maiden ladies." She was one of the wealthiest, smartest, most self-possessed young women in the city. Dante was immediately infatuated with her, but he didn't have the nerve to approach her. She was way out of his league. So he did what any self-respecting poet would do: He turned her into his muse. If he couldn't get to know her in life, he would fashion her to his liking in a work of art. This made for a great story, but her idealization obscured how impressive she actually was.

"You brought your sleeping bag, right?" I asked Carol.

She nodded. "But I think I might've forgotten my pillow."

"Don't worry," I said without thinking. "You can use mine."

We were getting close to West Wind. Mount Chocorua's rocky face was shrouded in dusky clouds, and the evergreens on the road's shoulder began to close in. We caught Route 113 and left the land of fluorescent lights and street signs behind. Why had I promised her my pillow? I asked myself. It made absolutely no sense. I *really* loved that beat-up thing. It was grimy and lumpy in all the right ways. Over the years, the down had slowly fallen out, so that it now squished right around my head like a little cave where I could escape the grimmer parts of my waking life. I wouldn't be able to sleep without it. Maybe she'd forget I had mentioned it.

"It's pretty spooky up here," she admitted.

West Wind *was* spooky for a newcomer. If I were Hobbesian about the whole trip, I wouldn't care how spooky it was for her. But somehow I did care.

DIVINE MADNESS

The library was pitch-dark when we arrived. We turned on the lights just long enough to arrange our things and hit the sack— separate sacks. The following morning marked the first of many spent exploring West Wind together. The boxes in dry storage represented but a small fraction of the library; there were still thousands that needed to be sorted. This day would be spent gathering the last of the rarest books and shuttling them up to North Conway for safekeeping.

Saving the rarest books often meant agreeing on how old a book had to be in order to be considered for storage. After extended deliberation we reached what, in hindsight, appears to be a random decision: 1845. These books would be stacked on the long oval table in the center of the first floor and would be trucked off to join the rest. We would eventually hire an appraiser to handpick the most valuable ones for donation. Further additions could be made on a case-by-case basis, but we would generally leave most of the nineteenth- and twentieth-century books behind. I knew that this meant missing dozens, if not hundreds, of valuable works, but for the time being, I couldn't see a way around it.

Carol paged through a slim, modest-looking volume of Emerson from 1878. According to our rule, we should have left this one for the mice. It was not Emerson's most famous work by any stretch of the imagination, but it was one of the more important ones if you were interested in his political views. A first edition of Emerson's *Fortune of the Republic* would bring enough at a Sotheby's auction to pay one of my students' tuition for a full year. And this one was inscribed by Emerson himself. It would be an exception to our rule.

Emerson gave this lecture for the first time in 1863, in the midst of the Civil War, and repeated it a dozen times over the next fifteen years, making revisions along the way. Unlike Hobbes, Emerson thought there were worse things than revolution, more dangerous things than the exercising of one's personal freedoms. To him, the American Revolution was the best thing that could have happened to this country because it signaled a final departure from external control. The Civil War provided equal, although different, opportunities. Carol opened to a random page, scanned it quickly, and read aloud: "'The end of all political struggle is to establish morality as the basis of all legislation . . . morality is the object of government. We want a state of things in which crime will not pay; a state of things which allows every man the largest liberty compatible with the liberty of every other man.'" This is even more radical than the thinking of John Locke, who said, "The end of law is not to abolish or restrain, but to preserve and enlarge freedom." For Emerson, political and legal order was not merely about protecting personal liberty but also—and always— about fostering the good life. The point isn't necessarily to live longer. It's to live freely and *well*. Carol smiled. "This is just like Kant," she said.

To Carol, the entire history of Western philosophy was about Kant. What came before him merely anticipated the philosophical moves that he would later master. And what came after him was either Kant warmed over or just plain wrong. She remains the only Kantian feminist I've ever met—every other feminist thinks he is completely irredeemable. In fact, American philosophers owed Kant a rather large debt. The diminutive professor from Königsberg, Germany, had initiated a massive philosophical project that the Transcendentalists and pragmatists extended through the nineteenth and twentieth centuries. Kant, unlike Hobbes and Locke, insisted that individual freedom—and therefore morality—was the foundation of social and political life.

Theorists prior to Kant were worried about political stability and the relative significance that personal liberty had in its pursuit, but for the most part they argued that moral theory had a relatively small role to play in political life. Hobbes and Locke diverged in many ways, but they agreed that people were generally moved by sensations, fears, and desires rather than by profound moral principles. For them, human reason was predominantly instrumental, an extension of an animalistic drive for self-preservation, and the wisest thing to do was to set up political institutions that could keep base instincts in check. Idealists such as Kant and Emerson, however, couldn't have disagreed more.

To Kant, human beings possessed unique capacities that separated them from the rest of the animal kingdom—the nasty realm of self-interest and beastly impulse. Kant argued that humans were not simply moved by the forces of their world but, at their best, were motivated by an internal, almost divine force he called rational will. Unlike porcupines and termites, humans had minds that were not buffeted by random sensations or experiences; they actively structured experience. Humans were creatures that could think and thereby self-legislate. By virtue of their active rational capacities, humans were the only beasts that could set duties for themselves, and therefore the only ones that could be morally responsible. The point of philosophy, for Kant, was neither to sublimate self-interest nor to construct systems that keep people in check, but rather to awaken individuals to their own active minds and thereby make them pointedly aware of their moral duty. This was a philosophical position many American thinkers could happily endorse. In 1842 Emerson tied American Transcendentalism directly to Kant, writing:

> What is popularly called Transcendentalism . . . acquired the name of Transcendental from the use of that term by Immanuel Kant, of Königsberg, who replied to the skeptical philosophy of Locke, which insisted that there was nothing in the intellect which was not previously in the experience of the senses, by showing that there was a very important class of ideas or imperative forms, which did not come by experience, but through which experience was acquired; that these were intuitions of the mind itself; and he denominated them *Transcendental* forms.

Ideas and imperative forms: Kant and Carol were all about them. These forms allowed us to escape the vicissitudes of human experience, to hinge our destiny to something a bit more stable than our own fragile lives. All we have to do is make good on our rational capacities and recognize the convincing force of moral duty.

There was, however, a substantial difference between Emerson and Kant, but at that moment, with a daunting amount of work ahead of us, I couldn't put my finger on it. Instead of arguing with Carol—an activity I relished almost as much as she did—I wandered into an unexplored nook of the library to begin the book hunt. To my genuine surprise, she followed me.

I'd been steering clear of this cubbyhole in the library for months. It was supposedly filled with several hundred volumes on metaphysics and religious studies, but one couldn't really tell, because it was also packed with easels, rolls of canvas, and other sundry painting supplies. Though Hocking himself had been a painter, these were owned by his great-granddaughter, Katie, who'd recently made this part of the library her summer studio. For some reason Katie and I had rarely crossed paths, but the signs of her presence were everywhere. Half-finished paintings and pastels were strewn about, and sketches hung from most of the bookcases on the east side of the building. I thought about the half-finished painting of Agnes in the foyer and made a mental note to show Carol the portrait at the day's end. I couldn't fault Katie for the mess; the library was hers, after all. And I could empathize with a person who became so engrossed in a project that she ignored the mundane affairs of tidiness. I hated cleaning up after myself, almost as much as I hated cleaning up after others. So despite my recent fascination with religious experience, I'd assiduously avoided these shelves. Carol had absolutely no interest in religion or metaphysics, but the prospect of handling old books was more than enough to pique her interest. So we cleaned out the corner.

We gingerly shifted Katie's things out of the way, discovering that she was not the first of her family to use this section of the library as a makeshift studio. Her paintings were intermingled with much older artworks—tapestries, ceramics, paintings, sketches, and statues. Hocking had been raised on the pragmatism of James, but his commitment to idealism ran deep. This meant, among other things, that he'd been taken by the neoclassicism that defined the architectural and artistic world of nineteenth-century New England. For a time, American intellectuals were in love with all things Greek. They saw something in classical antiquity that modernity pointedly ignored—the idea that human beings were only fully human when they aspired to truly transcendent ideals. I took hold of a large bronzed bust and thought how pretentious it would look in my study at home. But it fit in nicely here. It was a replica of a famous statue in the Vatican, *Laocoön and His Sons*. It had scared the hell out of me on my first trip to Rome, when I was twenty.

In the *Aeneid*, Virgil tells us that Laocoön was the priest of Poseidon in Ancient Troy. When the Greeks, hoping to put an end to ten years of trying to conquer Troy, constructed the famous Trojan Horse and sailed away, Laocoön was the first one to sound the alarm. He stood on the beach outside Troy, pointed at the massive horse that the Greeks had supposedly left as a parting gift, and warned his fellow Trojans against drawing it into the city. "Beware," Laocoön cried, "of Greeks bearing gifts!" But the Trojans wanted nothing more than to believe that the long, heinous siege they'd suffered was finally over and that the Greeks were on their way home. Laocoön's message fell on deaf ears. So he did what any true seer would do: He screamed it at the top of his lungs one last time and thrust his sword into the horse's side. This caught people's attention. It also caught the attention of Apollo, who sided with the Greeks and decided to shut him up permanently. Two sea serpents slithered up onto the beach, wrapped themselves around Laocoön and his two sons, and carried them off into the foam.

I looked into Laocoön's eyes, bulging in their deep-set sockets. He knew he was going to die, but not before he watched his beloved sons drown. John Dryden compares Laocoön's struggle to the torture of a sacrificial ox that doesn't have the good sense to die immediately on the altar: truth teller as mutilated beast. This is what happens to people who have the bad luck of being painfully honest. Maybe being less honest and alive was better than being self-righteously dead, I thought. My recent experiment with honesty had been rather brutal. I'd harbored secret doubts about my marriage for years, but as I edged toward thirty, it had become harder and harder to remain silent. Days before my birthday party I'd sold the ring. This, in turn, precipitated an epic fight with my wife that erupted in front of all of my friends who'd come to Boston to celebrate the occasion of my birth. Carol had been there and had watched the entire thing go down. As my mother shook her head, as only a mother with deep Calvinist roots can, I wanted nothing more than to be utterly dead. The next day, I told everyone we were getting a divorce, and once I did that, there was no going back. Our two families wrapped themselves around us and pressured us to stay together. In the end, I didn't die, but there were many nights I wished I could. I set Laocoön down gently on a nearby desk and placed a hand on his chilly head. Being punished for telling a lie made sense, but being sacrificed on the altar of truth seemed cruel.

I helped Carol move the last easel out of the way and surveyed the shelves. I had hoped to find a treasure trove of nineteenth-century commentaries on religious traditions—from Hinduism to Jainism to Christianity—that had fascinated William Ernest Hocking, and I wasn't at all disappointed. Max Müller's famous *Sacred Books of the East* (all fifty of them) were lined up on the top shelf. Müller, a German philologist born in 1823, had been responsible for bringing the Vedas and other sacred Indian texts to Europe in the second half of the nineteenth century. I scanned the middle shelves: Christian apologetics from A to Z. William James's copy of Augustine was sandwiched between Royce's copies of Meister Eckhart and a bunch of other German mystics. Both James and Royce were critical of institutionalized Christianity, but their critique did not entail ignoring the offending traditions. A vellum binding, bleached white, peered out from the shadows. *Cosmologia Generalis, methodo scientifica pertractata.* First edition, 1731. This was the *Cosmology* of Christian Wolfe—the natural theologian from the early eighteenth century—also once owned by James. Halfway through the shelf I began to slow down enough to realize what I was looking at.

American philosophy often gets pooh-poohed by the rest of the world's thinkers as having no historical basis; in their attempt to be original, classical American philosophers, like James, supposedly turned their backs on any meaningful intellectual inheritance. What I was looking at was a massive amount of evidence to the contrary. James wasn't one to worship the past, but he hadn't ignored it either. He knew that the fastest way to become passé or obsolete is to inadvertently repeat history. It's tempting to ignore the past, to pretend it never happened. But it did—and it will again and again if one isn't careful.

I squatted down next to Carol to look at the bottom shelf. It was dusty and tightly packed, as if it hadn't been touched for a century. Considering the contents, it probably hadn't. Outside of Harvard's Widener Library, I'd never seen a collection of Plato and Neoplatonism like this. Most of the texts had belonged to Royce and had been bequeathed to Hocking when Royce died, in 1916. I glanced up at the shelves that were stacked on top. For Hocking, Plato had provided the solid metaphysical and ethical foundation upon which all religions rested. This isn't exactly true (the Vedas were much older), and Hocking surely knew this, but Plato loomed large in his thinking and, for that matter, in the development of American philosophy. One of the first things Emerson ever wrote was the Bowdoin Prize Essay at Harvard, "The Character of Socrates," in 1820. He was seventeen. This was the young man who would go on to be called the "Yankee Plato," a moniker that amused Carol. I handed her an eighteenth-century translation of the Neoplatonist Plotinus. His was a form of idealism, but not the German sort she was used to. This was one of Emerson's favorites, I explained. He thought it contained the seeds of philosophical genius, so he called it a "spermatic book." She thought that was hilarious. I'd not genuinely laughed for a long time, but that afternoon in the corner of a moldy library I remembered the nature of true laughter, the kind that plants itself in the pit of your stomach and grows into something life-affirming. For the average philosopher who's used to controlling each and every mental function, it's a strange sensation. You're laughing—you just can't help yourself.

Plato and Kant both thought that the point of life was to live a good one. But they disagreed about how exactly we should embody this goodness. For Kant, it boiled down to recognizing and acting upon moral duty; to live well was to follow a set of well-thought-out and well-defined rules. Being free amounted to being rational. He wasn't much for laughter. Laughter and passion were additive, not constitutive, when it came to living a good Kantian life. I turned back to the shelf and, arming myself with one of Royce's copies of Plato, settled into one of the Stickleys. Kant might have been right, but he was dead boring about it, at least by my lights. Plato and Socrates thought the good life couldn't be defined in this hard-and-fast way. Life, at its best, wasn't always to be lived strictly by the book. There's more freedom and feeling—the stuff of actual *life*—in the Platonic dialogues. The pursuit of the good life, for the Greeks, was a profoundly personal, emotion-laden, all-consuming quest for a beautiful soul.

The beautiful soul was worth sacrificing everything for. Everything! Socrates stands before his neighbors and says the unthinkable—that there is something worse than death: living an ugly, wicked, boring life. This is not the stuff of Kant's "pure reason." It's the stuff of personal vision, insight, and a foolhardy courage to speak the truth. According to William James, who read his share of Plato, it's all about the "zest." It's the zest that makes life significant. This is what Emerson found so attractive about Socrates. Socrates believed that the pursuit of the Good was a kind of divine madness. I paged through the *Phaedrus* and found one of my favorite bits: "The best things we have come from madness, when it is given as a gift of the god."

I felt Carol behind me. The *Phaedrus* is a crazy dialogue. The craziest. She peered over my shoulder long enough to read both pages and see a passage I'd obsessed over for nearly a year: "There is no truth to that story that when a lover is available you should give your favors to a man who doesn't love you instead, because he is in control of himself and the lover has completely lost his head. That would have been a fine thing to say if madness were evil, plain and simple."

"That's not particularly Kantian," she whispered. "Is it?"

Laocoön kept faithful watch over us as we made our way through Hocking's shelves that afternoon, providing a constant reminder of the pains that attend dangerous truths. I knew the other version of the Laocoön story—where he was killed for having sex in a sacred place. With that thought, I forced myself to concentrate on the books.

The shelf packed with Plato was amazing. Hocking had ordered it chronologically, from the earliest dialogues, through the Neoplatonism of Plotinus and Proclus, to a curious group of seventeenth-century thinkers called the Cambridge Platonists. At the end of the shelf was a well-worn first edition of Samuel Coleridge's *Aids to Reflection* from 1825. I looked at this collection more closely. Emerson had never grown tired of these thinkers, writing in 1850:

> Out of Plato come all things that are still written and debated among men of thought. Great havoc makes he among our originalities. We have reached the mountain from which all these drift boulders were detached . . . every brisk young man who says in succession fine things to each reluctant generation,—Boethius, Rabelais, Erasmus, Bruno, Locke, Rousseau, Alfieri, Coleridge,—is some reader of Plato, translating into the vernacular, wittily, his good things.

Whosoever would be a Platonist must be a nonconformist. Being a follower of Plato meant never following anyone ever again. The philosopher Boethius was charged with treason in fourth-century Rome. There are a number of different accounts of his execution; he was either clubbed to death or chopped up in little pieces for conspiring against the Ostrogoths, who had taken control of the Roman Empire. The fifteenth-century French writer Rabelais fared a bit better, but only because he went into hiding to escape being condemned as a heretic for satirizing the Catholic Church. And then there was Coleridge. Rebel of rebels, hero of heroes, he occupied a special spot in my heart. Emerson loved him too—he had read Coleridge's *Aids to Reflection* as a young man; this is where Emerson picked up his early interest in Plato and Plotinus. Coleridge's Romantic interpretation of the ancients put the difference between Plato's bold drama and Kant's strict system into stark relief.

Coleridge—following a long line of Platonic thinkers—believed that Truth was realized through a sort of inner calling that granted each person partial access to the reality of the Divine. Every person could attend to this individual calling if he or she had the courage to take heed. For Coleridge, Socrates was courage personified; in the *Apology*, the Greek says that he pursues the Good and the True with the help of a *daimonion*—a "divine something"—that warned him against making bad decisions. Socrates listened to this *daimon* and therefore ended up living and dying nobly. The implication for Coleridge was clear: Those who fail to listen to the voices in their heads screw up royally. I knew all about these voices. One had warned me about getting engaged, and then about getting married, and then about staying married. If only I had taken its advice sooner. I'd watched Carol get married while my little *daimon* said all sorts of inappropriate things. My wife and I had traveled from Boston to Vancouver to hear my new colleague say her vows to another man. I'd forced myself to ignore the voice in my head, to lean over to my wife of the time and say in as convincing a voice as possible, "They're going to be happy together." I think I almost believed it at the time.

Listening to your *daimon* isn't necessarily easy. Coleridge gave it a go as a young adult. He had great plans to start what he

called a "pantisocracy," a coed agrarian commune based on principles of equality, of which his *daimon* silently approved. With
one of his Cambridge buddies, Robert Southey, Coleridge spent
months laying the groundwork for a utopian community in the
Susquehanna Valley, Pennsylvania. It would not be unlike the
Transcendentalist commune that sprang up at Brook Farm, outside
of Boston, in the 1840s. But Coleridge's idea was more than a
little insane—he had no experience farming and wouldn't have
survived a week on the eighteenth-century frontier. In prepara-
tion for the trip he married Sarah Fricker, the sister of Southey's
fiancée, in the belief that the foursome would form the core of their
new community. On this point, his *daimon* screamed at him to
stop, but he didn't have the guts to listen. After the wedding,
things quickly turned sour. Southey backed out of the pantisocracy, having decided that the simple life was untenable in the
modern world. Coleridge's idealism had led him to drop out of
Cambridge to raise money for this egalitarian society, so he was
left without a calling and with a wife he didn't really care for. In a
scathing letter to Southey he wrote, "You are lost to me, because
you are lost to Virtue." It was self-righteous anger born of the
frustration of an ill-suited marriage.

I thought for a moment about Coleridge's "Rime of the Ancient
Mariner," written months after his union to Fricker. Ostensibly it
is a poem about an old captain whose ship is lost at sea, but it's
actually a thinly veiled tale of a dismal marriage. It's no coinci-
dence that the whole ghastly poem is told to a group on their way
to a wedding party—it's a warning about what can happen in
such a union. The Mariner makes one really bad decision, and
the winds change, set the ship off course, and then fail to blow at
all. Motionless in the middle of nowhere:

> Day after day, day after day,
> We stuck, nor breath nor motion;

As idle as a painted ship
Upon a painted ocean.

Water, water, every where,
And all the boards did shrink;
Water, water, every where,
Nor any drop to drink.

Marriage can be something like this, and the albatross is always there, a sign of regret tied around one's tired, scrawny neck.

Many say that divorce is too easy today, but most of these people have never tried it. In my experience it's very difficult to shake the albatross. In Coleridge's day it was next to impossible. When he eventually got around to listening to his *daimon*, it told him to jump ship, and quickly. He did. He left his wife, and European Romantic poetry was born.

"I have to get a little air," I said, looking around to see where Carol was.

A voice answered from the middle of the library: "Okay, go on, I'll join you in a bit."

I grabbed a book, traversed the bookcase, and made my way toward the voice. She was hunched over a reading table that was stacked with dirty volumes, just underneath the portrait of Agnes Hocking. She looked up long enough for me to once again appreciate the uncanny resemblance, and she smiled and went back to work. I stepped out and took a long breath before wandering around the manor house through the uncut grass now covering nearly all of West Wind, and I looked down across the valley. At some point in the not-so-distant past the grassy stretch between the library and the mansion had been trimmed back so that the Hocking girls—now the Hocking women—could perform plays for the family on the lawn. I imagined a bunch of children assuming the roles of Shakespeare or Sophocles as their hyperintellectual

parents directed the whole affair. A scene of human culture, performed by babes, set in the vast expanse of nature. Coleridge
would've eaten it up with a spoon.

I walked across the back porch, laid my hands on the back
of a rickety Adirondack chair, and watched the sun pass slowly
overhead. My god, the light. It cast long, steady shadows down
the hill. I searched for my own among the shapes but eventually
gave up and turned my attention to Emerson. He met an aged
Coleridge in the early 1830s; Emerson was in his late twenties
and had escaped to Europe after the death of his first true love.
Coleridge's Platonism and Romanticism gave the young American
hope. As Socrates suggests in the *Phaedo* and the *Crito*, our physical existence is not the be-all and end-all. We should tether
our frail bodily lives to enduring ideals and hold fast, even if
doing so means giving up life. These ideals—the Real, the True,
the Good, and the Beautiful—were to be understood through
persistent reflection, the type of self-examination that Socrates
believed made life worth living. At the beginning of *Aids to
Reflection*, Coleridge states this clearly: "There is one art of which
every man should master, the art of reflection." Only through reflection and its product, self-knowledge, were self-determination
and self-possession possible. But self-determination wasn't just a
matter of looking back on your actions and wishing that you'd
paid closer attention to your *daimon*. For these Platonic thinkers
it was more mystical, more mysterious. Reflection brought you
into immediate contact with something beautifully transcendent.

I'd picked up a biography of Emerson—one of the very good
ones—on my way out of the library. The author, Robert Richardson, knew Emerson inside and out. I sat down and paged
through the biography slowly. Richardson had realized that
Emersonian self-knowledge wasn't the shallow self-help of the
twenty-first century, the solipsistic quest of a neurotic culture, but
rather an attempt to interrupt the neuroses of our society, to find
oneself in nature, and to consider the possibility that, in Emer-

son's words, "the currents of Universal Being circulate through me; I am part and particle of God."

As young men, Emerson and James hoped with all their being that this was true. A generation later, Virginia Woolf summed up Emerson's Romantic Platonism rather nicely: "[W]hat he did was to assert that he could not be rejected because he held the universe within him. Each man, by finding out what he feels, discovers the laws of the universe." This might sound like a bit of megalomania, as if the only thing in the world that matters is how one feels. But Emerson's message about nature and selfhood was equal parts empowering and humbling, restoring and effacing. As I sat in front of West Wind looking at the mountains in the afternoon's shadow and light, it made sense. It came close to William James's description of mystical experience as "a willingness to close our mouths and be as nothing in the floods and waterspouts of God." I sat perfectly quietly and listened. How did I feel? The question was a good one, which I'd not answered for a very long time. I found my answer when I looked over the ridge, to places where the trees had recently been clear-cut. New growth was already beginning to pop up, eking out a bit of life before the freezing temperatures set in.

Something strange happened to time at West Wind; it flew, or condensed, or simply vanished. I shook my head and pulled myself up from the Adirondack chair, shot a single glance at the sun, and blindly traced my way back to the library. Entering the library on a sunny afternoon was a bit like stepping into a dark, moist cave. Carol hadn't budged an inch in the last hour. She was still bent over, head down, writing furiously. "Are you okay?" I asked, mimicking her intensely strained posture. "How about a break?"

"No, it's okay. I want to finish this before dinner."

I wanted to tell her that there was no way to "finish this before dinner." In fact, I had the hunch that we'd never get our heads around West Wind. All you can do is pace yourself and enjoy the fact that there will always be something to do tomorrow.

"All right," I said, "but let's go to town in about an hour and have a drink." She didn't respond. I went and looked over her shoulder at the open title page: John Stuart Mill. *On Liberty*. London. 1859. First edition. I could now understand her concentration. This was a truly exceptional book. Along with Kant, Mill is one of the heroes of the liberal tradition. Unlike Kant, Mill was a thoroughgoing feminist who believed, like many American thinkers, that freedom was not simply a luxury for the chosen few.

I started to make some remark, but she told me to go back to my Plato.

It didn't take me long to lose myself in the shelves again. There were more than enough little mysteries to keep me occupied. The collection at West Wind was full of books from the personal libraries of American intellectuals, but the collection of Neoplatonic philosophy was different. I pulled out a surprising volume: Ralph Cudworth's *The True Intellectual System of the Universe* from 1678. First edition. The provenance was not American, but British. I guessed that Hocking had sought it out or, more likely, stumbled across it on one of his many trips to Europe. Turning the little masterpiece over in my hands, I wasn't sure that people would regard it as a collector's item, but they should. Ralph Cudworth, born in 1617, was similar to Hocking in that he was a nearly famous philosopher. He was part of the interesting group of thinkers known as the Cambridge Platonists, who took over two colleges at the University of Cambridge in the seventeenth century. Cudworth joined his more famous colleague Henry More as a fellow at Christ's College, which, along with Emmanuel College, was the stomping ground of the Puritans in Elizabethan times. I could draw some vague connection between the book and the formation of American thought, but making one between Cudworth and American philosophy was a bit harder. Christ's College is a weird nook of a college. It houses the smartest students at the university, as it has for the last three centuries. I remembered wandering through a parlor of Christ's while I was studying at

Cambridge (I was at Magdalene, a much more average college—but I liked to walk around and pretend), where I spotted a portrait of one of Christ's most illustrious students, Charles Darwin. Yes, this book must have had a rather strange history.

I stared down at the flyleaf: "T. H. Huxley," scrawled in what struck me as the tight script of a thirty-year-old. Over time, I imagined that Thomas Huxley's autograph loosened up a bit, as most of ours do, but it looked like whoever penned this signature was more than a little tightly wound. Huxley was the grandfather of Aldous Huxley, the author of the famous dystopian novel *Brave New World*, but he was more than just Aldous's grandfather. In the 1860s he was nicknamed "Darwin's bulldog," a name he came by honestly. He'd met Darwin in the early 1850s and was among the first to read *On the Origin of Species* when it came out in 1859. In November of that year he wrote to Darwin to express his adamant support:

> As for your doctrines I am prepared to go to the Stake if requisite . . . I trust you will not allow yourself to be in any way disgusted or annoyed by the considerable abuse & misrepresentation which unless I greatly mistake is in store for you . . . And as to the curs which will bark & yelp—you must recollect that some of your friends at any rate are endowed with an amount of combativeness which . . . may stand you in good stead—I am sharpening up my claws & beak in readiness.

Huxley was a ruthless defender of Darwin. I'd like to have friends like that—the type who would "go to the Stake" for me. What I found somewhat baffling was Huxley's willingness to defend Darwin while at the same time regularly and forcefully disagreeing with him. I couldn't conceive of a relationship like that, but Huxley and Darwin both fought and loved each other quite effectively. Huxley thought that Darwin's understanding of gradual evolution did not match up with the empirical evidence; he maintained that nature worked in leaps and bounds, through periods of evolutionary stasis followed by rapid spurts of growth. He also suggested that Darwin had downplayed the dangerous implications of his theory—namely, that *all* animals, including humans, had specific evolutionary histories. Darwin eventually got around to making this claim in *The Descent of Man* in 1871, but Huxley beat him to the punch by nearly a decade. In 1863 Huxley published *Evidence as to Man's Place in Nature* and became the first person in history to apply modern evolutionary theory to human beings.

I paged through the book. What was Darwin's bulldog doing reading Neoplatonism? It was possible that Darwin himself paged through this very book too. Improbable, but this was a time for indulging the improbable.

"Are you ready for that drink?"

"Nearly ready," I answered. I wanted to stay in the dimly lit library and figure out this little philosophical puzzle about Plato, Huxley, evolution, and American philosophy, but I wanted to get that drink more. My eyes and legs told me it was time to go; we could come back tomorrow. It was a long weekend, and I was happy that we wouldn't have to rush back to normal life. I thought Carol might want to go home after one night and was thrilled that I'd not completely alienated her in the last twenty-four hours. We picked up our belongings, packed the books, and headed for the door.

"Do you mind"—she paused, as if to acknowledge the strangeness of her request—"if we don't sleep at the library tonight? I actually didn't get much rest. Isn't there a place with a bed around here where two people could sleep?"

Yes, there were a bunch of shady motels on Route 16. They had "sordid affair" written all over them—one small bed per room, rented by the hour. But there was a place—I thought it might be called the Brass Heart Inn—at the base of Chocorua. I was sure we could find a room with twin beds or two small rooms. More appropriate for traveling with a married woman.

"Okay," I said, "no problem. But you have to promise me something."

"Oh?"

"You have to promise to wake up early to climb the mountain with me."

"Okay." She smiled. "Deal."

ON THE MOUNTAIN

"Carol—" I knocked at her door softly. "Carol, are you up?"

I waited for a good three minutes and then tried again in a forced whisper.

A little moan slipped under the door. "Seriously? The mountain? It's still dark."

I persisted, and after a few minutes the door creaked open. Carol, who is quite trim, emerged looking like the Michelin Man. She hadn't packed a pillow, but she'd apparently remembered an ancient puffy coat from her years in Canada. One of the few things Carol hates more than losing an argument or looking unfashionable is being cold.

"Not a word, colleague. This coat is warmer than dignity."

The roadside cafés in northern New Hampshire didn't open before dawn, so we were stuck with the pot of leftover coffee at the local gas station. We drove north on Route 16 through the tiny whitewashed town of Chocorua, past the James homestead tucked back a few hundred feet from the road. There's a rumor in town that his ashes are buried on the premises. James bought the farm in 1886, later adding land he purchased from William Ralph Emerson, Ralph Waldo's cousin and a partner at the nineteenth-century architectural firm Emerson and Fehmer. This Emerson actually built the James house on Irving Street in Cambridge.

After passing James's farmhouse on the right, we slowed to a creep. It was easy to miss the next turn, just an opening in the woods marked by a small wooden sign: BOWDITCH RUNNELLS STATE FOREST. Right before the sign, Scott Road veers off so suddenly that it's hard to tell it's a road at all. The year before, I'd learned this lesson the hard way—zipping to the trailhead in the dark, I'd blown by the turn and come frighteningly close to driving straight into the Chocorua River. This time I flipped on the high beams and covered the brakes. At some point in the past, massive hunks of granite had been dragged down the hill and assembled into what looked like a giant's house. It was Nickerson Mill, a sawmill that had been owned by Bunn Nickerson's family in the late nineteenth century. I'd heard that when the Bowditches— a family of Harvard intellectuals and conservationists—moved into the area, they bought the mill so that the Nickersons would quit polluting the stream and lake with sawdust. Now that I thought of it, Bunn's family owned much of the valley at one time. One of his distant relatives had run the Chocorua House, the town's earliest inn, in the 1860s. Bunn's comment to "go look around" on our first trip to West Wind now made a bit more sense. He had a feeling of ownership that came from having deep roots in the place.

A mile or so past the mill ruins, just before Scott Road deadended, I turned into a protected glen at the head of the Hammond Trail. Carol was now fully awake, but she wasn't ready to get out of the car. It was still dark, and the rustling of the leaves in the wind convinced her that the woods were haunted. Besides, there was the distinct possibility of meeting up with bears.

The first stretch of Hammond Trail, before it jogs up Bald Mountain and then to Chocorua, is covered with old beech trees that have a smooth gray bark. If you look at the trees in bear country, you can get a sense of the size of the creatures you're

dealing with. The previous year, I'd walked a mere ten minutes up
Hammond Trail before I saw a stand of trees with black pock-
marks in scattered sets of four at eye height on the trunks. This
beast wasn't huge, but it was big enough to mess up your face
without much trouble. I let this detail slide and avoided telling
her about Stonybrook, at the end of Scott Road. *That* place was
definitely haunted. It was one of the oldest farmhouses in the valley, built in the 1830s by my guess. It had been purchased by a
woman named Ellen Putnam at the end of the nineteenth century,
and it looked completely abandoned. Surrounded by beech and
hemlock, the stark white house looked like something out of
The Shining.

I suspected that any ghosts frequenting Hammond Trail would
have been quite pleased to have two philosophers trekking into
the forest again. William James, Henry Bowditch, and James Jack-
son Putnam had been colleagues in medical school in the 1870s.
Henry and William were fellow ghost hunters, séance sitters, and
psychical researchers (another tidbit I failed to tell Carol). Their
families vacationed together regularly and believed that woodland adventures and intellectual ones went hand in hand. Escapes
involved hiking, swimming, and sport—activities that allowed
American intellectuals of the time to convince each other that
they'd not gone entirely soft. Many of these excursions were also
meant as therapy to treat James's fragile psyche.

In the summer of 1875 the small group that James fondly
called the Adirondack Doctors traveled to Beede's Boarding
House, in Keene Valley in the Adirondacks in upstate New York.
After several summers visiting the mountains, the Harvard scholars
pooled their money and bought a tract of land and a few primitive
cottages. Their compound, Putnam Camp, was modeled on an
academic retreat set up by the previous generation of American
thinkers—"The Philosophers' Camp," which attracted members
of the Saturday Club, especially Emerson and the famous naturalist Louis Agassiz. James and his friends wanted to re-create

some of the Philosophers' Camp's glory in Keene. They managed handily, drawing their own unique crowd of luminaries: Carl Jung, John Dewey, Josiah Royce, and Royce's students, among them William Ernest Hocking, Richard Cabot, and Ella Lyman Cabot. Sigmund Freud, who visited the camp in 1909, reflected on his time there as the "most amazing experience" he'd had in the United States. From the very beginning, William James had similar feelings about the place. On his first trip in 1876, he remarked that creating the Putnam Camp was "the most salutary thing [he'd] ever [done]." Keene provided a setting where he could be his very best self—physically active, intellectually stimulated, and socially at ease. It was here, on a summer day in 1876, that James rendezvoused with Alice Gibbens, the woman who would later become his wife. In the summer of 1886 he and Alice decided to find another summer retreat near Chocorua, and the Bowditch and Putnam families came with them. I longed for a time when philosophy meetings took place in the outdoors—without the pretensions that come with conference rooms and titles.

I finally convinced Carol that it was no longer night, and we made our way slowly up the hill. It was still impossible to see the trail blazes, but the ascent, at least at first, was gradual and marked with rocks that one could make out in the gloaming. I looked up the hill at Carol's Michelin Man silhouette. I loved that silhouette.

The trail made its first switchback and turned sharply uphill. On a trip to Chocorua to visit his brother, Henry James had gotten lost on this trail, and even in broad daylight it took him several hours to make his way back to camp. The sun was still not up, and leaves had fallen the previous week, which meant that we could go badly astray or slip to our deaths. Thoreau might be right, I thought, that "an early-morning walk is a blessing for the whole day"—but only if one actually survives to see the day. So we found a little outcropping of rocks halfway up the mountain and sat down in the darkness. The sun would've been nice at the top, but there was something strangely magical about this time and place, a sort of "not quite" that lingered just long enough for one actually to savor the coming of dawn.

I'd heard about this mountain long before my acquaintance with William James. I grew up on the outskirts of Reading, Pennsylvania—a sad town that had never managed to reclaim its industrial glory days. But it tried desperately, which meant that students in town had to pay their respects to such authors as Wallace Stevens, who'd had the questionable fortune of calling Reading their home. Stevens had been Hocking's classmate at Harvard in 1901 and picked up the pragmatism of James that continued to circulate through New England at the turn of the century. Both Stevens and Hocking were drawn to the belief, held by James, Royce, and Santayana, that ordinary experience always pointed to some deeper, more meaningful reality. And sometimes to something genuinely sublime. Stevens had hiked Chocorua after graduating from Harvard; maybe he'd even felt his way through the morning gloom to this very perch. His poem "Chocorua to Its Neighbor" is disturbingly beautiful. It is, according to the literary critic Harold Bloom, "a morning-star poem, astral and Shelleyan, stationed in the difficult rightness of the moment when day is half risen." The difficult rightness of the moment—he had that right. I sat there in silence, listening to the mountain, reciting the poem in my head:

> I hear the motions of the spirit and the sound
> Of what is secret becomes, for me, a voice
> That is my own voice speaking in my ear.

The sound of what was secret quietly echoed in my ear, a tiny *daimon* voice. I should just tell her, it said. It wouldn't have to be grand or sublime. I would just—just once—be honest, and she could take it or leave it. It was a type of difficult rightness that should at the very least be faced. Stevens, however, knew that this was no easy matter.

I looked down the hill to where the gray birches were beginning to show themselves in the morning light. They didn't waver or shrink back into the shadows.

"I think we've officially missed the dawn," she said with a hint of disappointment. "Maybe we'll catch it next time. Let's keep going, okay?" I got up and turned to follow her. Maybe I could tell her at the top, or on the way.

Emerson was a walker. He believed that the plight of modern society could be traced to its inhabitants' inability to stand squarely on two feet. Thoreau "sauntered," and "having no particular home, [he was] equally at home everywhere." And William James hiked. Hard. For James, the point of climbing mountains was not to get to the top or to see the sun rise at a particular time; it was about the journey. James simply liked to tramp, to feel the dull ache in his legs, the burn in his lungs. And he just about died doing it. On July 7, 1896—in the summer after his address at Holden Chapel—he set out from the Adirondack Loj near Keene, New York, and, making for Mount Marcy, took the Van Hoevenberg Trail to the top. The fifty-four-year-old James had his sights on Panther Gorge, on the southeast side of Marcy, about seven miles away. He reached the lodge there just before dusk and spent the next few days scrambling up the High Peaks of the Adirondacks. I've spent days on these trails, and none of them is particularly easy. In hindsight James admitted that this weekend of exertion did something to his heart—it was never the same again.

But the story of James and Panther Lodge is not merely a story about hiking. It's a story about hiking and a woman who was not his wife. A twenty-four-year-old named Pauline Goldmark was the woman James had arranged to meet at Panther Lodge. Goldmark was the ninth of ten children of Czech and Polish Jewish immigrants. She'd just graduated from Bryn Mawr and would, according to the married James, "make the best wife of any girl [he knew]." There was nothing particularly scandalous about their meeting in the wilderness. Except that James loved her. On some level she probably loved him back. As far as I knew, they never consummated this probable love, but that didn't really matter. In a letter to fellow pragmatist F.C.S. Schiller, James described Pauline: "[She] is a biologist, has done practical philanthropy work among the poor in N.Y., is athletic, a tramper and camper, and a lover of nature such as one rarely meets, and withal a perfectly simple, good girl, with a beautiful face—and I fairly dote on her, and were I younger and 'unattached' should probably be deep in love."

Who was James kidding? Over the next twenty years he'd write eighty-five letters to Goldmark. In one of them he wished that his own twenty-one-year-old daughter could meet Pauline and thereby learn to be more like her. There was much to emulate: In the first decade of the twentieth century Goldmark would become the president of the National Consumers League, which fought for workers' rights against the forces of industrial exploitation. After that she became the associate director of Columbia University's School of Social Work. James's wife, Alice, knew all about Pauline: They were acquaintances, although Alice was understandably cool to the young woman. James made no secret of the feelings he had for her. That summer, he was preparing the Edinburgh lectures that would later become *The Varieties of Religious Experience*, and in Panther Gorge he had one of these experiences with Pauline. He wrote to Alice about the evening, which "turned out to be one of the most memorable of all [his] memorable experiences":

> The moon rose and hung above the scene before midnight, leaving only a few of the larger stars visible and I entered into a state of spiritual alertness of the most vital description. The influences of Nature, the wholesomeness of the people around me, especially the good Pauline, the thought of you and the children . . . the problem of the Edinburgh lectures, all fermented within me till it became a regular Walpurgis Nacht.

Walpurgisnacht, also known as Witches Night, can be confused with Halloween, but it shouldn't be: It is a gathering of spirits in late April to celebrate the coming of spring, a ceremony of rebirth. James and Pauline spent most of this night at Panther Lodge outside, presumably alone, save for the spirits that walk the earth on Walpurgis Nacht, the moonlight streaming down to light up the woods in a "checkered play." To James, it seemed as if "the Gods of all the nature-mythologies were holding an indescribable meeting in my breast with the moral Gods of the inner life." What a meeting it must have been: Pan and Dionysus and a bunch of satyrs gathering with the moral Gods of James's grandfather. James concluded that "the two types of Gods have nothing in common" but that this tension made the spiritual meeting "something worth coming for, and repeating year by year."

The sun eventually rose on James's Walpurgis Nacht, but the madness continued. Pauline was a tramper and camper, and James tried to keep up. Their party set off the next morning to the east and climbed Mount Marcy again, and then the 4,800-foot Basin Mountain, and then the Gothics. They finally reached the Putnam Camp just before dark, and the ten-hour trek almost killed William James. His heart gave him trouble from that day forward, but it was worth it. In 1902, when he traveled to Edinburgh to deliver the Gifford Lectures, which would later become *The Varieties of Religious Experience*, he wrote to Pauline, admitting that "[r]ather than be writing in Edinburgh, I would be sitting or lying on any summit in the neighborhood of K.V. [Keene Valley] with your adjacent soul." Many things had happened to James's heart on that arduous trip to Panther Gorge, and he would never be the same again.

A few small rocks spilled over a lip about ten yards ahead of me. I looked up just in time to see Carol climb out of view and to realize that I was falling behind. I quickened my pace. For a woman who hadn't wanted to get out of bed, she was making good time. I was reminded of Emerson's comment that "in the morning a man walks with his whole body; in the evening, only with his legs." She'd tied the puffy coat around her waist and now was making her way up the mountain with her whole body.

I managed to catch up before we reached the rocky cone atop Chocorua. Three hundred feet below the summit is a little cabin where campers can still spend the night, though it was empty when we arrived. We peeked our heads through the open cabin door and then took a seat on the rocks to survey the view of the lake below. The last ten minutes of the hike are the most demanding, and it is best to make a go of it when you're somewhat fresh. I, at least, needed a break. I realized that this was probably the longest stretch of time Carol and I had spent together without speaking. I turned to look at her, realizing that I'd been so busy catching my own breath and thinking about James that I'd failed to notice how tired she was. Her face was beet red, and her cheeks—not her forehead—were glistening with sweat. I handed her a water bottle and stretched back on the rocks behind us, peering up at the summit.

Four hundred years ago, according to legend, an Abenaki seer named Chocorua had thrown himself off that high cliff, probably landing right where the cabin now stands. Chocorua had welcomed the incoming English settlers, but when they killed his son, he was less hospitable. After avenging his son's death, he fled to this mountaintop, a number of Englishmen in hot pursuit. Instead of being captured, he opted for a fatal fall of several hundred feet. Before he jumped, the seer had placed a curse on the surrounding valley. "Evil spirits breathe death upon the cattle of the white man! Wind and fire destroy your dwellings! Panthers and wolves howl and grow fat on your bones. Chocorua goes now to the Great Spirit!" It was quintessential New Hampshire, quintessential American philosophy: live free or die. In a similar act of free will, Socrates chose hemlock over a life of imprisonment or exile. And in a more protracted but less dramatic decision, a middle-aged James hiked his way to a relatively early grave. For James, it was more a case of "live free *and* die." Better to die freely than to live in chains, or so the story went.

In the 1890s the wealthy Bostonians who vacationed around Chocorua thought it would be a nice idea to build a hotel at the top of the mountain. Carol and I were sitting about one hundred yards from where the hotel, called the Peak House, once stood. This single-gabled clapboard house was a precarious-looking thing, foundationless, perched on slick granite. In 1894 a thousand visitors signed the logbook, William James among them. It cost $13 to spend a week at the Peak House—just shy of $1,500 by today's standards. The Boston Brahmins were apparently happy to pay it. They returned year after year to make the rough trek up the mountain and then dine like royalty.

I stood and extended my hand to help Carol up. It was a three-hundred-foot scramble to the top. She was worn out, but she rallied, and we turned for the summit. I'd made the trek many times, but today I too was tired. And cautious. The wind was blowing, and I knew it could be very strong up at the top. The wind had actually taken down the Peak House in 1915, and it had never been rebuilt. Carol still wanted to make a go of it, but I suddenly realized that the wind was too strong. We could face the cone another day. She reluctantly agreed, and we carefully inched our way back down the mountain.

THE WILL TO BELIEVE

The days grew shorter and colder, and winter break approached. Carol and I went back to our separate end-of-semester slogs, and our weekend with Chocorua, James, and Coleridge slowly faded into the bleak grayness of New England snow. She left for the holidays, first with her husband in Toronto and then with her sister's family in Tuscany. I stayed at home. My *daimon* could protest, but it didn't change matters one bit: At the end of those short days I was still alone in my apartment. There was a horrible inevitability about the evenings, as if they'd been evoked by a force wholly indifferent to human needs. In *The Myth of Sisyphus*, Camus writes that human nature is marked by "the absurd," which he defines as the divorce between human purposes and a world that continually thwarts them. Sisyphus pushes his boulder up the hill, but gravity repeatedly gets the better of him. I filled the days as best I could—grading papers, doing my laundry, finishing my taxes, trying my best not to think about Toronto or Tuscany—but everything seemed so empty, so mechanical, so painfully Sisyphian.

I'd never brought any of the Hocking books back to Boston, but Huxley's copy of Cudworth had somehow followed me home and interrupted the monotony. I found it one evening on the backseat of the Subaru while unloading groceries: an unexpected but meaningful reminder of my—nay, *our*—last weekend in New Hampshire. Placing it gently in one of the flimsy market bags, I headed for my empty apartment. There was now plenty of time to think through the puzzle of Neoplatonism, evolution, and American philosophy.

The idea that the workings of the world are set out in advance, mechanistically determined, destined to pinball human beings from one tragic moment to the next, is one that has haunted the history of philosophy from its inception. This was the idea that Cudworth spent the better part of his life combating. I set the groceries and the Cudworth in the living room and slipped into the dimly lit bathroom. Looking in the mirror, I had to admit that the evidence for determinism was pretty convincing. I'd aged rather uncontrollably over the last year, with wrinkles, stubble, and gray hair appearing out of nowhere. I couldn't shake the feeling that I was becoming someone else against my will, and that I was looking more and more like my father. Returning to the living room, skirting the sofa that my ex-wife and I had squabbled over but I had eventually bought, I settled into the beat-up armchair, setting my feet on the coffee table where we had regularly eaten dinner in silence. I eyed the empty bottle of wine on the table. I'd split it with myself the night before. Twice. At that moment, with Cudworth in my lap, it seemed likely that I would live in this chair for the rest of my life.

Cudworth would have chided me for my fatalism. He'd been a defender of free will in an age when science was just beginning to show that life—including human life—was a function of hard-and-fast physical laws. Many philosophers, including Cudworth, raged against the indifferent machine of determinism. Others, such as Hobbes, just gave in. For Hobbes, like many of the scientists of his time, life was just matter in motion. In *De Corpore*, Hobbes describes human beings as natural bodies, as just one kind among others, like mice and porcupines. According to him, when it comes to choice, human beings are on the same footing as other sentient beings; their wills are determined by external forces. In the words of John Fruit, who summarized Hobbes's materialism in the 1890s, "Man is an automaton; the notion of personality, especially in its characteristic of self-determination, is excluded . . . [T]he argument is, that what are called voluntary actions are necessarily caused, for they are caused by the will, which in its turn, is necessitated." Cudworth went ballistic. This was not a world that the Cambridge Platonist could stomach. Without choice, the world was without morals and therefore—perish the thought—without God.

Glancing at Huxley's tightly wound inscription, I turned to the preface of Cudworth's *The True Intellectual System of the Universe*. Such a boring title to handle such a fascinating problem. Cudworth understood the implications of Hobbes's materialism: Determinism, which, in turn, implied moral subjectivism (the stance that moral goodness was simply a matter of self-interest), left the door open for atheism. In fact, Cudworth was one of the first writers to take Hobbes to task, initially in his *Intellectual System* and then in his defense of morality entitled *A Treatise of Free Will*. As an undergraduate, I'd read enough of the *Treatise* to get its gist; in fact, the book's opening claim sums up its conclusion: "We seem clearly . . . to be led to think that there is something in our own power, and that we are not altogether passive in our actings, nor determined by inevitable necessity in whatsoever we do." The philosophical battle lines were drawn.

Thomas Huxley was interested in the free-will debate in no small part because he was, in the middle of the nineteenth century, in the process of renewing it. He heralded the second coming of modern determinism. His philosophy, when coupled with that of Darwin and Spencer, was the flash point for a generation of classical American thinkers, such as Hocking and James, who wanted to preserve free will in a scientific age that threatened it. Despite being trained in modern biology and physiology, fields that made him sympathetic to the evolutionary hypothesis, William James would be Huxley's most nuanced American critic.

On December 26, 1859, Huxley published a five-thousand-word book review of Darwin's *Origin of Species* in *The Times* of London. With a few minor criticisms, Huxley's review, entitled "The Darwinian Hypothesis," was extremely positive. In subsequent years, as this controversial hypothesis was supported by empirical evidence, Huxley became Darwin's greatest supporter. Many people, however, were considerably less sanguine. These critics understood Darwinian evolution as providing evidence for the sort of materialism and determinism that Hobbes's philosophy had presupposed. The thinking was that life was not the product of divine creation or choice, but of the inevitable process of material variation and selection. This selection occurred through a struggle for survival that looked disturbingly like the Hobbesian "warre of all against all." Even more unsettling to traditional humanists was the idea that the seemingly transcendent aspects of human civilization—its art, its morality, its faith—were really just necessary outcroppings of this biological struggle. When all the ideology was stripped away, according to Hobbes, we were simply isolated animals, bloodied in tooth and claw.

Huxley thought that Darwin had shied away from the most radical and disturbing of his theory's implications—namely, that human beings were the direct product of evolutionary history. Huxley was resolved not to make the same mistake. In 1861 he was invited to give a series of lectures at the University of Edinburgh on comparative anatomy; here he made the charged claim that humans, along with every other animal, evolved through natural selection. Although he didn't come right out and say that we are descended from apes, he came close, suggesting that humans and other apes might have a common ancestor. In a letter to his wife, Huxley commented on the popularity of the lectures and joked about what this large audience might be learning: "My working-men stick by me wonderfully, the house being fuller than ever last night. By next Friday evening they will all be convinced that they are monkeys." Some of the members of his audience were happy with Huxley's argument, but others were not. A good friend of Huxley's satirized the utter terror that some of his audience experienced as they listened to his findings on comparative anatomy:

> The professor . . . had even got up once at the British Association and declared that apes have hippopotamus majors in their brains just as men have. Which was a shocking thing to say, for if it were so, what would become of the faith, hope and charity of immortal millions? . . . [I]f a hippopotamus major is ever discovered in one single ape's brain, nothing will save your great-great-great-great-great-great-great-great-great-great-great-greater-greatest grandmother from having been an ape too.

Huxley was blasted for his views. The lectures were described as the most "blasphemous contradiction to Bible narrative and doctrine" and "the most debasing theory that has ever been propounded before a civilized audience."

Despite the criticism, Huxley repeated the Edinburgh lectures in the fall of 1861 and then compiled them into *Evidence as to Man's Place in Nature*, which suggested that the proper place for human beings was right next to their primate brethren. This was the series of lectures that drew the attention of American thinkers, including William James. In Britain, the theologically minded rallied their troops to defend the special niche that God had set aside for human beings. The anatomist and paleontologist Charles Carter Blake suggested that Huxley's view was "indistinguishable from that of absolute materialism and even tends to atheism." Huxley had to admit that Blake had a point. The challenge for Huxley now was to advance a thoroughgoing material-

ism, one that implied agnosticism if not atheism, without jettison-
ing all semblance of morality and human meaning.

To many contemporary readers, Cudworth and Huxley seem to
be strange characters in a story of American philosophy—they
aren't even American. But Hocking understood that the question
of free will was *the* question of American pragmatism. James,
Dewey, and Peirce had cut their philosophical teeth on the British evolution debate of the 1860s, and in varying degrees, they
viewed Huxley as their principal interlocutor. In 1865, at the age
of twenty-three, William James published his first review in
the *North American Review*. It was on Huxley's *Lectures on the
Elements of Comparative Anatomy*, a version of the talks Huxley
had given in Edinburgh. James wrote approvingly of Huxley's
empiricism, praising him for holding "the view of the phenomena
of life which makes them result from the general laws of matter,
rather than from the subordination of those laws to some principle
of individuality, different in each case."

Like Huxley, James supported the Darwinian hypothesis, but
unlike Huxley, he was also deeply disturbed by it, writing that
the Darwinian framework is "hypothetically at least, atheistic in
its tendency, and, as such, its progress causes much alarm to
many excellent people." The scientific James had to stick to the
facts of biology and anatomy, but this left him in a bit of a fix.
He'd grown up with a father who had been an acolyte of the Swed-
ish mystic Emanuel Swedenborg, which meant, among other
things, that he wanted to leave space for the supernatural. In his
review of Huxley, James states, "Grant that [evolutionary] theory
leaves much of our moral experience unaccounted for, and is but
a partial synthesis,—grant that at present it turns its back upon
the Supernatural,—may it not, nevertheless, serve an excellent
purpose, and in the end, by introducing order into the Natural,
prove to be a necessary step in the way to a larger, purer view of
the Supernatural?"

In the end, maybe evolutionary theory would reveal the purer view of God. This was possible, but not likely, and James knew it. Concluding the review, he commends Huxley for his fierce defense of Darwin but thinks the Brit has gotten into a horrible quagmire. In a moment of gross understatement James assesses the whole of Huxley's argument and finds that "all this is somewhat problematical." James fell into a deep depression after writing this review. In the late 1860s he considered killing himself. "Somewhat problematical." The lesson that James gleaned from evolutionary theory was of an existential variety—human life was a natural process that began in the wailing of babes and ended in the pangs of death. In between was the seemingly futile struggle for survival. It probably didn't help that James spent most of the decade studying the workings of the biological world with the famous Harvard naturalist Louis Agassiz. He'd gone on Agassiz's expedition to Brazil, reflecting at the time that he was "body and soul, in a more indescribably hopeless, homeless and friendless state than [he] ever wanted to be in again." When he returned to the States, he took a post in Henry Bowditch's anatomy laboratory and got an even closer look at the nasty fate of humankind.

I thought back on the morbid sketches James had worked on during this time—dozens of gruesome bodiless heads. I could still remember the call number of the box at Houghton Library: MS Am 1092.2. A box full of dead people. I remembered being attracted to the darkly Gothic themes of James's doodles and ignoring a raft of drawings that didn't at the time seem to fit a narrative of existential angst. Specifically, there were lots of pictures of animals from his trip to Brazil and, more specifically, lots and lots of monkeys. It seemed that James liked monkeys almost as much as he liked dead people. On that bleak evening, alone in my apartment, the monkeys began to make more sense in the context of existential torment. In the end, evolutionary theory might reveal the purer view of God, as James once suggested. But more likely it would reveal that all of us, in the end, are just a bunch of dead primates. I looked up from my book to survey the messy cage I called my home. An eon of evolutionary development had delivered me to this miserable domicile in the North End, which I could scarcely afford. And here I was to remain for the rest of my life. *Somewhat* problematical?

Huxley's findings terrorized James through his depressive twenties. He managed to bootstrap himself out of depression and determinism only after reading the French philosopher-recluse Charles Renouvier, who argued that the best proof of free will turned on an individual's willingness to affirm its existence. In the months after my father's death, this idea had occupied no small amount of my mental energy, but it always struck me as oddly—if not viciously—circular. I eventually concluded that James, at the brink of emotional collapse, was grasping at philosophical straws. On April 30, 1870, James wrote of this turn toward Renouvier and away from Huxley:

> I think that yesterday was a crisis in my life. I finished the first part of Renouvier's second "Essais," and see no reason why his definition of Free Will—"the sustaining of a thought because I choose to when I might have other thoughts"—need be the definition of an illusion. At any rate, I will assume for the present—until next year—that it is no illusion. My first act of free will shall be to believe in free will.

This private moment of insight became the basis of his public affirmation of free will against Huxley's determinism. In 1874 Huxley published "On the Hypothesis That Animals Are Automata," which entertained and revived the hypothesis that Hobbes had affirmed in his *Leviathan*—namely, that living organisms bear an uncanny resemblance to machines. For Hobbes and Huxley, human beings, as living organisms, were bound to the mechanical laws of nature. "It is quite true, to the best of my judgment," Huxley concludes, "that the argumentation which applies to brutes holds equally good of men; and, therefore, that all states of consciousness in us, as in them, are immediately caused by molecular changes of the brain-substance." He maintained that mental life could be reduced to physical states and that "the feeling we call volition is not the cause of a voluntary act, but the symbol of that state of the brain which is the immediate cause of that act. We are conscious automata . . ." In his youth, James would have read these words with no small amount of fear and trembling, but he was older now, and armed with the philosophical tools of Renouvier, he was ready to put up a real fight. In 1879 he published his rejoinder to Huxley in *Mind*, an article that he entitled "Are We Automata?" This article put James on the philosophical map and served as the foundation for one of the most famous essays in American pragmatism, "The Will to Believe." In "Are We Automata?" James answered Huxley with feeling: No—no, we most certainly are not.

Feeling. For a split second I thought about Tuscany, about how I could max out my credit card in one fell swoop, buy a one-way ticket, and be there tomorrow. This sort of impulse—as emotionally vivid as it was absurd—buttressed James's argument against determinism. He argued that the feeling of freedom could not be analyzed away or reduced to a discrete set of physical processes. Feeling—immediate, personal, *free*—was not predetermined and had causal efficacy. Until science or philosophy furnishes evidence to the contrary, James argued, it was best to believe that free feeling was an active force in the universe:

When a philosophy comes which, by new facts or conceptions, shall show how particular feelings may be destitute of causal efficacy without the genus Feeling as a whole becoming the sort of *ignis fatuus* and outcast which it seems to be to-day to so many "scientists" (loathly word!), we may hail Professor Huxley . . . as [a] true prophet. Until then, I hold that we are incurring the slighter error by still regarding our conscious selves as actively combating each for his interests in the arena and not as impotently paralytic spectators of the game.

I didn't have enough money left on my credit card to get out of the state, much less buy the plane ticket to Italy that I found on Orbitz. But it didn't really matter. James's point still held. Feeling was not, in James's words, "destitute of causal efficacy." The will undoubtedly had limits on what it could accomplish, but it could, in fact, accomplish something. This anticipated James's position in "The Will to Believe," published in 1896, a year after his evening at Holden Chapel, in which he argues that there are many situations that cannot be thoroughly explained through empirical analysis. When certain questions cannot be settled on the basis of empirical evidence, we are justified in answering them through what he calls "voluntarily adopted faith." In other words, we are entitled to believe whatever we want. In the aftermath of my father's death I'd come to believe that such questions didn't exist, or if they did, they weren't really worth asking. To me, James's argument smacked of Pascal's Wager. In the seventeenth century the Frenchman argued that in the absence of proof, it is safer to believe in God (since you lose relatively little if you are wrong about his existence) than to adopt atheism (and face eternal damnation on the Day of Judgment). "Voluntarily adopted faith" struck me as a euphemism for willful ignorance, but I was slowly having a change of heart.

Shall I profess my love? Shall I be moral? Shall I live? These are the most important questions of modern life, but are also questions that do not have factually verifiable answers. For James such answers will be, at best, provisional. There are no physical signs that one is emotionally ready to become a lover or a husband, no auguries that suggest one will be any good at any of it. In fact, there is often a disturbing amount of countervailing evidence. But human beings still have to choose, to make significant decisions in the face of uncertainty. Love is what James would have called a "forced option"—you either choose to love or you don't. There's no middle ground. It would be convenient if science or logic could make sense of these forced options, but as James pointed out, "Science can tell us what exists; but to compare the worths, both of what exists and of what does not exist, we must consult not science, but what Pascal calls our heart."

I got up from the sofa, leaving behind another empty bottle of wine—which I tried to believe I had drunk freely—and surveyed my bookshelves. They weren't like those at West Wind, but they would suffice. I dug out James's "The Will to Believe" and returned to the quest Cudworth had initiated centuries ago. James had met Pauline Goldmark for the first time in September 1895, before he wrote and delivered the essay early in 1896. The precarious matter of love was clearly on his mind when he wrote about the possible "worths" of life and the causal efficacy of the will. Love was not decided by empirical study: It was instead a "maybe" that was decided by the heart. In "The Will to Believe," James thinks about the question that only volition could answer:

> Do you like me or not?—for example. Whether you do or not depends, in countless instances, on whether I meet you half-way, am willing to assume that you must like me, and show you trust and expectation. The previous faith on my part in your liking's existence is in such cases what makes your liking come. But if I stand aloof, and refuse to budge an inch until I have objective evidence, until you shall have done something apt . . . ten to one your liking never comes . . . In truths dependent on our personal action, then, faith based on desire is certainly a lawful and possibly an indispensable thing.

I really wanted to agree: Faith based on desire, on the feeling of volition, was an indispensable thing. In James's words, "The desire for a certain kind of truth here brings about that special truth's existence." I returned to my computer to check Orbitz again. Nothing had changed, but I'd keep my eye on tickets.

Setting Cudworth on the kitchen counter, I trundled off to bed with the thought that American philosophy had inherited an idealism and a sympathy for human feeling that made life slightly more bearable.

EVOLUTIONARY LOVE

Discovering Cudworth interrupted my daily routine and led me back to themes in American philosophy that I risked, once again, losing: the idea of freedom and the prospect of love. I woke, showered, shaved, cleaned up the apartment, and returned to my books.

After publishing "The Will to Believe," James faced a firestorm of criticism. He wrote to his friend and mentor Charles Sanders Peirce that he'd "been in a lot of hot water" over the essay. Peirce thought it was impressively original and admired James's defense of free will, but he had some serious reservations. James's argument for the causal efficacy of human volition was only a partial response to Huxley and other biological determinists. The question that continued to bother Peirce was about the *origin* of human freedom. Where did free will come from? What are freedom's metaphysical preconditions? Peirce's response to the problem of determinism had a slightly different emphasis than James's did. Whereas James sought to prove the existence of freedom through an act of Renouvier-inspired willfulness, Peirce, the scientist, wanted to carefully explore the degree to which "chance"—what he took to be the enabling condition of freedom—operated in the workings of the universe. Like James, Peirce had struggled with Huxley and Darwin through his student years at Harvard. In the 1860s he had criticized the biological classification systems of both Agassiz and Huxley, but on the whole he found the possibilities of evolution fascinating. Darwin's death, in 1882, provided the occasion for scholars, Peirce included, to assess the impact of evolutionary theory and to alter its course. Peirce thought that theorists working in the wake of Darwin had done him a great disservice by emphasizing the orderly design of evolution over chance and variation. At the end of 1883, in an unpublished manuscript entitled "Design and Chance," Peirce wrote: "It has always seemed to me singular that when we put the question to an evolutionist, Spencerian, Darwinian, or whatever school he may belong to, what are the agencies which have brought about evolution, he mentions various determinate facts and laws, but among the agencies at work he never once mentions *Chance*."

Peirce's interest in chance in the 1880s wasn't purely academic. He was in this period preoccupied with the chances for his personal life and, more specifically, for romantic love. "Design and Chance" was written as Peirce was considering taking the most radical chance of his life. He'd married Harriet Melusina "Zina" Fay many years before, in 1862, thereby temporarily quashing any chance of happiness. Zina was independent and smart and wouldn't put up with any of Charlie's dandyish and dilettante ways, and his family was extremely grateful when she began to straighten him out. Peirce, however, was not suited for the straight and narrow and, by the late 1870s, was looking for distractions. He found one in Juliette Froissy, a beautiful, diminutive actress whom he probably met in 1876 at the Christmas ball at the Hotel Brevoort in New York. "Probably" is the operative word here. No one—except Peirce and Juliette—seemed to know exactly where or when they first met. For that matter, no one really knew who Juliette was. Peirce claimed, well into old age, that he didn't even know her true family name. Some said she was a Hapsburg princess, others a Roma Gypsy, still others part of the French aristocracy.

The saddest part of many scandals is the cover-up, a lame attempt to mask the radical choice that has been made and to fit a moment of madness into the comfortable sanity of the everyday. I thought that Peirce handled his romantic affair bravely, if not entirely wisely. He didn't try to conceal it; in fact, he flaunted it for six years, traveling with Juliette while he was still married to Zina. I suspect he didn't relish being cruel or shocking, but rather enjoyed the feeling of freedom that came from doing something socially unacceptable. For a man plagued by the question of determinism, this moment of free love was probably a welcome relief. In April 1883 Peirce finally decided that he wanted out of his marriage, and he filed for what in that day and age was a rare divorce. Two days later he married Juliette. In a single impulsive act, Peirce initiated a death-do-us-part romantic commitment, proclaimed his love for the power of chance, and solidified his reputation as an academic and social pariah. The fallout from this illicit marriage was ugly. Peirce wrote "Design and Chance" in the next month, as if his life depended on it. It was a metaphysical defense of radical contingency. Human life—like the universe at large—did not operate solely by laws and orderly habits. It was defined by chance occurrences, the frequencies of which are inversely proportional to their magnitude: Cataclysmic ones happen rarely; less dramatic ones happen more often.

Peirce realized that his defense of radical chance was not without problems. Determinism denied free will by holding that every act—including those of human beings—was caused by an infinite series of prior events. Our decisions and behaviors are fated and therefore out of our control. But suggesting that the universe was defined by radical chance could lead to a similarly dissatisfying result. Peirce knew that chance could break the spell of the determinists, but it also could break the idea of causality itself. Chance, as a purely random or chaotic event, implied that there was no necessary causal relationship between our past and the present or, more frighteningly, between our present and the future. This strictly chaotic system was not altogether different from a deterministic one: It conceived of a world beyond our control. In order to avoid this conclusion, Peirce had to refine his definition of chance.

Chance can connote a random occurrence, but also, he observed, a rare opportunity, a possibility that is freely chosen. Discussing Peirce's argument with Hocking and Royce in 1903, Ella Lyman Cabot, one of the few women of classical American philosophy, put the point nicely: "Chance is always *my* chance!" For Peirce, chance was an opening for human beings to explore at their will, a space to be personally responsible for one's actions. The difference between Peirce's first marriage and his second is instructive. The first one, with Zina, was forced and expedient. It foreclosed certain possibilities and narrowed Peirce's angle of vision. The second, precipitated by chance, realized as potential, was most certainly free. He fell in love with Juliette, seizing an opportunity that flew in the face of societal expectations and traditional commitments.

Peirce's love had confounded me for nearly a decade. Theirs wasn't always—or even mostly—a happy marriage, but he and Juliette remained together for nearly forty years. The later years of Peirce's life were absolutely miserable. The facial neuralgia that had plagued him for decades took a turn for the worse, and he became addicted to the drugs—alcohol, morphine, and cocaine—that he used to self-medicate. His finances were terrible—he remained on the edge of poverty during his last twenty years. And he exhibited all the hallmarks of someone suffering from psychological afflictions—from Asperger's to bipolar and depressive disorder. But he didn't abandon Juliette as his life slipped out of control. They squabbled over money, and he would occasionally carp about her housekeeping, but for the most part he remained firmly in love. When Juliette fell ill in 1889, he made it clear that he'd staked absolutely everything on the relationship, stating with classic Peircean melodrama: "If I should lose her, I would not survive her. Therefore, I must turn my *whole* energy to saving her." And he did. Despite admitting that her husband could be "perfectly awful," Juliette returned the favor and kept Peirce alive much longer than his self-destructive tendencies—drinking, drug abuse, overwork—should have allowed. If life was going to be a disaster, at least it would be *their* disaster. They were companions in misery to the very end.

I ate my breakfast—the same banana and toast I'd eaten for a decade—and wondered how philosophy had managed to lose its personal character. In graduate school I was taught to carefully ignore the personalities that gave rise to philosophical arguments. But this was almost impossible when it came to American philosophy. The first page of *Walden* is explicit: "In most books, the *I*, or first person, is omitted; in this it will be retained; that, in respect to egotism, is the main difference. We commonly do not remember that it is, after all, always the first person that is speaking. I should not talk so much about myself if there were anybody else whom I knew as well. Unfortunately, I am confined to this theme by the narrowness of my experience."

Peirce's papers are not exactly like *Walden*. Most of them are covered with equations and charts, but insofar as they reveal Peirce's personal character, his unpublished manuscripts were thoroughly Thoreauvian. His writings are mercurial—logical formalisms and metaphysical speculations interspersed with intimate anecdotes and private confessions. These personal tangents were signs that Peirce had been brought up under American Transcendentalists who held that philosophy should be woven into the conduct of life. Autobiography was the outgrowth of serious philosophical reflection. Peirce's philosophical system was a reflection of a person who willingly got sidetracked. Beneath his formal critique of determinism was a living, breathing person whose life defied any prescribed logic. And beneath his technical metaphysical system was a man who craved intimacy and love.

Darwinism and determinism, according to American pragmatists, overlooked the importance of chance but also produced a worldview that precluded the possibility of meaningful relationships. For thinkers like Huxley, the arena of life was just that—one where people were destined to be pitted against one another in a gladiatorial fight. Despite his occasional fits of rage, Peirce didn't want to live in this sort of world, so he fashioned a philosophical one more suited to his desires.

For him, the cosmos was neither held in gridlock by mechanical necessity nor a chaotic mess of competing forces. Instead, it was a "multiverse," or a "pluriverse," defined by complexity and held together in improvisational harmony by individuals freely pursuing a more perfect union that was always in the making—an ideal, never achieved but always pursued. To the extent that the world realizes this more perfect union, it does so loosely, provisionally, by means of what Peirce would call "evolutionary love." This was not the self-love that drove the evolution of Darwin, Huxley, and Spencer. Peirce held that that sort was no love at all. He explains that evolutionary love, or *agape*, is characterized by the willingness to "sacrifice your own perfection to the perfectionment of your neighbor." According to Peirce, it is the decision to hold our own selfish interests in abeyance and give ourselves freely to another. This is not easy, but it is also not impossible. "Love," according to Peirce, "recognizing germs of loveliness [even] in the hateful, gradually warms it into life, and makes it lovely." The movement of this love is "circular, at one and the same impulse projecting creations into independency and drawing them into harmony." Peirce realized this later in life, but it would be too late for Zina. As an elderly man, he argued that *agape* is the basis of creative evolution that begins by chance but grows as individual purposes harmonize and sympathize over time. Gardening, a pastime the Peirces enjoyed together on their estate in Milford, Pennsylvania, was Peirce's favorite example of loving care. There is, according to him, a certain purpose or *telos* to gardening; the results can be influenced but not controlled or guaranteed, nor are they predestined. A master gardener lovingly encourages her plants to grow as they may. The best that a person could do in life was to cultivate a garden of her own. Peirce's belief in the generative force of love influenced thinkers who carried the torch of American philosophy into the twentieth century. Writing in 1913, in *The Meaning of God in Human Experience*, Hocking continued to maintain that "love of this sort is the one thing in the world that is creative." Hocking, following Peirce, understood love to be a reasonable principle for change because of its ability to hold opposites together in a kind of productive tension, encouraging the interplay of necessity and chance.

"The world," according to a rapidly aging Peirce, "lives and moves and has its BEING in a logic of events." This "logic of events" was not your standard deductive or inductive variety; it was a logic that had to accommodate chance and variety, but also purpose and intimacy. It was the "logic" of love. Peirce borrowed his words from the book of Acts, where it is said that humans "live and move and have our being" in God. As he developed his essay "Evolutionary Love" in the 1890s, he came to the belief, expressed in the Gospel of John, that "God is love." On April 24, 1892, Peirce entered St. Thomas Episcopal Church on Fifth Avenue in New York City and came as close as he ever would to experiencing this firsthand. On that New York morning, Peirce was drawn into a religious experience that revealed the unseen but unmistakable affections of the world. He was not a churchgoer, but on that day he felt compelled to visit, and he later wrote to the rector at St. Thomas that he entered the church and approached the altar rail "almost without my own volition." The "almost" is important. Every act of communion, of Emersonian "give and take," of affectionate love, is a certain kind of choice. This *agape*, or divine love, according to Peirce, was just the way the world worked, and it was up to us to participate. Peirce had long criticized institutional religion and the idea of transubstantiation, but he suddenly, freely gave himself over to "the Master." "I have never before been mystical," Peirce writes, "but now I am." The experience of divine love, according to Peirce, was not constrictive or inhibiting. Rather, it gave him the will to carry on through another difficult decade.

I'd spent more than enough time thinking about determinism. I finished my toast, cracked my laptop open, and resolved to get in touch with the outside world. But first I would read "Evolutionary Love" one more time. I was so immersed in my Peirce that I barely registered the ping of my email notification. It was Carol, asking for a ride back from the airport. Tuscany had been beautiful, but she was ready to come home. The email went on for a few paragraphs, with no mention of Toronto. This probably meant little more than there was nothing to report about her husband. I assumed that their relationship was strong enough and habitual enough that she didn't have to mention him to her colleague. This was not pleasant to think about, but if Peirce was right, it was best to embrace the objectionable whenever possible—to, in his words, warm the hateful into loveliness. So I'd pick my colleague up and try to make the best of it.

PART III

REDEMPTION

A PHILOSOPHY
OF LOYALTY

Her plane was forty-two minutes late. I'd wandered around the terminal at Logan for more than an hour. I wanted to see Carol more than I had any right to, and at this point I was beginning to worry that I'd already missed her.

Early in Agnes O'Reilly's acquaintance with Hocking, months before they were married, she had traveled to Italy. In one of his many letters to her, Hocking wrote, "For one reason I am glad you have gone away. It gives me the chance to realize you . . . I like to see you from time to time mentally . . . and say, 'She is a friend of mine.' I am proud of it, dear, way down in the bottom of my heart."

Maybe Carol was downstairs in the baggage claim. I headed for the escalator and glided downward to continue the search.

"John. Hey, John!"

I turned around and spotted Carol's curly head at the top of the escalator. I hadn't missed her, but I was going the wrong way. I about-faced and made a dash against the mechanical flow. She caught me at the top. The hug started out professional enough, but my hand somehow ended up on the back of her head and gently pulled it into my neck. She didn't pull away. And then she whispered something I could hardly hear.

"I'm getting a divorce too."

Peirce never tells us about meeting Juliette for the first time or exactly what it felt like when she fell ill. And he never tells us what happened in his religious experience at St. Thomas's or exactly what his communion with the Absolute was like. All he tells us is that he was radically, irreversibly changed: "I have never been a mystic before; but now I am." Some things are better left unsaid, and others can't be said at all. Carol and I drove home together in silence. We had dinner that night. And the next night. And the night after that. For many nights. And then we went back to West Wind.

Decisions that once seemed completely foolhardy now made perfect sense, so a month after Carol's return, we decided to brave the awful weather and drive north toward Madison through a growing blizzard. We took our time and laid our plans for the coming years. The Hockings were open to the idea of donating a large collection of the books, and Carol and I were intent on finding them a proper home. We'd have to get the books appraised, but before that, we'd finish the cataloging. The appraisal and subsequent donation could happen in the warmer months, but the cataloging would be done in the unpredictable New England winter. This didn't bother me at all. In fact, for the first time in my life I was singularly unbothered.

The mid-February snow was deep, making the unpaved roads nearly impassable. As we finally hit Route 113 and crept toward the Hocking estate, our conversation faded, and I was left listening to the low hum of the Subaru on unplowed snow. Carol was fast asleep. I too was tired. It was a little after noon, but it felt much later. I guided the car through the final turn with deliberate care and made the final ascent to West Wind. The library looked like an igloo; it was going to be absolutely frigid in there. I parked the car but kept the engine running. I'd let Carol sleep and enjoy the warmth of the car for a few more minutes.

The snow was only ankle-deep, but the wind had blown drifts that covered most of the library's stone walls. Over the years, I'd learned a bit more about those walls. In 1926 Hocking, with the help of a friend, Fred Frost, had begun to gather the granite from the hills of West Wind. They devised their construction technique from one of the first DIY building manuals, *Build a Home: Save a Third*. The book outlined what is called slipform masonry, a method developed in the early 1920s for making reinforced concrete with stone facing. The slip form itself is just a greased wooden frame that can be filled with rock, cement, and reinforcing metal bars. When the concrete sets enough to stand by itself, the wooden forms can be slipped off and arranged to construct the next level.

By the time Hocking undertook the building of West Wind, he was already a master carpenter: Before starting his career in philosophy at Berkeley in 1906, he'd joined the American Federation of Labor—one of America's earliest unions—as a carpenter-contractor to help rebuild San Francisco after the great earthquake. "We were using fresh-sawed redwood lumber," Hocking recalled, "all the dry stock long since used up; our boards were so wet that the sap would jump out of them if we hit them with a hammer. Our faces were caked with the inescapable ash-dust blown by incessant winds." In 1910 William James wrote "The Moral Equivalent of War," in which he argues that college-educated men should be conscripted for several years of hard public service. In taking on this sort of manual labor, privileged youth would, in James's words, "get the childishness knocked out of them, and come back into society with healthier sympathies and soberer ideas." Hocking didn't need to be conscripted. He volunteered.

A decade later, after Hocking returned to Harvard, he interrupted—or rather augmented—his studies of ethics and metaphysics to join the army. He was one of the first Americans to enlist in the Citizens' Training Camp at Plattsburgh, New York— an outgrowth of the Preparedness Movement, spearheaded by

Teddy Roosevelt in 1915 as a response to the escalating war in Europe. "When the time came for choosing a specialty [at Platts- burgh]," Hocking later explained, "I took military engineering where my earlier experience would come into use." The military is usually regarded as specializing in destruction, but Hocking's experience in the armed forces told another story—it could also be a place of construction, or at least preservation. He perfected his engineering skills at Plattsburgh and was on the first transport of U.S. Army civil engineers to reach the Western Front in the summer of 1917. Hocking went as an "observer" and entered the trenches at Croisilles, a town on the Hindenburg Line, a German defensive position that stretched through much of Flanders and northern France. He'd been invited to oversee the British war effort by the now-defunct British Ministry of Information (MI-7), in the hope that he could advise the Americans as they joined the fighting.

Being an observer didn't mean that you couldn't be killed, and Hocking observed combat for much of that summer. During this time he was forced to think through the relationship between de- struction and preservation rather carefully. Trench warfare de- pended in no small part on the expertise of engineers. Trenches had to be surveyed, framed, and reinforced, much like the walls at West Wind, and when Hocking returned to the States in 1918 and took over the ROTC program at Harvard, this is what he taught his students to do. But there was another side to army en- gineering that Hocking never wanted to talk about.

The British counterattack against the Hindenburg Line, in the summer of 1917, marked the single most devastating engineering project in the history of nonnuclear warfare. Hocking was sta- tioned on Kemmel Hill, overlooking the Belgium town of Ypres and the nearby Messines Ridge, where German forces had built extensive fortifications. In the previous months the British Royal Engineers had tunneled under the Axis defenses. They were the most extensive tunnels ever built for the sole purpose of being destroyed. Under Messines Ridge, engineers laid 450 tons of high explosives. When the mines were detonated on June 7, they created craters, the largest being the size of a soccer pitch. The low boom of the explosion could be heard as far away as Paris and London. Many say that the Battle of Messines was one of the turning points of the war, one of the reasons that the free world was kept in one piece. Hocking knew firsthand the devastation required for this act of preservation. In September 1917, at the end of his time at the front, he wrote to Agnes: "I have had my baptism in this immense business of war making and war thinking, and now I can come back and do my work with a deepened understanding."

I surveyed the grayish-blue landscape surrounding the library. It was barren beneath the snow—rugged and largely uninhabitable. Yet Hocking had decided to put down roots here. "The essence of military engineering, as distinct from 'regular' engineering, consists in doing everything with nothing," he'd once remarked. West Wind was really something—to Hocking, it was everything—and it had grown out of virtually nothing. The essence of military engineering, I imagined, also consisted in the knowledge that everything could be laid to waste once again. The task was to build something from nothing and then carefully protect it.

I turned the engine off, leaned over to Carol, and gently brushed the hair out of her face. She opened her eyes slowly. "Oh," she said after a moment, taking my hand, "here we are."

"Yes," I agreed. *"Here we are."*

It's amazing how powerful these three little words could be. I wasn't the first to find them philosophically and personally significant. Alfred North Whitehead—one of William Ernest Hocking's more famous friends—placed them at the center of his philosophical system. "Hang it all!" Whitehead once exclaimed in the midst of a Harvard seminar, *"Here we are!"* Hocking was co-teaching this seminar and loved the expression. The "we" was definitive: Both of these thinkers developed an idealism of togetherness. Hocking quoted Whitehead, somewhat ironically, long after the Englishman was gone, recounting the "here we are" moment in his 1956 *The Coming World Civilization*: "When my colleague Whitehead, in one of our joint seminars, throws out an amiable aside, 'Hang it all! *Here we are*: We don't go behind it, we begin with it,' he has implicitly brushed aside one of the theoretical bases of modernity . . . [O]n Descartes' ground, which is modernity's, we must all . . . be solipsists in theory." Descartes had fixated on, and defended, the sole existence of the unitary "I." Whitehead and Hocking were much more concerned with the existence and feeling of a "we."

"Here we are" was Whitehead's response to the Cartesian *cogito ergo sum*. By the time Whitehead began writing his magnum opus, *Process and Reality*, in 1926, Descartes had dominated epistemology and metaphysics for almost three hundred years. Whitehead thought that was long enough. Following Hocking, he traced modernity's hyper-individualism, its tendency to slip into uncaring solipsism, to Descartes's philosophical position, which implied that we had, at best, limited access to the thoughts and feelings of other people. For Descartes, there could be no meaningful meeting of the minds, and people were destined to be strangers. Other people be damned—nothing else was as certain nor as preciously intimate as the existence of one's own mental life. Whitehead and Hocking couldn't face this philosophical loneliness. Extending a long line of American thinkers, they set out to overcome this alienation and instead argued, in Hocking's words, for "an intersubjective Thou-art, inseparable from each subjective I-am, serving to bind their several experiences together in such a way that the loose suggestion of shared experience with an identical object is defined and confirmed."

Whitehead would have never gotten his Harvard appointment

at the age of sixty-three had it not been for Hocking. Whitehead made a name for himself in logic and mathematics when he and his student, Bertrand Russell, wrote the *Principia Mathematica* in the first decade of the twentieth century. Yet Hocking was attracted not to Whitehead's expertise in logic, but to the intellectual move he had made toward metaphysics and philosophy in the 1920s. In 1918 Whitehead lost his son, Eric, in World War I, a tragedy I'd always interpreted as the reason he went on to broaden his intellectual life beyond the confines of formal logic. After the war, Whitehead's philosophical interests took an idealist turn, and he developed a metaphysical system that looked uncannily like the philosophies of Peirce and Royce. In Whitehead's system, the world doesn't consist of discrete billiard ball–like objects that knock against one another. Instead, parts of the universe live and move *together*, and have their being in a logic of events in which individuals freely participate. The task of philosophy was not to secure an individual's solitary existence, divorced from all other beings, but to affirm a shared life in a common place. The experience of this shared life was not unlike James's appeal to the "varieties of religious experience" that temporarily quelled the fear of existential isolation. In Whitehead's words, "[I]n its solitariness, the spirit asks, What, in the way of value, is the attainment of life? And it can find no such value until it has merged its individual claim with that of the objective universe."

Hocking liked this sentiment, in no small part because it reminded him of his own philosophical system, developed in *The Meaning of God in Human Experience*. His insistence that Whitehead be brought to Harvard permanently in 1924 reflected Hocking's desire to have a philosophically kindred spirit in a department that was quickly being handed over to philosophers who wanted nothing to do with idealism. Hocking courted Whitehead for several years and finally invited him to deliver the prestigious Lowell Lectures at Harvard in 1923, which were subsequently published as *Science and the Modern World* in 1925. The presentation copy of this book had been wedged into a rusty file cabinet at the back of the Hocking library, signed, "To Agnes and William Ernest, with love, Alfred North Whitehead." *Process and Reality* was published four years later; a first edition of the book, inscribed by the author, was still tucked away on its shelf when we entered the icy library. I found it and placed it next to the pencil sketch Hocking had done of Whitehead in the 1930s. Both of them could sit on the mantel this weekend.

Carol was already happily ensconced at Hocking's old desk, surrounded by volumes that needed to go into our catalog. She didn't give a hoot about Whitehead. Or about metaphysics, for that matter. But she'd done her part in helping me beyond self-imposed loneliness, not least by giving me a book by David Foster Wallace when she returned from Tuscany. I'd devoured *Infinite Jest* almost against my will and then turned to his much less intimidating pieces, memorizing his famous commencement speech, "This Is Water," in a week and internalizing his argument for the "intersubjective Thou-art." According to Wallace, we're not fated to be "imperially alone" at the center of our little "skull-sized kingdoms," but have the rare and precious choice to venture outside with others. Whether we do is completely up to us, but this choice of togetherness beckons even, and most importantly, when we feel the most cut off.

In the previous months of working at the library I'd moved chronologically through the first editions of West Wind: from Spinoza and Descartes to Hobbes and Cudworth, Paley and Malebranche, Locke and Hume. Now we'd finally reached Carol's bread and butter: Kant. Hocking had collected the first editions of every major book Kant had ever written, starting with the *Critique of Pure Reason*, published in Riga in 1781, and finishing with the *Critique of Judgment*, released a decade later. Carol was intensely interested in Kant's middle works, particularly the moral theory of the *Groundwork for the Metaphysics of Morals*. She was slowly fingering through this ambitious yet skinny volume. Our cataloging of Kant was going to take a long time, but we didn't need to hurry. We could come back to West Wind as often as we needed to. The Hocking sisters had met Carol the previous year and had immediately fallen in love with her.

Carol looked up for a minute. "What are you doing?"

Looking at you, I thought. "Same thing you are, colleague. Cataloging."

She worked through the *Groundwork*—collating a book that most people would describe as a mere pamphlet. As the pages turned, she peered in for a better look, as if to decipher the whole of Kant's deontology in a few pages of German. She was one of the few scholars I knew who allowed Kant to be exactly as formal and morally exacting as he'd intended. Deontology—one of the three great moral theories of the West—was all about duty. Duty to others and duty to oneself. Most of my friends who wrote about American pragmatism thought that Kant's sense of duty was so rigorous and inflexible that it didn't fit with human experience. For Carol, this wasn't a problem—she believed that when people fail to conform to universal moral principles, it's the people, not the principles, that need to be fixed.

Kant thought it important to establish certain obligations to others even when we don't especially like them. Moral obligations arise from the ability to recognize others as rational agents who can set and pursue ends for themselves. It was irrational, and thereby morally impermissible, to impede the rational projects of one's neighbor. This all made good sense to Carol, who was especially taken by Kant's view of self-respect—he argued that each of us has moral obligations to ourselves to protect our own powers of self-determination and dignity. I always suspected that Carol's divorce could be traced to this Kantian duty of self-respect, which, on her reading, usually trumped conventional moral commitments. In any event, as I peered over her shoulder at the *Groundwork*, I decided never to test my hypothesis about the importance of her self-respect. I put my hands on her shoulders, we stood together for a long moment of contemplative silence, and then I slipped around to the other side of our desk.

Hocking had been more skeptical than Carol about Kant's project. He believed in treating others with respect, but he was concerned that Kant failed to move beyond the "problem of other minds" set up by Descartes. In the course of Kant's formal—some might say tedious—analysis, he never gets around to explaining how we could overcome this solipsism. He does his best to set up a clear system of moral duties, but articulating our most intimate connection with others was not something the bachelor from Königsberg was prepared to address. In Hocking's words, the modern age was "infected with the relativity and the warping of the disparate egos, whose problem of togetherness Kant himself never squarely faced."

I knew that Carol would want to pore over the Kant, to make sure that every page was fully intact. Even if I inspected a few and cataloged them, she'd still take the time to go through everything herself. My eyes wandered around the library. West Wind had changed since I had first come here two years earlier. Once a resting place for "pestilence-stricken multitudes," it had slowly become a place where what was on the brink of destruction could be preserved. As Shelley had once said: destroyer and preserver. I thought about the chesterfield where I'd inhaled the mouse droppings more than a year before. Maybe that was where Carol and I would be sleeping tonight. I looked up to the portrait of Agnes, who now seemed to smile down on us with those cool, all-knowing eyes. I was no longer ashamed in the face of her omniscience.

"You're not really interested in these books, are you?" Carol asked in a way that was only slightly accusatory. As I stammered some excuse, she laughed and gave me a look suggesting that nothing could be more important than Kant.

"I was thinking about you and Agnes." I pointed to the portrait. "I'm going to go work on the Hegel. I assume you want to stay put?"

"You assume correctly, love." That was a nice and unexpected addition to our repartee. "Love." It sounded vaguely English, like something from Carol's Canadian past, and more sincere than I could have hoped.

The Hocking library was partitioned by its bookshelves into cozy nooks, little intellectual crannies where a scholar could set up temporary residence for an afternoon or a week. Each nook, consisting of shelves on its two opposite sides and a wall of windows, was approximately six feet wide—just large enough that a person of my size could sit at the desk, facing the window, and reach for books from either wall without having to get up. The post-Kantian philosophy was in the southwest corner at the front of the library and was in surprisingly good shape. I'd spend the rest of the afternoon there, plucking out first editions that were interspersed with family photo albums.

One of the first books I came upon was *Differenz des Fichteschen und Schellingschen Systems der Philosophie*, published in the German university town of Jena in 1801. When it came to the greats of German idealism, there was Kant, and then there were Schelling and Hegel. This was the first printing of Hegel's first publication: *The Difference Between Fichte's and Schelling's Philosophical Systems*. The first editions of Hegel's famous *Phenomenology* and *Encyclopedia* had already made their way to dry storage, but I'd missed this early volume. It was tucked behind a number of newer volumes, as if it had been hidden there for safekeeping or meant as the backdrop for the rest of German idealism. Something else was back there, but I'd have to remove all these books to reach it. With them came the customary centimeter of what I hoped was only dust. Pinched behind was a postcard-size tome, no thicker than my wallet. I opened it and read—or tried to read—the filigreed eighteenth-century German. *Ueber die Möglichkeit einer Form der Philosophie überhaupt* (On the Possibility and Form of Philosophy in General), published by a nineteen-year-old Friedrich Schelling in 1795, his first book.

I thought about calling out to Carol, but thought better of it. She was happy with her Kant. I paged through the tiny volume, past words that looked archaic and menacingly long. With a dictionary and a lot of trouble I'd slogged my way through it once in graduate school. Hocking, however, could've breezed through this text without any problem. In 1902 he had traveled to Göttingen, where he became the first student to study with Edmund Husserl, the father of modern phenomenology, a school of European philosophy that, like pragmatism, believed that philosophical speculation should attend to human experience. Sixty-two pages of Schelling wouldn't have intimidated Hocking. It wouldn't have fazed his Harvard mentor, Josiah Royce, either. Royce, who was practically Teutonic, had made his own pilgrimage to Heidelberg and Göttingen in 1875 and 1876. Royce and Hocking—two of the last idealists at Harvard—were profoundly indebted to Hegel and Schelling, a fact that emerged repeatedly in the course of their philosophical lives. Royce lectured on post-Kantian idealism hundreds of times, and his lectures were so accessible, so thorough that many of them were published, first as *The Spirit of Modern Philosophy* in 1892 and then posthumously in *Lectures on Modern Idealism* in 1919.

I slipped out of the nook and returned with a copy of Royce's lectures on German idealism. To understand American philosophy, you needed to get a sense of its European roots, but to understand certain bits of Continental philosophy, you sometimes needed to find a very good American teacher—such as Royce.

Josiah Royce was not exactly tall and not exactly handsome. As a philosopher, when you look like this, you have one of two options. You can sanctify all things lonely and unbecoming and head out to Walden with your neck beard. Or you can follow Royce's lead and push beyond your awkwardness to fight the isolation that you seem almost fated to suffer.

Royce was elfish and a little pitiful, but his philosophy was grand and systematic. Many of his students even called it beautiful. Like Hocking, Royce was brought up far from the circles of the Harvard elite. Born in 1855 in Grass Valley, California, a tiny mining town between Reno and Sacramento, Royce didn't share the pedigrees of Peirce and James. He was an outsider, and he felt that way his entire life—loneliness and discontent were not philosophical abstractions for him, but a way of life he desperately tried to escape.

As a boy in Grass Valley, Royce would hike up a deserted hill at the back of his house and sit for long hours at the solitary gravesite of a miner who'd lived and died long before an odd mixture of evangelical faith and lust for gold had inspired Royce's family to trek to California. Royce read Edgar Allan Poe as a twelve-year-old and wrote a gothic essay, "The Miner's Grave," in his last year of high school. For Royce, the grave represented a life so insignificant that it hardly mattered when it flickered out: "Affection's hand had not been present to erect anything by which the memory of the deceased might be kept up," observed the thirteen-year-old Royce. "Only a little mound of earth . . . and a shingle, with a half-effaced inscription, distinguished the spot from the common earth around it." Even in his youth Royce was terrified of being this sort of nobody. He entered the University of

California at age fourteen and immediately became the brunt of his classmates' jokes, including a graduation skit featuring him as a "fiery-haired Jehovah" with an enormous head and cartoonlike pot-gut. Not all teased kids become philosophers, but I suspect that all philosophers, at one point or another, were teased kids. When Royce went to study in Germany at the tender age of twenty, he was in search of genuine companionship for a way to escape alienation. He found what he was looking for in the post-Kantian philosophy that dominated the academy in Heidelberg and Berlin.

I flipped to Royce's lecture on Hegel. Modern philosophy, from Descartes to Kant, reflected deep-seated and extremely problematic dualisms—the divide between mind and body, between the human and the natural, between subject and object, between individuals and their neighbors. Cartesian solipsism was the outgrowth of several of these philosophical divides, and philosophers writing in the aftermath of Descartes had been relatively unsuccessful in their attempts to overcome this legacy. So Schelling and Hegel, writing at the dawn of the nineteenth century, set out to develop an idealism that would unify the seemingly disparate parts of the universe. Royce, more than James and Peirce, was interested in this type of harmonious worldview. He wanted togetherness, a way of mending his broken world. And he wanted it more than almost anything else. He'd been brought to Harvard in 1882 as a replacement when William James was on sabbatical, and he spent the next thirty years ensuring that the insights of German idealism would not be forgotten.

Royce's lectures on German idealism began where all philosophy does—in biography. Hegel and Schelling met as students at the Tübinger Stift, a seminary in Tübingen where many of the greatest young minds of Germany came to study. These two "Stiftlers" (as students were fondly called) joined the poet Friedrich Hölderlin in 1789, and the trio embarked on a not-so-simple quest to transcend Kant. They shared a room at the seminary, but compared with his two friends, Hegel was a philosophical late bloomer; for much of his adolescence, he assumed a backseat to Schelling. In Royce's words, "Nobody had yet detected any element of greatness in Hegel . . . during all these years Hegel matured slowly and printed nothing. The letters to Schelling are throughout written in a flattering and receptive tone." I looked at Hegel's first attempt at a book. It was largely and obviously derivative, a gloss of Schelling's system.

Although Hegel would distance himself from Schelling in his later life, he was initially attracted to the idea, espoused by his mentor, that there was some "absolute identity" underlying and unifying all things. Individuals were never irretrievably lost; they are always, and have always been, an aspect of divine creation. In Schelling's words, "The *I* think, *I* am, is, since Descartes, the basic mistake of all knowledge; thinking is not *my* thinking, and being is not *my* being, for everything is only of God or of the totality." This was supposed to be reassuring, but Hegel was never fully satisfied with Schelling's answer. Hegel agreed with Schelling that Descartes's *Cogito* was the wrong way to think about personhood or individual identity. Individuals did not experience the world as solitary thinking things, but rather as relational, intersubjective beings. In his lecture Royce explained, "[For Hegel] I know myself only in so far as I am known or may be known by another . . . leave me alone to the self-consciousness of this moment, and I shrivel up into a mere atom, an unknowable feeling, a nothing." I thought about the morning, now many months ago, when I'd gone swimming alone in the frigid pond below the library. I'd once assumed that self-reliance entailed total isolation. But when I tried to identify the self I was supposed to rely upon, I was never particularly happy with my findings. Royce's lecture on Hegel told me why:

> We are all aware, if we have ever tried it, how empty and ghostly is a life lived for a long while in absolute solitude. Free me from my fellows, let me alone to work out the

salvation of my own glorious self, and surely (so I may fancy) I shall now for the first time show who I am. No, not so; on the contrary I merely show in such a case who I am not. I am no longer friend, brother, companion, co-worker, servant, citizen, father, son; I exist for nobody; and ere-long, perhaps to my surprise, generally to my horror, I discover that I *am* nobody.

I'd made this unpleasant discovery in the early days of my divorce. In wresting myself from the shackles of marriage, I thought I'd discover personal fulfillment. But in Royce's words, "My freedom from others is my doom, the most insufferable form of bondage." Being romantically untethered had unintended consequences: I'd floated aimlessly for more than a year without even an albatross to keep me company. The point of life, for Hegel and Royce, was not to lose oneself on the high seas of existential freedom, but to seek out and find oneself in wider and more meaningful communities.

Ultimately Hegel's notion of unity parted ways with Schelling's. Schelling's "absolute identity" was an underlying substratum that silently brought together the various parts of the world. This struck Hegel as overly simplistic and out of touch with experience. Human experience was undeniably defined by tragedy that didn't admit of Schelling's underlying oneness. Hegel argued that unity is achieved *through* conflict, that conflict and differentiation are necessary steps in achieving oneness. I knew on some intellectual level that this strange contradiction was the heart of the Hegelian dialectic, but it took destroying my life—and partially reconstructing it—for the lesson to come home. As Royce puts it, "Life consists everywhere in a repetition of the fundamental paradox of consciousness: In order to realize what I am, I must, as I find, become more than I am or than I know myself to be. I must enlarge myself, conceive myself as in external relationships, go beyond my private self, presuppose the social life, enter into [the inevitable] conflict, and, winning the conflict, come nearer to realizing my unity with my deeper self." This made better sense than Schelling because it explained the tumultuous life of individuals and their communities, but did not preclude the possibility of greater or more meaningful synthesis as a result of conflict. Unity is not the static substratum of Schelling; it is achieved through a difficult process, something like climbing a mountain. It was something to be accomplished by people—even, and perhaps especially, by people like Royce.

In 1908 Royce attempted to translate Hegel's conception of interpersonal meaning and self-overcoming into a language for nonspecialists, into what he called *The Philosophy of Loyalty*. Loyalty: It is the most two-faced of virtues—one that is absolutely necessary for one's moral growth but also extremely easy to pervert. Hard to create and easy to destroy, it is a word for the downtrodden, for the hope, however slim, that one is not lost. According to Royce, loyalty was not a Kantian call to duty, but a heartfelt sense of belonging to a greater whole. Loyalty was the animating spirit of love and the power that could spare individuals from their feelings of quiet desperation. In the face of calamity, loyalty enters the scene, and though it might not save the day, it can make the day so much more bearable.

When Royce arrived at Harvard in 1882, he'd hoped to find himself a suitable home. By that point Harvard was widely regarded as the promised land for American thinkers, but Royce was far from satisfied. G. H. Palmer, who worked down the hall from him, referred to his younger colleague's "afflictions sorted, anguish of all sizes." In the first years of the twentieth century, Royce's afflictions multiplied. His son, Christopher, was diagnosed with "acute abulia," a mental disorder characterized by paralyzing apathy. Christopher was placed in Danvers State Hospital on January 9, 1908, two months before *The Philosophy of Loyalty* was sent to press. In a letter to James written in the spring of that year, Royce conceded that they'd lost the battle against this mental illness: "We have fought our fight and lost. We shall keep on fighting and try not to make an outcry . . ." I'd read this note several times during my own dismal year at Harvard. What was it to fight, and lose, and keep on fighting? Royce closed the note with the hard truth about his son: "The poor boy will probably never see any of the light that I have been hoping and longing for him to see." Christopher died in Danvers on September 21, 1910, on the brink of his twenty-ninth birthday. "And the way is a long and dark one for us all," Royce continued. Loyalty was his way to find the strength to fight the darkness, with the sense that one isn't, despite evidence to the contrary, alone.

The Philosophy of Loyalty was written not in an attempt to save Royce's lost soul, but as a moral and spiritual instruction manual on how to save individuals like his lost son. Royce worried about the growing number of "detached individuals," many of whom professed to be free, but only to the extent that they were alone. Echoing Hegel, he argued that the false freedom of "unhappy consciousness" was overcome only when we are loyal, when we willingly devote ourselves to a cause. For someone like me, brought up on the philosophical ideal of rugged individualism, this was initially off-putting. But in *The Philosophy of Loyalty*, Royce voices a question that I'd failed to silence fully in my years studying Thoreau. "What worth," Royce asks, "could you find in an independence that should merely isolate you, that should leave you but a queer creature, whose views are shared by nobody?" With Carol a few feet away, now closer than she'd ever been, I was hard-pressed to find any worth in it at all.

Royce's classes were notoriously close-knit, and at the end of the nineteenth century he became one of the few Harvard professors to invite women into his classes. In fact, many a romantic relationship bloomed between his students as they listened to him extol the virtues of loyalty. Richard Cabot, the son of Emerson's literary executor, James Cabot, was one of Royce's disciples in the early 1890s. Cabot had become reacquainted with Ella Lyman in one of Royce's seminars, and they would spend the rest of their lives crafting a sexless marriage based on Roycean principles. I'd stumbled across Lyman's papers at the Radcliffe Institute for Advanced Study before my father died and, in my first year teaching, successfully distracted myself from the book I was supposed to be writing about Peirce by writing one about her.

Ella and Richard's relationship was a fascinating mix of religious piety, philosophical sophistication, and artistic inspiration. They'd decided to forgo having children so that they could fulfill God's purposes more fully, but this was the God of Emerson and Thoreau, which meant that they were free to pursue their own consciences and life projects. They fostered dozens of children, wrote dozens of books on topics that ranged from education to medical ethics, and sponsored—mostly with Ella's family fortune—the arts and sciences at Harvard (Cabot Library and Science Center at Harvard is dedicated to their family). In her spare time—which was admittedly slim—Ella helped Richard organize a Cambridge choral society that rehearsed and performed at their home at 190 Marlboro Street in Boston. At a holiday concert on November 17, 1903, they invited William Ernest Hocking. He arrived twenty minutes before the concert started and met another early arrival: Agnes O'Reilly. "Our conversation," Hocking reminded Agnes in a love letter written later that year, "began with candles [that adorned the Cabot house] and continued with flames."

In the "flames" the couple discussed philosophy and the fact that Agnes had an interest in the subject but little opportunity to study it. After the meeting, William wrote to her: "Have you then a discontent with your thought-horizon? If it is not a mere discontent but at the same time an earnest aspiration, there are goods in store for you whether you seek them among the mountains of philosophy or elsewhere. I wish I might lead you to some peak of vision, but it is seldom that I feel myself more than a wanderer—a climber."

Hocking agreed to tutor Agnes on Descartes. She found Descartes boring, but eventually fell in love with her tutor. William Ernest and Agnes were married the next year, and they turned to Royce, repeatedly, for marital guidance. Royce might not have been particularly qualified (his own marriage was not unproblematic), but he was happy to oblige. This was an extended philosophical family—with all its lasting loyalties and dysfunctional intimacies. Royce drew a particular type of acolyte. His best students were just like Royce himself: They came from devoutly religious families and they were also wickedly smart, which meant they typically had serious misgivings about institutionalized religion. In short, they were perfectly equipped to be loyal servants, but they lacked an object of loyalty that could satisfy their intellectual sensibilities. Royce's philosophy fit the bill perfectly.

Hocking's Methodist roots meant that devotion came naturally to him. He was a loyal Roycean, and he dedicated himself, from beginning to end, to his gnomish teacher. He participated in the philosophical conferences of 1903, informal weekly meetings of faithful students organized by the Cabots, often held on Sunday evenings at Royce's Irving Street home. James, who lived two doors down but attended only one of these philosophical meetings, joked that "the conference [was] a queer illustration of [the students'] inability to live without Royce." Most likely, this was a slight that stemmed from the fundamental disagreement between James and Royce. The individualism of James's pragmatism, which had become hugely popular, stood against any form of community that might stifle free expression. For James, "experience" was the philosophical watchword, and he worried that Royce's near obsession with community would sacrifice individual experience on the altar of devoted service. Hocking was well aware of the tension between Royce and James, and while he was intensely loyal to

Royce, he acknowledged that James had a point. Sociality was important, but unless you could articulate the *experience* of community—immediate and intimate—your loyalty would remain a mere abstraction. If you wanted to overcome solipsism, it wasn't enough to argue for the necessity of community; you had to tap into the personal experience of togetherness. "Solipsism is overcome, and only overcome," in Hocking's words, "when I can point out the actual experience which gives me the basis of my conception of companionship." This would become Hocking's philosophical mission.

Hocking's works—many of which had been written at West Wind—were scattered throughout the library, placed hopefully, insistently (presumptuously?) among the truly monumental works of Western philosophy. As a graduate student interested in Royce, I'd read Hocking's first book, *The Meaning of God in Human Experience*, but at the time, I was too obsessed with my own academic and marital woes to understand its message, even though the whole point of Hocking's book is to move beyond one's own narrowly personal obsessions. To achieve this end, Hocking had to show that genuine communion with others was possible.

I hunted for *The Meaning of God* for a few minutes and discovered it in Hocking's desk drawer. "I have sometimes sat looking at a comrade," Hocking says, "speculating on this mysterious isolation of self from self. Why are we so made that I gaze and see of thee only thy Wall, and never Thee? This Wall of thee is but a movable part of the Wall of my world; and I also am a Wall to thee: we look out at one another from behind masks."

Sitting down in his seat, opening his book, reading his words, I was, for the first time, ready to face the question that Hocking put to his reader: "How would it seem if my mind could but once be *within* thine; and we could meet and without barrier be with each other?" The romance of this had been completely lost on me when I first read it, but now I knew that Hocking's "comrade" was Agnes. The rest of the passage rushed through me suddenly:

And then it has fallen upon me like a shock—as when one
thinking himself alone has felt a presence—But I am in
thy soul. These things around me are thy experience. They
are thy own; when I touch them and move them I change
thee. When I look on them I see what thou seest; when I
listen, I hear what thou hearest . . . This world in which I
live, is the world of thy soul; and being within that, I am
within thee. I can imagine no contact more real and thrilling than this . . .

I walked to the center of the library and looked up at the portraits
I'd encountered on my first visit to West Wind. Ernest and Agnes
faced each other from across the foyer. They weren't looking down
at me at all. They were looking at each other.

I shifted past the table where Carol was working and returned
to my desk. I could barely see her where she sat behind the piles
of philosophy, but I could see that she and I were of one mind
about this place. It was our library now—we could be kicked out,
it could be sold or destroyed or forever lost, but it would remain
ours. As she shifted the books from one shelf to another, I was
moved to believe that a person, even a philosopher, could, in the
words of Gabriel Marcel, "surmount solipsism." Carol had re-
arranged the library, and it, in turn, continued to rearrange me. I
agreed with Hocking: "The lover widens his experience as the
non-lover cannot. He adds to the mass of his idea-world, and acquires thereby enhanced power to appreciate all things." There
was a reason why Dante didn't make the long journey toward salvation all by himself, why Virgil and Beatrice had to accompany
the poet. It's because salvation can't be accomplished in isolation.

ON THE STEPS

Writing *The Meaning of God* was not a solitary project. Agnes had helped her husband draft it and often referred to the chapter on prayer as "my chapter." It was the last one, and I was now ashamed to admit I'd only skimmed it. In fact, it wasn't just about prayer, but about "prayer *and its answer*," prayer being the active and deliberate form of worship, its answer being the passive, effortless reception of the divine. "The best known of all experiences of [this] mystic type is that of discovering the individuality of another person." The basis of prayer had nothing to do with folding your hands and speaking into the void. It had to do with falling in love. "At times," Agnes wrote, "we are granted something like a mystic vision: it seems that we come into the presence of the individual and have seen the miracle as such." It was absolutely quiet in the library, save for the occasional sound of Carol turning her pages of Kant. I didn't look up, but I could picture her with a vividness that the rest of life somehow lacked: "The vision in fact begins to work upon us," the Hockings explained. "We cannot forget it: we no longer attend to it with voluntary effort, but it forms a part of our consciousness and begins to make us over after its own pattern, as if it were active and we were plastic before it."

I flipped to the end of the book: 586 pages. It took a lot of words to overcome solipsism. The volume barely fit in the desk drawer. I was about to put it back, but before I did, I performed a ritual I'd learned during my time at West Wind: I grabbed *The Meaning of God* gently by the spine, turned it over, and shook it in case something was left or intentionally tucked inside. A carbon copy, folded in quarters, slipped out of the back. It wasn't an original letter, but Hocking, or perhaps his son Richard, had taken the time to duplicate it before shipping it off to the archives at Harvard. It was from Robert Frost.

Frost had visited the Hockings in April 1915 and had at that point picked up a copy of Hocking's magnum opus, which he called a "feat of poetry." And he gives a suitably poetic comparison: "Let me say," Frost began, "in Tennyson's poetry what it reminds me of: *'A ninth wave gathering all the deep / And full of voices, slowly rose and plunged / Roaring, and all the wave was in a flame: / And down the wave and in the flame was borne'* Well. Something Incarnate. It is the humanity of it all—the insight." Incarnate. Like freedom, togetherness, happiness incarnate. At the end of the letter Frost ribbed Hocking for the weightiness of *The Meaning of God*, writing, "Let me thank you for so <u>much</u> book . . . You mustn't smile when you see the size of the book I am sending in return."

There was really only one book that Frost could have sent in 1915, the one Yeats had called "the best poetry written in America in a long time." *A Boy's Will*, Frost's first collection of poetry. It had been published in Britain in 1913 and in the States two years later. It had to be here. I called out to Carol, and we looked for it everywhere. Behind file cabinets, in the eaves, under the stairs. After an hour we gave up and she went back to her Kant. The Frost wasn't in the library. It also, to my dismay, was not in the inventory of stolen books that the FBI had compiled upon arresting the man from Berkeley. I flopped down on the chesterfield to mourn the loss of a masterpiece, when I realized it must be in the house.

I was out the door before Carol could ask where I was going.

There were bookcases on the first floor of West Wind; they were reserved for family heirlooms and poetry. By now I'd been given keys and free rein over large parts of the estate, but entering an empty house that was not my own still evoked the strange sensation of trespassing. I entered slowly and moved through a surprisingly small kitchen into the two large sitting rooms that overlooked the mountains. The spaces were magnificent, beautifully proportioned. And nothing had been moved in a century. A grand piano loomed in the darkness. From the library, I'd heard Penny's husband playing Chopin many afternoons. The rooms smelled a bit like cool old leather.

The books were tucked behind the French doors that separated the two parlors—two narrow built-ins, stuffed with poetry. I scanned slowly, but found nothing. I'd worked through the second shelf and got to the bottom one when I found what I was looking for in blue cloth, gilt. *A Boy's Will.* I flipped to the flyleaf: "Prof. & Mrs. Hocking from Robert Frost with thanks for their book." Frost's words are famous for their understated power, their ability to convey a great deal in a mere gesture. I'd never thought that the word "their" could mean so much. *The Meaning of God* had been "their" book, "their" task. I later found out that Agnes had insisted that her husband rewrite the introduction a dozen times. She probably wrote much of the conclusion. The Hockings' book was not an argument against solipsism. It was a demonstration, a performance of intersubjectivity, one that I now desperately wanted to try. I sat down on the tight spiral staircase Hocking had designed and built. I opened up to Frost's "Revelation," a little poem that echoed the basic message of Hocking's massive philosophical project:

> We make ourselves a place apart
> Behind light words that tease and flout,
> But oh, the agitated heart
> Till someone find us really out.

Most cloistered misanthropes have the secret desire to be heard. We keep it secret out of fear or anger or anxiety, but it bothers us no end. We want to be found out, even, and perhaps especially, when we're most hidden. Frost, another American thinker plagued by depression, knew this all too well. He closed "Revelation" with two seemingly optimistic couplets:

But so with all, from babes that play
At hide-and-seek to God afar,
So all who hide too well away
Must speak and tell us where they are.

The words seemed hopeful—too hopeful—for Frost. He had eventually come out of emotional hiding and, in 1895, proposed to Elinor Miriam White. She accepted, which initiated a series of events that showed how tragedy can occur even on the path of revelation. The Frosts' first son, Elliot, died of cholera in 1904, at the age of seven; they buried their infant daughter, Elinor, three years later. Their daughter Marjorie caught puerperal fever after childbirth, and died at the age of twenty-nine. Carol, their remaining son, killed himself in 1940. Frost, who lived until 1963, endured all of this. I'd heard that Frost was hard to get along with. At least he had a good excuse. Sometimes the best-intentioned revelations can lead to the most disastrous consequences.

I looked down at the page and saw something very strange. I hadn't turned on a light after letting myself in, and I had struggled to scan the shelves, but I was somehow able to read Frost. The staircase was the brightest spot in the house; the stairs curled around and ended on the second-floor landing. But it didn't look that way. From where I sat, they appeared to go straight up to heaven. Hocking had designed the staircase around an oval skylight. It opened up and out and had no end.

WOMEN IN THE ATTIC

In *Waiting for Godot*, one of Samuel Beckett's characters blurts out something that had haunted me since I was a child: "Nothing is certain." For a long time, I thought that marriage was supposed to be the exception, but I was wrong. It is, at best, an adamant hope—a hope against hope—that two people can weather the tumultuous uncertainties of life without killing or leaving each other. At some point in the spring of 2011 Carol and I began to hope.

The snow melted, the books thawed out, and we moved in together. My thoughts no longer gravitated toward William James's chloral hydrate or broken tire irons or my ex-wife, who was now apparently happily married in Minot, North Dakota. But as Carol and I began our new life in Boston, our work at West Wind temporarily stalled. The trustees of the Hocking estate—like the members of any large family—didn't agree on everything. They couldn't settle on a plan for the books, much less the entire estate. Six months passed. All the while, the family seemed to hemorrhage money, and the principal of their trust dwindled. When the books were mentioned at all, they were described as a potential source of revenue. The thought of the library being scattered to the wind, to auction houses around the country, made us ill—so

Carol and I reconnected with the Hockings and resumed our efforts to get the books valued and donated to the University of Massachusetts Lowell. We hired an appraiser, a quiet Vermonter who had devoted his life to rescuing literary remains.

It was the end of summer, months since our last trip. Carol reminded me of finding the Frost, and we spent a number of days sifting through the books in the main house before making a final pass at the attic of the library. We wanted to make sure that the appraiser had all the valuable books at hand. Carol insisted on going through everything again, even the boxes shoved way back in the eaves. It was in the attic, under the rafters, that I learned something about redemption: Not all people get a first chance, much less a second, and the proper response to the chance of redemption is unadulterated gratitude.

We started early on an August morning before the sun was up. We climbed the stairs together and donned the requisite headlamps. "You know what this place is missing?" Carol said as she reached the top. "Women," she jabbed. "There aren't any women on the shelves down there. They're all up here." It was true. I remembered the sad, dark evening I'd spent with Whitman and John Boyle O'Reilly. At the time, I'd wholly overlooked the women who had been banished to the attic.

I'd picked up my share of Hocking family lore over the years, much of which suggested that Agnes Hocking had regarded her husband as a demigod, or at least God's gift to philosophy. When they were in public, Agnes would refer to him deferentially as "Ernest Hocking." One evening on her way back from Cambridge, legend has it, she forgot her train fare. Sailing through the turnstile, she breezily told the guard, "Ernest Hocking will give you the five cents tomorrow."

West Wind was there to keep him happy, to shield him from

the mundane affairs of everyday life. It was a library of his books. I'd been right to think that the library was a sacred space. It was sacred because he worked there. Hocking's granddaughters, well into middle age, called him Grandfather in a manner suggesting that he was still alive and ruling West Wind. Now an anecdote from Marian Cannon Schlesinger (Arthur's first wife and an acquaintance of the Hockings) struck me. According to Marian, Agnes attended her husband's graduate seminars at Harvard, but not as a student. Later in life Hocking took up painting, and Agnes, "ever a worshipper at his shrine," would bring his paintings to class. "She would creep," in Schlesinger's words, "silently across the platform in front of the lectern where he stood speaking, doubled over in order not to interfere with his flow of words, with one of his paintings clasped to her bosom. Having reached the other side, she would snatch up another painting in exchange, and noiselessly repeat the exhibition." According to onlookers, Professor Hocking scarcely noticed and "carried on the discussion of the evening as though it were the most natural happening in the world." Schlesinger was obviously being a bit harsh, but even for the 1920s this was, at least from the outside, weird: a husband holding forth at the front of a lecture hall while his fawning wife shuffled back and forth across the stage showcasing his artistic side projects. As if the conventional format of a lecture alone couldn't express his genius.

I'd never given any real thought to Schlesinger's story of idol worship. Instead, I'd fixated on the abstract concepts Hocking had developed over the course of his lengthy career. When I eventually focused on the biographical tidbits of the Hocking legacy, I found that they were usually the parts that fit perfectly with the subtle chauvinism of a professed liberal. But as Carol and I had discussed West Wind over the previous six months, she'd made me see what a mistake that was. Philosophy shouldn't stem from the theories of others or from a collection of convenient facts, but from a careful evaluation of the widest range of experience.

This pragmatic method sometimes forces one to have unpleasant thoughts—for instance, that Ernest had allowed, even encouraged, his wife to humiliate herself—but it was precisely these unsettling possibilities that deserved our attention. Unpleasantness can be instructive, something Royce recognized in *The Sources of Religious Insight*: "Those who, like Dante, have looked upon hell, sometimes have, indeed, wonders to tell us." Hocking himself had a name for this philosophical method of trial and error: "negative pragmatism." He didn't buy the pragmatic idea that truth was that which works, but he did endorse the converse, that untruth or falsity is that which doesn't. The Nobel Prize-winning physicist Richard Feynman, yet another of Hocking's many famous friends, resuscitated the idea in his Cornell lectures from 1964. "We never are definitely right," said Feynman, "we can only be sure we are wrong." The story of Agnes and Ernest was wrong, one of thousands of examples of the sexism that plagues American philosophy. And yet their life together lasted a long time and, for the most part, happily so.

I peered out of one of the attic's two small windows: Though I couldn't see it in the dark, I knew Mount Chocorua was out there. Men had scaled it, and fallen off it, for centuries. It was easy to forget the women who'd played a part in the mountain's story. For instance, Chocorua's name would never have made it to the nineteenth century were it not for a writer who was arguably the first woman of American philosophy. In 1829 Thomas Cole painted *The Death of Chocorua*, a sublime Romantic piece that depicted the fate of the Abenaki chief. The painting was promptly lost, but an engraving of it was published in an 1830 gift volume called *The Token*, which had somehow made its way to the attic at West Wind. Next to the engraving was a story called "The Curse of Chocorua," written by a young author named Lydia Maria Child.

Before Margaret Fuller, Susan B. Anthony, or Jane Addams, there was Lydia Maria Child. The abolitionist William Lloyd Garrison called her "the first woman of the Republic." This was no exaggeration. Child was born in 1802 and became the grande dame of American Transcendentalism. She was friendly with most of the thinkers who circulated through Concord and Boston; and many—including Emerson, Thoreau, Fuller, and Garrison—admired her as a philosopher and social reformer. "The Curse of Chocorua" was a foray into a life of social and political activism, one of many attempts to advocate for the rights of the oppressed. In her rendering of the story, Child suggested that European arrogance was largely to blame for the tragedy that befell Chocorua, a view that ran directly against the prevailing political grain. She championed the rights of women throughout her career, emphasizing the ways that women, rather than their male counterparts, could be self-reliant. After all, Child argued, women *had* to be self-reliant—cooking, cleaning, raising children, keeping a house, making ends meet—because ultimately they were expected to take care of the men.

Thoreau was enough of an iconoclast to admire her argument. He'd read at least three of her novels in his undergraduate days, and his experiment in simple living at Walden took its cues from Child's 1829 *The Frugal Housewife*, in which she argued for the virtues of humble living in the face of modernity's decadence. These positions made her work controversial but also popular. Then, in 1833, she became the first person in America to write a comprehensive history of slavery in the United States, *An Appeal in Favor of That Class of Americans Called Africans*. This was no longer palatable controversy. Garrison loved it, remarking that any "heart must be harder than the nether mill-stone which can remain unaffected by the solemn truths it contains." William Ellery Channing, who was the most prominent Unitarian minister in America and soon to be its most vocal abolitionist, walked from Boston to Roxbury to thank Child for sending him the book. But everyone else hated it, and Child's book sales plummeted.

She hardly flinched. Throughout the 1830s she attended Emerson's seminal lectures and occasionally blasted them for turning a blind eye to injustice. She eventually published most of these criticisms in 1843 in her *Letters from New-York*. Child listened to Emerson's lecture on "Being and Seeming" in the winter of 1838 and wrote a review that began, "In the course of many remarks, as true as they were graceful, he urged women to *be*, rather than to *seem*." On the face of it, this was commendable—the suggestion that women should not be fixated on appearances—but Child discerned a less-than-noble motive in Emerson's words: "He told them . . . that earnest simplicity, the sincerity of nature, would kindle the eye, light up the countenance, and give an inexpressible charm to the plainest features."

Light up the countenance? This was too much for Child to stomach. The sage of Concord, along with every other man in New England, was a sexist. Emerson's advice amounted to telling women that being rather than seeming would make them more pleasing for men to look at. "The advice was excellent," wrote Child, "but the motive, by which it was urged, brought a flush of indignation over my face. *Men* were exhorted to *be*, rather than to *seem*, that they might fulfil the sacred mission for which their souls were embodied, that they might, in God's freedom, grow up into the full stature of spiritual manhood; but *women* were urged to simplicity and truthfulness, that they might be become more '*pleasing*.'" Men were expected to please God, but women were just expected to please men. Child was furious: "What weakness, vanity, frivolity, infirmity of moral purpose, sinful flexibility of principle—in a word, what soul-stifling, has been the result of thus putting man in the place of God!"

Men, made in God's image, were to exist for the sake of themselves, for the sake of their self-reliant souls, in the face of the divine. Women, on the other hand, were to exist merely for the pleasure of their husbands, who had conveniently placed themselves in the role of the Almighty. A hundred years after the publication of *Letters from New-York*, little had changed in the relationships between men and women. I thought about Hocking's paintings strewn around the first floor. Agnes must have carted some of them in front of her husband's lectern, making sure not to disrupt his presentation. Many of them were self-portraits, so very carefully executed. Hocking had read enough Dante to know that self-love was the reason that most souls ended up in Purgatory. And he'd desperately tried to overcome his solipsism, but I wasn't sure he'd entirely succeeded. Most men of Hocking's age fell in love at a very early age. With themselves. And the women they loved were expected to deal with this belief acquired in their youth—that they were the absolute center of everyone else's universe.

Carol and I backed into the eaves, where I'd once found the literary remains of Walt Whitman and John Boyle O'Reilly. With two headlamps we could see things I'd missed on that evening I'd done my best to forget. Our beams darted around the attic for several minutes, dancing across the walls, casting shadows on an even stranger corner of Hocking family history, one that would remain intentionally hidden until I could figure out how to face it. We cast our attention elsewhere, finally settling on a small blanket chest next to the O'Reilly books. It was empty save for a single leather notebook and a handful of clippings strewn across the bottom. The notebook looked like something from the turn of the nineteenth century and was filled with handwritten poems. I flipped through quickly, but I could not make sense of the anonymous poems, with only a few titles. Carol dug through the clippings and after a minute handed me an obituary from *The New York Times* dated July 21, 1882: "The Death of Fanny Parnell: The Sister of the Irish Leader Dies in Bordentown."

At the height of the Irish nationalist movement in the 1870s, its leader, Charles Stewart Parnell, was deemed the "un-crowned king of Ireland." Fanny was Charles's sister, and one of the founders of the Ladies' Land League, which—despite its innocuous title— was one of the more radical nationalist organizations in Ireland. Fanny, called the "Patriot Poet," was best known for her writing, which was published on both sides of the Atlantic and frequently called "war propaganda." This soiled notebook contained the handwritten manuscript of nearly all her poems. Many had been published in O'Reilly's *Pilot*—then the most famous Irish paper in the United States.

Fanny had come to the country in 1874 and died eight years later at the age of thirty-three. In her short life she'd seized the imagination of Americans, who could still vaguely remember their own call to revolution. Irish Americans in Boston were especially enamored of her and paid tribute to her for decades after she was gone. "It became a habit in Boston," according to the historian Roy Foster, "to make a pilgrimage to Fanny's grave on Memorial Day, with speeches, floral tributes, and a general demonstration of grief . . . Her influence and inspiration were of a unique type during her lifetime; she remained a cult figure after her death." I leafed through the notebook. The American War of Independence, American abolitionism, and the Irish Land War were battles not only for freedom, but battles for a room of one's own. Sixty-seven pages of poems with one message: It's better to die than to be stripped of one's homeland. I turned to "Hold the Harvest," Parnell's most famous poem, written out in a quick yet oddly controlled hand. This one had been quoted as evidence against Irish nationalists of the time, proof that they were violent hooligans. Fanny extolled her Irish brethren to "hold their harvest" from absentee landlords:

Now are you men or cattle then, you tillers of the soil?
Would you be free, or evermore in rich men's service toil?
The shadow of the dial hangs dark that points the fatal hour

Now hold your own! Or, branded slaves, forever cringe
    and cower!

Fanny's sister Anna was even more militant. When her brother
Charles faced imprisonment in 1881, he charged the Ladies'
Land League with keeping the home fires of Irish nationalism
alive. Fanny stayed in the United States, raising thousands of dollars for the Irish cause, but Anna went back home to Ireland and
trained women in the subtle acts of civil disobedience. She encouraged women in the rural areas to leave their houses, protest
in the streets, resist the authorities, and boycott.

Many bids for freedom, however, end tragically. O'Reilly published Fanny's poems but secretly bad-mouthed her writing. Even
her obituary provided hints of derision: "Having travelled exten-
sively in Europe, and always moving in a refined atmosphere, she
had acquired a large store of information, which would be more
highly prized by philosophers and poets than by the gentler sex."
To the end, the Parnell sisters were viewed not as intellectuals or
heroic freedom fighters, but as extremely uppity women. When
Charles Parnell signed the Kilmainham Treaty in May 1882,
functionally ending the Irish Land War, the British demanded
that he disband his sisters' Land League. He obliged, and women
were, once again, written out of the battle for independence.

In Irish poetry, women weren't people, but icons—much like
Dante's Beatrice—meant to be revered or rescued by men. Irish
women were to be seen and worshipped, but certainly not heard.
They were embodied in "old mother Ireland," to whom her valiant
sons devoted lifelong service, but when Irish sisters got together
and did something on their own, they became the targets of a
deeply misogynistic culture. Fanny's fame grew after her death,
and she lived on, as so many famous women do, in posthumous
mythology. Men who couldn't have controlled her in person managed to control her memory quite nicely. Carol handed me Fanny's

"Ireland, Mother," a short, biting piece that would have galled her brother:

> Vain, ah, vain is a woman's prayer!
> Vain is a woman's hot despair;
> Naught can she do, naught can she dare,—
> I am a woman, I can do naught for thee;
> Ireland, mother!

Carol and I dug through the various obituaries, many of which had been written by O'Reilly. For three months after Fanny's death her body was carted around the major Irish centers of the Northeast—Philadelphia, New York, Boston—and tens of thousands came out to join the macabre circus. In New York, her body was processed up Broadway from the Fifth Avenue Hotel at Twenty-Third Street to Grand Central Station. People packed the sidewalks every inch of the way to watch Fanny be carried off into history. A huge funeral was arranged at Mount Auburn Cemetery in Cambridge, and O'Reilly wrote up the proceedings in wrenching detail. He might have found her annoying in life, but in death Fanny could do no wrong: "her lyre would only respond to one breeze—nationality," and her "noble heart-work" had "a magnetic and almost startling force." What was truly depressing was how Fanny subsequently vanished from the history of Irish independence. In 1912 James Joyce likened her brother Charles to "another Moses," who had "led a turbulent and unstable people from the house of shame to the verge of the Promised Land." By that point, however, most people had forgotten Fanny.

After many minutes in the darkness Carol shook her head. "That," she said, turning away from me, "is sad."

My hands skimmed the bottom of the chest. Nothing left. But memory, when it speaks, insists that nothing is ever fully gone. I sat down on the dusty floorboards and let Carol wander off to the other side of the attic toward a more hopeful set of books. I couldn't shake a guilty feeling, as if I were somehow personally responsible for Fanny's fate—for all the Fannys of the world— culpable for the misogyny and disrespect they'd faced and to which they'd eventually succumbed. Of course this made the guilt sound almost heroic, which was my first and only hint that I was still, after all these years, lying to myself. The truth was much simpler and less attractive: I'd recently left a woman, and though I hadn't felt regret at the time, now, on these unforgiving floorboards, I found myself terrified by the thought that I might do it again. I cherished my public persona as a Really Nice Guy, but the fact was that in my heart of hearts, in my own personal attic, I frequently viewed other people as mere things—to be avoided, to be managed—not as other people whose inner lives could possibly be as immediate and vivid as my own.

Suddenly my grandmother came to mind—a slight, saintly woman from a small coal town in Pennsylvania who had once, long ago, picked me up from elementary school. On the drive home she'd been cut off on the freeway and had leaned over into the passenger seat to tell her eight-year-old grandson a secret. "Hell, my love," she said quietly, "ain't half full." As a child, I'd been pretty sure she was right, and sure that my father—who drank too much, yelled too much, and abandoned his family—was going to do his part in filling it up. If I did nothing significant in life, if I was a complete and utter failure, I'd sworn that at the very least I would avoid becoming him. Two decades later, in the middle of an especially loud argument and on the brink of divorce, my wife took off her wedding ring and hurled it across the bedroom. Then she burst into tears, crawled on her hands and knees to find it, and promptly sold it on eBay. In case I had any doubts about the matter, she assured me that I'd become my father. As if to offer my confirmation of that fact, after she went to sleep that night, I went out and drank myself into oblivion.

These were memories I could no longer suppress or rewrite. As Schopenhauer put it, "[I]n his powers of reflection [and] memory . . .

man possesses, as it were, a machine for condensing and storing up . . . his sorrows . . . [I]t develops his susceptibility to happiness and misery to such a degree that, at one moment, the man is brought in an instant to a state of delight that may even prove fatal, at another to the depths of despair and suicide." I couldn't go back in time to make Hocking understand how shortsighted he'd been, how his entire philosophical legacy would be lost in the hinterlands of New Hampshire, and how he shouldn't have let his wife fawn all over him. But suddenly I wished I could. And I wished similar things for my own past. Lines from the canon of American philosophy, written more than a century ago, continued to haunt me. One from Royce's *The World and the Individual* stuck in my head and refused to budge: "The most notable feature of the past is that it is irrevocable . . . unchangeable, adamantine, the safest of storehouses, the home of the eternal ages." Adamantine: an unbreakable metal from the mythical past. According to Virgil, the gates to Tartarus are made of the stuff. Milton says that the Devil himself is bound up in adamantine chains.

According to Royce, who'd witnessed his son's psychological collapse, our histories are full of adamant atrocities. After Christopher died, Royce maintained his conviction that "salvation comes through loyalty," but he was, for the rest of his life, plagued by the question of how one might be saved if he had willfully failed to be loyal to his cause. Disloyalty was an act by which one "should violate the fidelity that is to me the very essence of my moral interest in my existence." It was, in his words, an act of "moral suicide." Royce wasn't the first writer to make this point: Dante had beaten him to it by several hundred years. The Archangel's sin, what gets him banished to a frozen lake at the very bottom of hell, is one monstrously traitorous act. How could one live with this sort of betrayal? Painfully. Royce, however, suggested that this pain could, under certain circumstances, be meaningful: "No baseness or cruelty of treason so deep or so tragic shall enter our human world, but that loyal love shall be able in due time to oppose to just that deed of treason its fitting deed of atonement."

In the end, my ex-wife and I had split on surprisingly good terms. After the yelling and ring throwing, we'd been able to say our goodbyes amicably enough. But one of the "good" terms of our divorce was that we agreed never to speak to each other again. In that dusty attic I had the almost irresistible urge to call her, to write her a letter mapping the contours of my traitorous mind, to ask for her forgiveness. But I also knew this was something I would never do. At least I'd keep this promise. I pushed the chest full of nothing back under the eaves.

The point of Roycean atonement isn't to seek forgiveness, and it isn't to nullify the act of disloyalty—the first is often shallow and the second is always impossible. For Royce, after the devastation of moral suicide, atonement brings "out of the realm of death a new life that only this very death rendered possible." It was a phoenixlike second chance that, until now, had always struck me as too convenient. "The world, as transformed by [atonement]," according to Royce, "is better than it would have been had all else remained the same, but had that deed of treason not been done at all." Agnes, Lydia, and Fanny deserved another shot at freedom and homecoming, but somehow, by some act of cosmic injustice or infinite mercy, I was the one who was granted a second chance.

In the best-case scenario, if we had remained married, my first marriage would have been miserable, the archetypal life of quiet desperation. I'd broken with the woman, but I imagined that we were both better off for it. Royce would not have been happy with this rationalization. It reeked of a warped sort of hubris about making moral commitments—that promises could be broken so long as one could master the art of post hoc justification, when it was actually just immature and self-deceptive. Atonement was something else entirely. Atonement was to recognize that you'd freely, consciously done the wrong thing, and then to exercise your freedom, in light of that mistake, to try to make the

world a slightly better place. To be clear, this isn't the banal plat-
itude that one has to learn from one's mistakes or, more galling,
that suffering is necessary for our moral education. It's the attempt
to integrate the past, with all its not-so-little tragedies, into a more
promising future.

I turned away from the chest, toward the rustling on the other
side of the attic. Disloyalty was to be avoided, but if you commit
treason against a cause, according to Royce, this treachery is an
occasion to deepen, rather than abandon, your ties of loyalty. I
thought about a letter from George Herbert Palmer, another of
Hocking's Harvard professors. Early in his relationship with
Agnes, Ernest had confided to his mentor that he and his new wife
were having a little trouble. Palmer responded with an appeal to
genuine loyalty: "Differences are an enrichment, if in every jar
you can take refuge in one another." During my first trips to the
attic, in the midst of a disintegrating marriage, I'd wholly missed
this possibility.

I made my way out of the eaves and straightened to my full
height. Something cool brushed across my cheek, a metal chain
hanging from the ceiling. I grabbed it and pulled gently. The entire attic lit up. Years of fighting darkness with headlamps, and
only now was I discovering the lights.

I left Fanny behind and joined Carol where she was rooting
through a shelf of books written by a woman who had only recently
regained her rightful place in the canon of American philosophy.
Earlier that week, Jennifer had suggested that we explore the corner of the loft that held the "Addams stuff." I knew who Jane Addams was: the founder of Chicago's Hull House in the 1880s and
one of the very few women who is now regarded as an American
philosopher. But I didn't know she had a Hocking connection. In
the late 1880s, Jennifer explained, Addams and her friend Ellen

Gates Starr envisioned a settlement house that was modeled on Toynbee Hall, in London, established in 1884. But Addams's house would be for women, and her settlement would grow in tandem with the progressive educational ideals being developed at the time by John Dewey at the University of Chicago. It was a good plan, but they needed a building. They finally got one when a wealthy woman, Helen Culver, decided to first rent and then donate the Hull family home, on Halsted Street in Chicago's Near West Side, to Addams and Starr. Culver's nephew, Charles Hull Ewing, continued to oversee the Hull House Association at the turn of the century. Ewing's daughter, Katherine, married Richard Hocking in 1939, making Ewing Jennifer's grandfather. The "Addams stuff" were all the clippings, letters, and books Jane Addams had sent to Culver.

Carol and I tucked ourselves under the eaves and inspected the lower shelves. Just as Jennifer had promised: a pile of first editions of every book Jane Addams had ever published, each flyleaf bearing a personal dedication to the author's benefactor. News clippings from the opening of Hull House and Addams's interactions with luminaries from Leo Tolstoy to Teddy Roosevelt were neatly stacked around the books, interspersed by inventories, letters, and settlement house contracts—a hidden shrine to what philosophy had once been able to accomplish. Addams had been living proof that freedom could be far-reaching and should be exercised in responsible, loving ways.

Addams opened Hull House at the age of twenty-nine and did most of her philanthropic work and writing after she turned forty. She was prolific, writing ten books, hundreds of articles, and thousands of letters. In 1908 *The Ladies' Home Journal* named her "America's First Woman." Five years later the New York Twilight Club (a literary club founded by Twain and Emerson, among others) sent three thousand ballots to representative Americans asking them who they thought was the "most socially useful American." Addams won by a landslide, handily beating out Teddy

Roosevelt and Thomas Edison. She went on in 1931, at the age of seventy, to become the first American woman, and the only American philosopher, to win the Nobel Prize.

I'd learned most of what I knew about Addams from my friend Marilyn Fischer, a professor at the University of Dayton and a careful scholar, fastidious in all the right ways, who insisted that one needed to know the history and culture of a time in order to understand its philosophy. And she *knew* the history of American philosophy. "Of all the American thinkers you like to talk about, John," Marilyn once observed, "Jane Addams has the strongest claim to national and even international superstar status." But today Addams remains only slightly more famous than Fanny Parnell. Both women ended up in the attic at West Wind.

Born in 1860 in Cedarville, Illinois, Addams started off doing what most young women born in tiny midwestern towns did, which is to say not much. She contracted tuberculosis when she was four, and it twisted her spine in all sorts of unnatural ways. Despite this difficulty, she had great expectations for her life, primarily constructed from the Dickensian fiction that she devoured. For most of her childhood, however, these expectations remained the stuff of fantasy. Addams was bright enough to aspire to attending Smith College in Northampton, Massachusetts, but her father, John Addams, a wealthy agricultural businessman who thought that women should stay close to home, didn't like that idea at all. So his daughter went to Rockford Female Seminary, right down the road. This, an evangelical training ground for overseas missionaries that didn't even award proper college degrees, wasn't the place for Addams. She initially hoped that her stellar grades would convince her father that the seminary was too easy for her, that she was ready for a real education in the East. These hopes were promptly dashed, and Jane was left to her own devices at Rockford, where she struggled to convince her teachers to act as if they were at a respectable college. But in 1881, after she completed her course work at Rockford, Addams's father died. Jane worshipped her father, but his death meant an inheritance of $50,000 and her freedom. She, along with the rest of her family, left Illinois at once. In Philadelphia, at the Women's Medical College, Addams pursued her dream of going into medicine, a profession that appealed because it would let her live among the poor. Although she'd objected to the missionary mentality of Rockford—overbearing, insensitive, proselytizing—its ethos of self-sacrifice was deeply ingrained in her psyche. Her studies went extremely well, but she grew increasingly dissatisfied with the process of dissecting life in order to make it better. She realized that many of the problems of modern medicine had nothing to do with biology and much to do with the social and psychological conditions of patients that many doctors of her time had failed to understand.

In 1882 Addams slipped down a path charted by Thoreau, O'Reilly, James, and Royce by having a serious mental breakdown. It was bad enough that she spent time at Weir Mitchell's hospital in Philadelphia. Mitchell was famous—some might say infamous—for the "rest cure" he prescribed to late-Victorian women to treat their "hysteria," a catchall diagnosis that ranged from a mild case of being "uppity" all the way to full-blown schizophrenia. But the treatment was always the same: relax, put your mind at ease, do as little as humanly possible. The "rest cure" was somewhat effective for some overworked women, but most middle-class neuroses were not the effects of hard labor, but rather a result of repression and oppression. Rest was the last thing in the world that bright, ambitious women such as Addams and Charlotte Perkins Gilman (who resided at Hull House for a time, and whose "The Yellow Wallpaper" documented the absurdity of this supposed "cure") needed. They wanted, more than anything, to have something meaningful to do. When Mitchell's treatment didn't work for Addams, she returned to Illinois, acting on the prevalent but often mistaken belief that being closer to home can settle the nerves. When that didn't work, she left for Europe. Again, to get some more rest.

By the time Addams reached London in 1883, she was desperate to escape the mind-numbing pleasantness of relaxation; and the plight of London's workers—"pestilence-stricken multitudes"—gave this midwesterner something to *do*. At first, according to Addams, she "went about London almost furtively, afraid to look down narrow streets and alleys lest they disclose again this hideous human need." But she eventually conquered her fears and realized—in a way that many philosophers never do—that the things that frighten us the most are usually the ones that deserve our greatest attention. Addams's was not an academic interest in the general character of urban poverty, but an ongoing response to its concrete and horrible particularities. She quickly came to the opinion that "the first generation of college women had . . . developed too exclusively the power of acquiring knowledge and of merely receiving impressions; that somewhere in the process of 'being educated' they had lost that simple and almost automatic response to the human appeal, that old healthful reaction resulting in activity from the mere presence of suffering or of helplessness."

This was a very early articulation of what the pragmatist John Dewey, a close friend of Addams's, would later term the "philosopher's fallacy," a pernicious case of overintellectualization. Abstractions and generalizations were inappropriately substituted for the flesh-and-blood realities of individuals and their communities. For Addams, London wasn't the place for sentimental abstraction but for moral activity and social activism. There was no better place to do that kind of work than at the newly opened Toynbee Hall, the first of many settlement houses in London. Toynbee Hall served the working poor of London's East End and was meant to provide some much-needed guidance to a community that was on the verge of being irretrievably lost. Addams's frequent visits gave her an understanding of the settlement movement, and she began to envision how it might take shape in an American context. First of all, it would have to lose its Christian trappings. It also wouldn't be formed strictly around working *men*. Masculine hierarchies were largely responsible for the economic inequality and political violence of the nineteenth and twentieth centuries, so a solution to injustice would have to be found elsewhere. As an alternative, she founded a relatively egalitarian community where men and women worked and lived side by side.

Hull House opened its doors in Chicago in 1889 and immediately became a testing ground for social progressives of the nineteenth century, a place where diverse urban populations could not just live in proximity, but also cohabitate and thrive. Addams's house would turn into the intellectual and political epicenter of the Windy City. Today, activists and social workers are occasionally invited to give lectures at distinguished universities, but in the 1890s, faculty from the University of Chicago were invited to come to speak at Hull House. John Dewey and George Herbert Mead, two of the most famous members of the Chicago school of pragmatism, were regular visitors to Addams's community. Both of these men, following Plato, took education as the starting place for political reform. Education was not something that you "get," the way one gets a diploma or a jelly doughnut. It is something you experience, a process you live through—spring training for the rest of your life. Dewey, Mead, and William James came to think of Addams's reform movement as pragmatism in action.

Hull House was built at the crossroads between theory and practice, a place where ideas could be implemented and tested by a diverse set of individuals facing common problems. Throughout the 1890s Addams led open philosophical discussions with residents of Hull House, most of them women. One of these seminars had centered on Royce's *The Religious Aspect of Philosophy*. Royce had spent his entire career talking about the need for loyal and reverent communities, but Addams worked tirelessly to actually maintain one. By the turn of the century she was widely regarded as one of the best academic sociologists in the United

States, and she used sociological hypotheses to negotiate the interpersonal dynamics of Hull House. She was empirical and experimental and, above all, sensitive to the situation of her fellow community members. James, who shared this intellectual sensibility at least in principle, read Addams's first book, *Democracy and Social Ethics*, with "deep satisfaction" and claimed that "[i]t seems to me one of the great books of our time." Dewey's *Democracy and Education*, which argued for the vital link between a free society and education, stemmed from his time at Hull House, and his *Liberalism and Social Action* was dedicated "to the memory of Jane Addams." Dewey's daughter, Jane, was named after her.

In the fallout of my divorce I'd reached out to my friend Marilyn—who'd helped me understand Hull House—for a bit of moral support. Appropriately for someone who'd dedicated her life to reading Addams, Marilyn listened to me patiently for months, her empathy embodying Addams's belief that "sympathetic knowledge is the only way of approach to any human problem." I whined and sniveled and went on and on about the frustrations of being alive and the inescapable hellishness of living with others. After too many days of my Sartrean bellyaching, Marilyn wrote me a little note, two quick lines that made all the difference: "Not long after my first child was born I knew in my bones that I could not die, that my daughter's life depended on my being responsible every single minute. Existential angst turned into a luxury item enjoyed by those who did not have ground-level responsibility for others' lives." And that was the end of my whining. At first it sparked into righteous indignation but soon died down into acceptance and finally admiration. Maybe I didn't have to have kids—that still seemed like a total impossibility—but perhaps my life would be more bearable if I didn't go it alone, if I was willing to be responsible for others.

Addams's books—from *Twenty Years at Hull-House* to *Newer Ideals of Peace*—should never have been packed away and separated from the rest of the history of philosophy. Carol and I, without even saying a word to each other, packed them up and prepared to do something that the Hockings had avoided for a century—take them downstairs and put them with the rest of "Grandfather's books."

I KNEW A PHOENIX

By the time we lugged the last of the books to the first floor, the sun was directly overhead, so we broke for lunch. Afterward Carol packed her things to go for a walk, and I headed up the stairs one last time.

There was one more woman in the attic: Agnes Hocking. I wanted to think that Agnes's books had once been intermingled with Ernest's, but even if they had, by the time I came across them, stuffed haphazardly in Budweiser boxes at the far end of the attic, they'd been forsaken for many years. Her jottings and letters were upstairs as well, and although I thought that she'd been the one to initially organize the attic, she'd taken great care with all the family's papers except her own.

I remembered Jill's remark that growing up at West Wind, surrounded by her grandfather's treasures, she'd always been interested in philosophy but had never felt at liberty to pursue it. Apparently it simply wasn't considered an option for the "gentler sex." In the 1980s Jill's father, Richard, had carefully copied and collated Ernest's letters, eventually paying Harvard no small amount of money to house the collection. I imagined Richard visiting the archivists at Harvard, pronouncing "Father" with the same strange mix of reverence and terror that the granddaughters said "Grandfather." Saving Ernest's papers was, for Richard, a monumental act of filial piety.

In a telling act of self-effacement (or humility), Richard, himself a proficient philosopher who'd had a long career at Emory University, placed his own books in the lower barn in the field below the library. This was the real place where things came to perish. If the scat was any indication, it was home to generations of mice, raccoons, and porcupines. A structure at once enormous and rickety, it was supported by hulking wooden beams that were in turn secured by a massive reinforcing chain. The chain wrapped around the rafters, and the internal supports appeared to be the only thing holding the barn together. Inside the building was a rusted-out Model-T, dilapidated farm equipment, and enough waterlogged antique furniture to furnish another West Wind. Plus seven thousand of Richard's moldy books. The hierarchy was clear: William Ernest Hocking's books were in the library, Richard's were in the barn, and Agnes's were in the attic.

Had Agnes had a library of her own, it would have been full of poetry and fairy tales. When Plato, in *The Republic*, says that the poet is a "light and winged and holy thing," he may as well be describing Agnes Hocking. By many accounts, Agnes was quite eccentric—the woman actually believed in fairies—but she was also absolutely steadfast in her personal loyalties and intellectual commitments. She was, from beginning to end, an educator.

In 1916, when the Hockings "could find no suitable instruction for their young children" in the schools of Cambridge and Boston, she founded Shady Hill School. I rummaged through the attic debris: clippings and invitations and long notes and grocery lists—the sorts of things my own grandmother had kept in troves in her house. Agnes and my grandmother, Hazel, were pack rats, brought up in an age when nothing—not even the trash—was wasted.

Under the wreckage was a set of *Atlantic* magazines carefully wrapped in newspaper and bound up in twine. A dozen copies of the same issue from December 1955. Someone had taken great care in wrapping these, so I took equal care in unwrapping them. This wasn't a first edition of Hobbes or Descartes, but it had been precious to someone. I settled down on a crate to read the article on page 63: "Creating a School" by Agnes and Ernest Hocking. Ernest had churned out hundreds of publications over his professional career (294, to be exact), but this was, I imagined, one of Agnes's cherished few.

"Cambridge is a school bearing town," the couple explained, "and justly proud of it." But in 1915 the Agassiz School, which had for decades educated the children of Harvard professors, planned to close its doors. Agnes and Ernest recounted, "Our eight-year-old son, Richard, began to bring home caustic teacher's reports; long division was getting him down. What could a parent do? . . . [T]his was no moment for us to start a school . . . but if circumstances required, one of us was ready to meet the challenge."

More specifically, Agnes was ready to meet the challenge. At first it didn't look like much—just twenty kids gathered Montessori-style on the back porch of the Hockings' home at 16 Quincy Street in Cambridge. But this was the start of the "Cooperative Open Air School," which would become Shady Hill School, a model of the "experience curriculum" of twentieth-century education. Enrollment grew steadily, and soon the fledgling school had outgrown the porch. Agnes and Ernest floated the idea of establishing an experimental school at Harvard (modeled after John Dewey's school at the University of Chicago), but this plan was quickly abandoned. The Hockings would have to go it alone with the financial backing of Richard Cabot, Paul Sachs (of Goldman Sachs), and Mrs. Edward Forbes (of *Forbes* magazine).

In the summer of 1916 Agnes had raised $9,750 (which may not sound like much, but is in fact the equivalent of about a quarter of a million dollars today) and purchased land for the new school from the old Charles Eliot Norton estate, Shady Hill. This was the next best thing to being affiliated with Harvard—and no small plot for a midwestern couple to lay claim to. The Norton estate was the heart and soul of Harvard, and its owner was widely regarded as the most cultivated man in America. Before 1874, when he was appointed professor of the history of the fine arts at Harvard, Charles Eliot Norton acquired a reputation as a Dante scholar, one matched only by James Russell Lowell. Norton had followed Emerson in translating *La Vita Nuova* in 1859, and his prose version of the *Divine Comedy* remained in wide circulation after the turn of the century. Shady Hill was the place where classicists, Transcendentalists, and up-and-coming pragmatists would gather: Emerson, Lowell, Agassiz, Chauncey Wright, Henry and William James, Royce, and Santayana. And now Agnes and Ernest Hocking.

The Shady Hill School might have looked a bit like a Montessori school, offering the type of progressive education that encouraged students to pursue their own interests instead of following a strict curriculum, but looks could be deceiving. Yes, Agnes had a "constitutional aversion to textbooks," but this did not translate into pedagogical laxity or an educational free-for-all. Agnes Hocking believed that bringing young children into contact with original literary sources—Homer, Shakespeare, Dante— would go a long way in cultivating mature and sustaining intellectual interests. (Shady Hillers still read *The Iliad* and *The Odyssey* in fourth grade.) The Hockings wrote that they

> were often classified as progressive—chiefly, I suspect, on the ground of a certain informality in our procedures, which led to the supposition that, like the typical progressive school, we were consulting and catering to the existing "interests" of children. Our principle was the exact reverse of this. Interest was of course of first importance, and we secured it; but not by bending our work to what was on the surface of children's minds. We expect children to take an

interest in what was worthy of their interest; and with teachers who cared for their subjects, they did so.

The Hockings objected to what they called the "yielding morass of progressivism," the idea that still holds sway in certain educational settings that children should be given free rein over their intellectual destinies. This freedom, often self-serving and self-centered, was, according to the Hockings, no freedom at all. Education was not about satisfying the interests that children already had, but about awakening them to the possibility of pursuing broader and more meaningful ones. In the words of Mary Williams, one of its former students, the lessons at Shady Hill were "over our heads at all times. But within our reach. We were always pulling ourselves up to exciting new levels." It sounded to me a bit like purgatory—torturously inspiring. In Ernest's words:

> Poetry class is Mrs. Hocking standing on the front porch in spring with eight children at her feet with Doric columns. She swayed as she recited to us . . . Over our heads she would wave her hands, gloves flying . . . Her voice conveyed excitement. Presently we looked up, too. By then the world had become bright with images, rich in feeling. To us it was not necessarily coherent; it was rapturous. Like poetry, Mrs. Hocking aroused an exuberance that was supra-rational.

This was Plato's divine madness and the definitive argument that it could, and should, be at the heart of education. As one of the original brochures for the school made clear, Agnes's suprarational exuberance had a pointedly rational aim: to "provide life with all possible richness and fullness; to secure freedom <u>with</u> self-control." This sounds grave and boring—with Kantian undertones Carol would have loved—but it wasn't. Shady Hill was a

place where children fell happily in love with both this educational aim and their headmistress.

May Sarton adored Agnes Hocking. In the 1970s Sarton would
become one of the most popular women writers in America, an
icon of feminist and lesbian literature, one of the first women ever
to write a journal—*Journal of a Solitude*—that became a best-
seller. But in 1917 Sarton was five years old and one of the youngest pupils at Shady Hill. I poked around the stacks of books
in the attic until I found Sarton's memoir, *I Knew a Phoenix*, and
returned to my crate. "There is no doubt," Sarton wrote, "that
[my] creative mind stemmed in those early years from the genius
of Agnes Hocking, the school's founder and moving spirit." It was
such a relief to read those words. I was so tired of hearing about
Agnes's submissiveness, about how she'd been, in the words of
one of Ernest's biographers, "an excellent practitioner in the
wifely art of ferreting out ambiguities and opaque passages in a
husband's work." Sarton had a very different take on Agnes and
her work: "The school was born of [the] marriage of poetry and
philosophy, and though philosophy was worshipped, poetry ruled."
If there were even a sniff of misogyny at Shady Hill, Sarton would
have been the first to let us know. She'd made her career articulating the subtle and not so subtle injustices of gender bias, so I
couldn't imagine that she would have given the Hockings a pass.
Sarton went on about Shady Hill for many pages, and at the end
of the chapter, I'd begun to think that Agnes was in fact the
"phoenix" Sarton had known in her youth.

   Being an Irish Catholic woman in the early twentieth century
was not particularly easy on Agnes. The Protestant-Catholic
union between Ernest and Agnes was at the time widely regarded
as a "mixed-race" marriage; it was controversial in some social

circles and downright blasphemous in others. They were, in Ernest's affectionate words, "two odd sticks." Odd sticks who decided to spend their honeymoon summer teaching at George Junior Republic School in Freeville, New York. This was not a posh summer camp, but a correctional facility for what Hocking termed "'delinquent' youth, male and female, at the point where education in the usual sense merges with correction." Hocking would later remark, "I do not especially recommend this as the best way to spend a honeymoon; but for us it opened a new chapter, and an essential angle, of the whole educational undertaking." Over the years, the Hockings managed to make something together—first Shady Hill, then West Wind, and all their other meaningful projects in between.

At Shady Hill they wanted to bring idealism up to date, "to give every child an experience of the inner glory of a physical task done with love and with a wish for perfection." This is what they had done for Sarton. They'd also brought Sarton into connection with Robert Frost. Owing to his friendship with the Hockings, Frost came to Shady Hill on a regular basis and read his poetry to students, their parents, and faculty. Agnes, who I later found out was even closer to Frost than Ernest, took a special pleasure in introducing her friend to the next generation of American writers.

Yet in the midst of this intellectual high-mindedness, something bothered me. I went back to the *Atlantic* article. Ernest and Agnes had coauthored it, but the voice wasn't Agnes's. I flipped to the end of the article: "There was just one person who had the heart and will to hold the threads [of Shady Hill] together . . . How Agnes Hocking, who always disclaimed 'executive capacity,' carried all this, God only knows." Agnes was supposed to be an author of this article, yet she was just a character described in the third person. Ernest had written her into the story, idealized her like Beatrice. Like so many men, Ernest hadn't let his beloved speak for herself. Disgusted, I grabbed the *Atlantic* and trundled downstairs to meet Carol. We ate dinner in the library—two gas-station sandwiches and a bag of stale chips—and, discussing Agnes, reaffirmed our refusal to repeat the past.

Early the next morning I slipped out of bed without waking Carol and shuffled through my cramped book bag, which was stuffed to the brim with articles I'd resolved to at least skim before the appraiser arrived. If I couldn't sleep, at least I could read. From Ernest Hocking's presidential address given to the American Philosophical Association in 1927: "There is some analogy between philosophy and biography . . . A good biography must be something better than faithful to fact: it must be a work of art and imagination. It must be so, in part, because without imagination it cannot be true."

This was my permission to interpret West Wind as I saw fit, and it was my warning not to abuse its history. Philosophy, according to Hocking, could err in two ways: "If it falls into bare chronicle, or if it substitutes the writer's vision for that of the subject, it is so far false biography."

I eased myself into the armchair across from our bed. Carol and I were to meet the appraiser in a few days at the library, and he would try to tell us what it was worth. I was dreading it. For the past few years I'd been able to live with the idea that these books were priceless. Putting a value on them somehow seemed to diminish their import, and I imagined that this might be even more difficult for Hocking's granddaughters. Despite their grandfather's heavy-handed rule of West Wind, it remained a place of gracious memory. Agnes and Ernest had gotten married in 1905 and remained married for fifty years. Their children, children's children, and children's children's children regarded West Wind as the center of family life. On Agnes's headstone, nestled on a discreet plot of West Wind, she'd requested the following words:

"Agnes O'Reilly Hocking, who loved life, her family, and this farm." No fanfare or philosophical system. Just a straightforward account of a life I'd always regarded as particularly beautiful.

I was still mildly annoyed at Ernest for his apparent slight in the *Atlantic*, so I went to take another look. Why hadn't he let Agnes write it? It was 1955, not 1655—by that time, on the brink of genuine civil rights, there was already a raft of women authors, and she was a very good one. Then it clicked: Agnes died in May of that year, and when the article had been penned, she was likely on her deathbed. I'd imagined the set of *Atlantic*s being wrapped up by Agnes, carefully preserving one of her few pieces of professional writing. But perhaps the *Atlantic* article had been a eulogy, the best kind. The kind that might still be read by the soon-to-be-departed. In subsequent months I discovered that Ernest had in fact planned to write an entire book about his wife's impact on modern education. The project was never completed, but its beginnings are still to be found in the archives at Shady Hill. Among those papers is also a copy of a letter Ernest Hocking had written about Agnes's last days:

> Her death was like the definite flickering out of a candle, not in pain, but in growing limitation. She had long been without words; but these silent weeks are to me among the most precious of my memories. For her utterly simplified self, with nothing but a sign language—perhaps a faint smile, perhaps a pressure of the hand—was still so entirely herself: it was she and no other, and she knew that I was there. And now, while there is no "there" where I can find her, she is still un-losable.

I crawled back into bed and inched my way closer to Carol, where I would remain as long as possible.

EAST WIND

The appraiser turned out to be as dry and dusty as the books he'd spent his life appraising. His hands—perfectly clean, slightly plump—made their way over the treasures of the Hocking collection. He worked at a glacial pace, which made me absolutely furious until I realized that he—unlike me, with my haphazard approach—was being appropriately careful. History was delicate and, if mishandled, could be irreparably damaged. It could also be incredibly valuable if it was kept in the proper condition. Unfortunately, most of the Hocking books hadn't been kept in any condition whatsoever. The appraiser thumbed through the first edition of Hobbes's *Leviathan*. "This," he pronounced slowly, "is less than ideal." He placed a tape recorder on the desk in front of him and gave the diagnosis: "First edition, first printing. With engraved title leaf laid down and the folded table (stained), but lacking the letterpress title; boards scuffed and spine worn; joints cracked; bookplate; edges shaved; pages 395–396 laid down: nearly good overall, but imperfect." He was right, of course, but it was still a little hard to hear. He gently closed the book and pushed it off to the side of the desk. He stopped the machine and then pushed "play." The recorder echoed his evaluation in a

tinny, deadening voice. The machine rolled on, and he reached
for the next volume: "Rudolf Carnap. *Der Raum: Ein Beitrag zur
Wissenschaftslehre*. Berlin: 1922; original printed wrappers; near
fine. First edition. Presentation copy, inscribed to W. E. Hocking
on the front wrapper by the author. Carnap's dissertation, published in a supplemental issue of *Kant-Studien*. Current fair
market value: twenty-five hundred dollars." And then another:
"*The Year-Book of Spiritualism for 1871*. Boston: 1871. First edition. Annotations by William James to text, especially at front,
with marked list of texts at rear. Current fair market value: fifteen hundred dollars." He kept going (for hours), but I couldn't
bear to watch. It was revolting: philosophy, that epic love affair
with wisdom, summed up on a spreadsheet for the purposes of a
tax write-off; Hocking's lifework carefully tabulated by a complete stranger; William James's explorations of the spirit world
documented in the least spiritual way possible. I turned to
Carol, excused myself, and made a beeline for the opposite corner of the library.

There was one place I'd avoided out of respect for the Hockings, one drawer of one file cabinet that I'd not checked out. When
I first tried to open it, I'd been with Penny Hocking. She'd laughed
softly and promptly closed the drawer. "Those are the Buck letters," she explained. "Buck," as in Pearl S. Buck, the Nobel lau-
reate. The drawer had remained closed throughout the years I'd
been coming to West Wind. As the months passed, I'd been sorely
tempted; Buck was worldly and an international celebrity after
she'd won the Pulitzer for *The Good Earth* and the Nobel in the
late 1930s. I'd briefly imagined Hocking cheating on Agnes with
the eminent author. I'd given Penny the impression, however, that
I'd restrain myself, and I wanted to honor that unspoken promise.
This hadn't kept me from going to Houghton Library to look at the
three hundred letters between Hocking and Buck stored in the
archives. The Houghton letters had been redacted by Richard

when he delivered them to Harvard, but they still gave me some sense of the mystery.

To this day, American philosophy is regarded as provincial and narrow in its focus, just another by-product of the nation's political and cultural exceptionalism. And to some extent, that characterization is spot-on. Emerson and James wanted to escape the strictures of traditional philosophy, which occasionally meant downplaying or criticizing the intellectual resources of the rest of the world. But a quick walk through West Wind revealed a slightly different story: American thinkers were in constant contact with European and non-Western philosophy. There was Emerson's *Indian Superstition*, an early commentary on the Vedas. And there were James's copies of *Buddhism in Translation*. Hocking had carefully collected these books; they were pieces of evidence suggesting that American philosophy could be, and in some sense always had been, intercultural. As Western expansion exhausted itself at the beginning of the twentieth century, Americans—and the philosophers in their midst—began to more explicitly set their sights abroad. Such thinkers as Addams, Dewey, and Hocking, who lived through World War I, argued that American philosophy could not fulfill its potential if it remained narrowly American; its ideals of self-determination, pluralism, and loyalty should be employed in structuring the modern international community. Their recommendations often stood in marked contrast to long-standing norms of American diplomacy, which is to say that they were often ignored. But on rare occasions they had their say, dramatically affecting U.S. foreign policy.

Hocking met Pearl S. Buck in Nanking in 1931. He was touring China as chairman of the Laymen's Foreign Mission Inquiry, a group of laymen and scholars organized by John D. Rockefeller to conduct an extensive study of American Protestant missions in Asia. Today the task of evaluating missionary work might sound like a small-time operation, but in the early years of the twentieth century, Christian missionaries were the ties that bound a surprisingly large number of Americans to the lives of foreign nationals. Pearl's father, Absalom Sydenstricker, was one of these missionaries; he'd transplanted his family—a small clan of fundamentalist Presbyterians from West Virginia—to the Chinese interior, where he and his wife had attempted to convert the members of its rural communities. Absalom, along with the rest of the American missionaries, was largely unsuccessful. He regarded the Chinese as a bunch of hopelessly backward heathens, and most of the Chinese he encountered thought he was the craziest white person they'd ever met. Pearl, originally filled with religious fervor, lost it when she hit her teenage years. Her father, in Buck's words, was "a spirit made by that blind certainty, that pure intolerance, that zeal for mission, that contempt of man and earth, that high confidence in heaven, which our forefathers bequeathed to us." He was a painfully misdirected idealist. It is not altogether surprising that Buck ended up falling in love with another type of idealist, one who might right her father's wrongs.

When she met Hocking, he was in the midst of preparing the commission's three-hundred-page report, *Re-thinking Missions: A Laymen's Inquiry After One Hundred Years*, which provided a systematic and ultimately devastating critique of the Protestant missionary system. When it was published in October 1932, the book was hotly debated and immediately featured in *Time*. It was not Hocking's magnum opus, but *Re-thinking Missions* was the book that made him famous. The report was grounded in empirical social science—teams of academics, led by Hocking, had conducted a year of field research in Japan, India, and China—but after all the data were collected, it was Hocking who interpreted and passed judgment on the findings. He concluded that most missionaries, so intent on saving the Asian horde from eternal damnation, were in fact dangerously out of touch with the local populations they hoped to rescue. Some attempts at salvation, according to Hocking, were not only counterproductive, but absurdly so. He observed that most missions were just a lot of talk: preaching, moralizing, proselytizing, more preaching. According to him, salvation turned on one's willingness not to talk, but to *do*. Missionaries should assume a pointedly ecumenical posture, give up their self-righteous sermonizing, and emphasize the meaningful similarities between world religions. Instead of holding forth on Christian ideals of humility, charity, duty, and love, missionaries should try to embody them. Rural Chinese didn't need scriptural lessons or warnings about the tortures of hell. They were all too familiar with the tortures of earth. What they needed were basic social services.

Buck couldn't have agreed more. "I am weary unto death of this incessant preaching," she wrote in a glowing review of Hocking's book in *The Christian Century*, "[it] deadens all thought, it confuses all issues, it is producing in our Chinese churches a horde of hypocrites." For Buck, preparing *The Good Earth* for publication in 1931, the issues of mainland China were perfectly clear: People were dying of starvation and disease in unprecedented numbers, Western imperialism had undermined local political authority, and modern economic inequalities heightened the effects of traditional Chinese hierarchies. All the while, Christian missions attempted to do their "good works" in saving the godless millions. *The Good Earth* was arguably the first book to bring average Americans into close contact with rural Chinese, and its social realism was jarring to an American public and a Protestant clergy that had grown accustomed to either exoticizing or patronizing foreign populations. It also shocked Chinese officials, who in 1937 refused to release the original MGM production of the film owing to its depiction of crime, poverty, and the treatment of refugees by the Chinese Republican Army. Pearl was just sticking to the facts, but sometimes the facts get you in a passel of trouble. In a stern rebuke, Courtenay Fenn, executive secretary for China of the Overseas Missionary Board, wrote to Buck after the book was published: "[T]he fact that a thing is 'true to life' is not a sufficient reason for its publication." When Buck gave the book to her father, he thanked her kindly and then told her he'd be too busy with his missionary work to read it. These were the first signs of what would become a large-scale dispute between Buck and the Presbyterian Church that eventually forced her to part company with its Overseas Missionary Board.

Hocking and Buck were kindred intellectual spirits, much more similar than Buck and the spouse with whom she had chosen to spend her life: John Lossing Buck, whom Pearl had married in 1917, who expected her to play the part of the good wife, a role this feminist writer was never particularly able to fill. When *The Good Earth* won the Pulitzer in 1932 and Buck received the attendant professional accolades, the marriage went from bad to worse. Three years later they were divorced. My guess was that Pearl and Ernest might have dallied around in the early 1930s, but as their letters had been redacted, there were no traces of any impropriety. It seemed that Ernest was happy with Agnes, and Pearl, from all appearances, remained loyal to her soon-to-be ex-husband. Ernest sent Buck a single letter during the early years of their friendship, a note of support on April 30, 1933, when Pearl left the Presbyterian Mission Committee. "I am writing to lend you a helping hand during this time," Hocking had written. According to the letters at Houghton, it would be another three decades before he received one from her. In the interim, Hocking became almost as famous as Buck, a true presence in American philosophy. He delivered two of the world's most prestigious lecture series—the Gifford Lectures in 1938 and, in the following year, the Hibbert Lectures, entitled "Living Religions and a World Faith." During these years Hocking constructed a systematic philosophy of religion to ground the liberal theology of *Re-thinking Missions*. It was, as philosophical systems go, wildly popular. On one of my first trips to the Hocking library I'd flipped through a *Life* magazine from 1944 only to find a full-page picture of a seventy-year-old Hocking peering out from his desk at West Wind. A five-page article followed, in which this elderly idealist set out "America's World Purpose." His bio from the *Life* article was telling: "Professor Hocking is one of those rare men who combine an ability to think with a practical knowledge of the world . . . One of his many intellectual achievements has been to grasp the essential character of all the world's great religions and to distinguish in his books (notably *Living Religions and a World Faith*) between the things that really divide members of mankind, and the things that really link them."

By this point American pragmatism was in decline. Academic philosophy had begun to make its unfortunate ascent to the penthouse of the ivory tower. The idea that philosophers might have something useful to say about foreign policy or religion or even life was slowly going out of fashion. Hocking sensed this trend and fought the dying of philosophy's light for more than half a century. From a little library in the White Mountains he corresponded with virtually every major American political figure of his day: Franklin and Eleanor Roosevelt, Dean Acheson, Henry Luce, Lyndon Johnson, John F. Kennedy, and so many more. There were 7,236 correspondents in total. On one sad afternoon several years earlier I'd tried to count the folders of Hocking's letters, and I gave up at 17,895. Many of these letters were from the twilight of Hocking's life, from the last two decades he'd spent at West Wind. This was the case with his letters to Pearl S. Buck.

Henry James's "The Middle Years" is not about the middle years at all. It is a short story about the end of life. An ailing writer, not unlike Hocking or the James brothers, comes to realize that his many books—some quite popular—were just the prelude to books that he'll never have the time to write. He'll be snuffed out, silenced, just as he is on the verge of acquiring an artistic voice that is actually worth listening to. When you come to the end of life, all you have are the middle years, those fallible middle years that you haven't spent altogether wisely. In the last passages of the story, James's hero, Dencombe, exclaims, "A second chance—that's the delusion. There never was to be but one. We work in the dark—we do what we can—we give what we have. Our doubt is our passion and our passion is our task. The rest is the madness of art." What we call a "second chance" is really just working in the dark, hand over hand, to make good on our first and only one. We give what we have, nothing more, nothing less. And we get to do this right up until the very end.

Ernest wrote to Pearl in 1960, five years after Agnes's death. He was eighty-seven, she was sixty-eight. Buck's second husband, Richard Walsh, had died earlier that year. This might not have been a second chance at love, but it was as close as either would come. The correspondence started out on a formal footing: Hocking wrote to pass along his condolences and at the end of the note suggested that Buck come to West Wind on her next trip to Vermont, where she frequently vacationed. Pearl accepted, and in September, Hocking thanked her for her company, closing the note, "Bless you, dear: I love you." When I first read the letter, I thought that this was probably just a turn of phrase. But the letters continued and became increasingly passionate.

In October 1961 Hocking informed Buck of a recent visit he'd had from the religious studies scholar Huston Smith and the French existentialist Gabriel Marcel; he explained that Marcel wanted to meet Buck when he came to her hometown of Philadelphia. Hocking also told her that he missed her terribly. The feeling was mutual. She confided that she'd always admired Hocking's philosophical work, but "now to the respect and admiration is added—the immeasurable." The immeasurable? Really? In March 1962 she wrote to the ancient Hocking as if he were a young man. At the end, she exclaimed, "Well if this sounds like a love letter—*well it is!*"

Between 1962 and 1964 Pearl (who was still very mobile) took every opportunity to see Ernest, often visiting while his family was at the estate. She came on the pretext of working in the library, but admitted that she really just wanted to be close to him. In late September 1962, as the leaves were changing, she hatched a "mad idea" to take Ernest, on the brink of his ninetieth birthday, to Vermont, "just you and I." She was crystal clear about the isolation of her house: "[T]he chauffeur stays in Manchester on call." There is nothing titillating or shocking about this. It is simply a matter of two people—one at death's door—deciding to linger a bit longer in each other's company. Hocking was extremely careful not to make the mistakes of Pearl's former partners. He didn't try to control her. In fact, when he wrote "my darling" in a letter, he also wrote "('my,' not in the sense of ownership, but of companionship)." On February 5, 1964, Pearl wrote to Ernest: "I love you and you love me and *that* is wonderful."

Wonderful enough that their love ended up being immortalized in that "madness of art" that we call fiction. Buck wrote *The Goddess Abides* in 1972, six years after Ernest's death, a story about a widow from Vermont and her decision to either love a young man named Arnold or a philosopher thirty years her senior, named Edwin. She ends up loving both of them. It is also, by Buck's own admission, autobiographical. Arnold is a young dance instructor she fancied. Edwin is of course Hocking. Edith, the widow in question, was a student of Edwin's when they both were still married. Now that they both are free, Edwin pursues her as aggressively as any octogenarian can. And Edith loves him in return and eventually invites him into her bed.

"Each experience of love," Edwin had said one night in the darkness, "is a life in itself. Each has nothing to do with what has taken place before or will take place again. Love is born, it pursues its separate way, world without end, transmuted into life energy."

"I doubt I shall ever love anyone else," she had replied in the darkness. At that moment she had deeply loved the beautiful old man. Never had she known such a mind as his, crystalline in purity. That was the amazing quality. Even when he held her against him, the quality was not changed.

I couldn't remember the rest of the story. Perhaps I didn't need to. I heard Carol sneak up behind me and realized that I was still looking dumbly at the unopened file cabinet.

"Are you going to look inside?" she asked.

I shrugged as I followed her out the door into the afternoon sun. I wasn't sure. It was one of those known unknowns, a mystery that seemed to invite further consideration. But as the voice of the appraiser faded away, it struck me as a rather lovely mystery that might be best kept that way.

THE MYSTERY OF BEING

Carol and I set out for the upper field above West Wind. We'd
been inside all day with the appraiser, so we decided to spend the
night in the open air. I'd often camped on the upper field, the
place where Bunn once told me he'd learned how to downhill ski,
where I'd picked up Lyme disease and decided to get a divorce. In
the autumn the grasses turned dry and brittle, but in late August
they were still green and smelled fresh, which I only later realized was the smell of dead things turning over.

On July 7, 1895, when William James wrote his brother Henry
from Chocorua announcing that he'd read "The Middle Years,"
he asked Henry why it was bound in a collection that he'd titled
Terminations. Having spent the summer hiking around these New
England mountains, the elder James seems to already have had
some inkling. "I know nothing more redolent of poetic sentiment,"
he wrote to his brother, "than this little chary New Hampshire
nature with its aromatic elements. All tender and pathetic and
suggestive of dead things." "But that is all over," he continued,
"and a small amount daily of muscular exercise has set me up
wonderfully." In the twilight of his life, William James had turned
almost Whitmanesque.

Carol had been a Girl Guide back in Canada and had plenty

of experience camping. We reached the very top of the field, over-looking the Sandwich Range, and I proudly presented our supplies: food, wine, firewood, sleeping bags, sleeping mats, pillows (two of them), toothbrushes, organic toothpaste, bug repellent, water, more water, and a tent. I'd remembered everything, except tent poles. Carol assured me that we'd be fine, that it wasn't a big deal, we would just sleep under the stars. It would be romantic, and I couldn't have agreed more. I remembered Gabriel Marcel's comment that "[l]ife is not a problem to be solved but a mystery to be experienced," and I was almost positive that Marcel had come to this position on his famous trip to West Wind.

He and Hocking had been in correspondence for nearly four decades, but they met for the first time at West Wind in 1959, two years before Marcel came to Harvard to give the William James Lectures. One of the founders of modern existentialism, Marcel had read *The Meaning of God in Human Experience* when it first came out in 1913 and was immediately taken by Hocking's understanding of freedom and human meaning. In Marcel's words, "It is no exaggeration to say that Hocking gave me the key to a prison in which I was afraid I would suffocate." At first it was difficult for me to believe that Marcel, a French existentialist, came to understand freedom through the writings of an American midwesterner—just about as hard as believing that Jean-Paul Sartre, *the* French existentialist, was an avid reader of William James and George Santayana. But all of this was true, and Hocking's philosophy was decisive for Marcel. "For this reason," Marcel admitted, "perhaps no meeting in my entire life has ever been happier and more moving than the one which I had with him . . . at his beautiful woodland home in Madison . . . [T]he presence of this older man to whom I owed so much gave me a distinctly filial feeling—indeed, it was even more than that, so that I dare to believe that we shall be companions for eternity."

In the 1930s Marcel organized a Saturday-night reading group—some might accurately call it a soiree—of young, up-and-coming philosophers at his home in Paris. Young philosophical giants such as Sartre, Simone de Beauvoir, Emmanuel Levinas, and Paul Ricoeur came to chat with a middle-aged Marcel about the future of freedom in an age of dehumanization and totalitarianism. Marcel loved these little gatherings, but he loved his visit to West Wind, to see a ninety-one-year-old Hocking, even more. Marcel and Hocking shared the sense that contemporary philosophy—defined by its hyper-analytic technicalities—had sold itself short. The love of wisdom was not bound in academic journals that no one read; it rather permeated all aspects of human existence. After meeting Hocking at West Wind, Marcel wrote, "The problem I consider essential is that of the relationship between philosophical research and life." Hocking was the product of a philosophical age that embraced this problem and inspired Marcel to hold out against the professionalization of philosophy in the middle years of the twentieth century. This was, at least in part, what made the trip to West Wind so memorable for Marcel.

Marcel, however, was indebted to the elderly American for another, more important reason: Hocking helped him find God. At one point Marcel and Sartre had been, if not friends, at least civil acquaintances, but by the end of their lives they pretty much despised each other. The fissure reflected (because it partially caused) a rift in twentieth-century European philosophy between theists and a growing number of atheists. Sartre, who quickly became one of the most recognized philosophers on the planet, used Marcel's soirees as a forum to air what would later become his formal philosophical position—namely, that human individuals are completely alone in this world and therefore radically and unshakably free. There was no one—not your mother, not your boss, not your führer, and certainly not your God—who could make you do something against your will. This freedom was nonnegotiable. For Sartre, one of the greatest difficulties of being free, of being "condemned to be free," is that we have to be free while at the same time being surrounded by others who desperately, conniv-ingly, unconsciously want to enslave us. Being condemned to be free wouldn't be so bad if we weren't also subjected to the "hell [of] other people." When it came to misanthropy, Thoreau had absolutely nothing on Sartre. Of course neither Thoreau nor Sar-tre would have called it misanthropy, just hard-nosed realism about the human condition. But Marcel, with Hocking's help, came to disagree, and he went on to take Sartre to task at every turn for most of his professional life.

Marcel agreed with Sartre about the basic method of philoso-phy: It should be realistic. Existentialists stood against those thinkers from the history of philosophy who had completely aban-doned the ground of human experience, taking off into ever more distant spheres of abstraction, never to be seen again. Marcel maintained that a philosopher should start from the concrete stuff of life, instead of from abstractions, and then work "up from life to thought and then down from thought to life again, so that [one] may try to throw more light upon life." Marcel got this idea of philosophical reflection directly from Hocking's *The Meaning of God in Human Experience*, and for him, it revealed something that Sartre never saw clearly. In Marcel's words, "My reading of *The Meaning of God* was to show me once and for all that it is actually in experience, grasped at its center, that we find the means of transcending that experience."

I'd always regarded experience as the most personal of things, the one thing that makes me who I am. Experience was, by defini-tion, immanent, always "right here"—the only thing that could not be taken from me. Experience was always *my* experience. And the freedom of my experience depended on it remaining, unequivo-cally and forever, not yours. So even if it were possible to transcend my experience, it would be far from preferable to do so. For many years I had embraced this Sartrean view and faced its attendant interpersonal failures. Marcel, following Hocking, following Royce, Addams, and Peirce, told a different story. And I was beginning to get a sense of it. Experience is always, even when we fail to recognize it, transcendent. Individual experience is not a form of solitary confinement, precisely because it is never strictly "mine." In Marcel's contribution to Hocking's *Festschrift* (a thick book long out of print, checked out from the Harvard library exactly once in the last fifty years), he writes, "as Hocking sees it, for the individual, *being* is originally and, in a permanent way, *being with*." For Marcel, the existentialist's obsession with individual freedom was to be tempered by the equally mysterious power of love.

Carol was right: Our camping under the stars was, by any standard, romantic. For a philosopher like me, it was just shy of a miracle. I'd like to say that we fell asleep in each other's arms—"companions for eternity" like Marcel and Hocking. I'd like to say that the whole thing ended in one perfect consummatory moment of "being with." But it wasn't exactly like that.

The truth is, I fell asleep with her in my arms. And she woke me up an hour later. She couldn't sleep. It was a breezy night, and there were noises in the trees behind the meadow. She was sure there was "something in the darkness." She was also sure that she could sleep if I would keep watch until she drifted off. She was absolutely right. As soon as I roused myself, she fell asleep, and I was left all by myself with "something in the darkness." Of course, now *I* couldn't sleep. At all. It's amazing what you hear when you actually listen, unsettling what you see when you actually keep watch.

Marcel said that our modern age was a special one, but not in a good way. Never in our history have human beings lived with such a profound sense of existential disjointedness, a dark unease felt at the very pit of our being. We moderns live in what he called a "broken world." Marcel argued that the Industrial Revolution, mechanized warfare, and genocide had conspired to fracture our sense that the world was a place to be inhabited and revered. But I always suspected that Marcel's sense of our brokenness was more immediate and autobiographical—the result of losing a parent at an early age.

His mother had died when he was four. Looking back on her brief and sudden illness, he wrote, "Strange as it may seem I recall absolutely nothing of those two desolate days . . . Yet I retain a rather definite memory . . . I still seem to hear the murmurs of Granny and other members of the family who had come to extend their condolences." When he was eight, on a walk with the aunt who had assumed the job of raising him, the young Marcel asked if there was any way to know if the departed continue to live on in some way. "When I grow up," exclaimed the child, "I am going to try to find out!" His entire philosophy can be understood as the attempt to escape and then to mend his broken world. Philosophy provided ample chances to escape: "On the plane of ideas alone," Marcel admitted, "was I able to create a shelter from these wounding contacts of everyday life." Later in life, his position on the value of philosophy began to shift: The point was not to escape, but rather to engage the deep mystery of being human. In philosophy, for Marcel, "the unity of a broken household was reconstituted."

I was attracted to philosophy for similar reasons. My father left us twice: first when I was four and then, permanently, when I was twenty-nine. I can hardly recall the day he first departed, but I still have a definite memory of my mother telling my brother and me that he wouldn't be coming home. It was in our furniture-less playroom, adjacent to the garage, where my brother and I usually spent the evenings dancing to folk music, one of the few things that my parents, at the end of their marriage, both liked. A beige Berber rug—the kind that lasts forever—covered the floor. My mother sat us down, and I remember pushing my little fists into the rug to see the imprint it left on my knuckles. My mother and brother, neither of whom I'd ever seen cry, sat on the rug and wept. I watched them for several minutes, slightly confused but mostly just embarrassed, and then crept into the other room to watch cartoons. I could hear them from the other room, which seemed, even at the time, very far away. I turned up the volume, and eventually the crying and the afternoon faded away.

My mother was right: My father was gone. But his absence remained. I now understand that it eventually drove me to philosophy, to study the writings of men who worked at figuring everything out, who could tell me the meaning of life, who could help me make sense of my place in a difficult world. At least at first, to philosophize was to compensate for something, for someone, I'd lost. I was, unsurprisingly, drawn to the fathers of American philosophy, obsessing about the intimate details of their lives, hanging on their every word, hoping they would explain themselves and the world to me.

I adjusted my sleeping bag and peered out into the night. I'd done this before. In bed, with my erstwhile wife, I'd stared at absolutely nothing for hours, unable to sleep, unable to shake the problems that I blamed for my unhappiness. What if I became a real drunk? What if I sabotaged yet another relationship? What if I became a father or, more frighteningly, *my* father? For a moment I tried, once again, to problem solve, but then I remembered Marcel's suggestion that this reaction to existential angst isn't the appropriate, much less the only possible, response to our human condition. Framing the universe—and our estrangement from it—as a problem to be definitively solved has the unintended consequence of distracting us from our ongoing participation in what Marcel called the "mystery of being." And this participation, according to him, is about the best we humans can hope for. "A mystery," in Marcel's words, "is a problem that encroaches upon itself because the questioner becomes the object of the question. Getting to Mars is a problem. Falling in love is a mystery."

I was so busy with my problems that I almost didn't notice the faint light beginning to creep up from the East. On an intellectual level I knew lots of things about the moon—that it actually didn't give off light, that it moved very quickly, that it came up in the East and set in the West—but I'd never truly experienced it before. I'd just have to wait a few more minutes and the upper pasture would be bathed in light. As the moon rose, I thought it would take care of the darkness, but it simply let me see it more clearly. Long, strange shadows—the kind that weren't supposed to be cast at night—pitched down the hillside and quivered in the breeze. This wasn't some deus ex machina that would save me from my situation; it was one of those Walpurgis Nachts that do nothing to solve our discrete, often petty problems but to cast them in the proper light. Little woodland creatures—satyrs, fairies, angels, werewolves—scurried about in the thicket behind us.

James described his night in Panther Gorge, surrounded by spirits and thoughts of Pauline Goldmark, with such romantic flair, but I'd be shocked if he wasn't a little overwhelmed by the dark. James's mentor, Peirce, might have been right that the "world lived and moved and had its BEING in a logic of events," but that night on a hillside in New Hampshire convinced me that it was not the sort of logic humans could ever fully master. It wasn't supposed to be mastered at all. It was supposed to be experienced. We play a role in the living and moving and being, and we are free to participate, but never simply as we see fit.

In June 1904 Hocking wrote to James to thank him for a course Hocking had attended on the concept of "pure experience." Hocking had learned many lessons that term, "one of these . . . [being the] lively sense of how big the truth is, and how little any philosophy which flourishes its solution in a few formulae is able to do it justice." Defining the whole truth of experience was much like describing this moon: perfectly impossible. "There is nothing more paralyzing," in Hocking's words to

James, "than an even remotely adequate sense of the complexity of the truth."

I lay motionless on the grass. Somewhere in the last hour I'd given up on the thought of sleeping and become lost in questions about how I'd come to this hill above the Hocking library. I remembered Whitehead's comment, borrowed from Plato: "Philosophy begins in wonder. And, at the end, when philosophic thought has done its best, the wonder remains." Wonder remains the origin, animating force, and ultimate end of philosophy. It is what keeps us, intellectually and spiritually, on the move. In 1951 Marcel wrote *Homo Viator* (Man, the Wanderer). Royce, whom Marcel deeply admired, would have been happy with the traditional Christian connotation of "Man, the Pilgrim," but it still chafed me. I'd stick to the wandering, though not aimlessly. My own attempts to describe the journey to myself seemed incomplete, and were aptly explained by Marcel in *The Mystery of Being*:

Consider what happens when we tell our friends the very simplest story, the story, say, of some journey we have made. The story of a journey is told by someone who has made the journey, from beginning to end, and who inevitably sees his earlier experiences during the journey as coloured by his later experiences. For our final impression of what the journey turned out to be like cannot but react on our memories of our first impression of what the journey *was going to be like.* But when we were actually making the journey, or rather beginning to make it, these first impressions were, on the contrary, held quivering like a compass needle by our anxious expectations of everything that was still to come.

I was, like the rest of these shadows, quivering. And had been for a long time. I tried to stop, to control myself, to put my thoughts and memories in order: Buffalo, Holden Chapel, James, trespassing, prison ships, leaping, falling, willing, love, gray eyes, Agnes, Carol. It was no use. It had been, and still was, one monstrous quiver. I took a deep breath and held it as the night continued to move in its perfectly inexplicable way.

Freedom and love. For Marcel, those were the two quintessential mysteries of the human condition. At the end of *The Mystery of Being*, he concludes that the point of life is not to figure them out, but to remain open to them, in touch with them despite their utter perplexity. "Man can touch," according to Marcel, "more than he can grasp." I pulled a blanket around Carol's shoulders and settled in next to her. In the months before their marriage, Hocking had written to Agnes, "[Y]ou are with me nearly always. How incredible it all is. I spend most of my time trying to realize it—and giving it up."

Dante's *Divine Comedy* ends in a similar way. At the end of his epic journey through hell and purgatory and paradise, he finally arrives at the Empyrean, the everlasting abode of God. When I first read the poem, I thought that I'd done so to get some concrete answers about divine love and freedom. The Empyrean was the place where all this reading was supposed to pay off. At the time, I'd been deeply disappointed. In the last stanzas of the poem Dante tries to understand how the highest spheres of heaven fit together. Because they really must, after all, fit together, but he doesn't have the words to articulate their majesty. Dante looks up at the divine orb that lights the sky, tries to explain it, and finally concludes that such a venture "is not a flight for these wings." A decade ago I'd thought that the whole point of Dante's journey was to reach the end. But there was no definitive ending:

> The will roll'd onward, like a wheel
> In even motion, by the Love impell'd,
> That moves the sun in heav'n and all the stars.

It is the best ending one can hope for. Freedom and love. Perhaps not to have and to hold, but rolling onward.

We were married in the fall of 2011, and Carol got pregnant on our honeymoon. "Are you a man *entitled* to wish for a child?" Friedrich Nietzsche asks. "Are you the victorious one, the self-conqueror, the commander of your senses, the master of your virtues? . . . Or is it the animal and need that speak out of your wish? Or loneliness? Or lack of peace with yourself?" Or, one wants to add, all of the above? As fathers, we're expected to be "self-conquerors," to have ourselves fully in order before we start giving directions to children. That might be a reasonable expectation, but one that nobody seems able to meet. After my time at West Wind, I expected that parenting, like falling in love, meant never again having yourself in perfect order, but facing the mysteries of intimacy as best you can. As a young child, I had feared my father, and years later, I feared becoming him. But in the end, he helped me learn very important lessons about being a parent—and about being alive. He taught me that William James was probably right about the meaning of life: It is up to the liver.

As we waited for our daughter, Becca, to arrive, the Hockings decided to donate part of the library to the University of Massachusetts Lowell. On the day we were to move the books, Carol was still enduring the trials of the first trimester, and she decided to stay home. So I picked up a U-Haul with my buddy Mark, and we slowly clunked up the hill to the library. The Hocking sisters met us in the driveway, and we made a last pass through the first floor before caravanning out to North Conway Dry Storage. Jill was excited: The thought of the books being used by real, live philosophers was thrilling to a woman who could have easily been one herself. Jennifer was relieved: She'd never felt at ease with the books, and a small part of her, I think, was happy to see them go. Penny wept. The books were the heart and soul of this place and—although they had to be preserved—their removal would destroy an essential part of West Wind.

Mark drove the U-Haul, and I hopped into Jennifer's beat-up Saturn along with her sisters. As we pulled out of the driveway and made our way over to the storage locker to load the books, I asked the question that had bothered me from the start:

"Why was this place called West Wind?"

Penny reassured me that my guess about the Shelley poem was a decent one—"Ode to the West Wind," the destroyer and preserver. I hunkered down in the backseat to consider the strange paradox of the poem:

> Drive my dead thoughts over the universe
> Like wither'd leaves to quicken a new birth!
> And, by the incantation of this verse,
>
> Scatter, as from an unextinguish'd hearth
> Ashes and sparks, my words among mankind!

Penny cleared her throat in the front seat. She wasn't finished. She'd just paused to think.

"I could be wrong," she said, "but I also think it was the nickname of my grandmother, Agnes. They used to call her West Wind."

EPILOGUE:
THE CULT OF THE DEAD

Today, a few hundred of the Hocking books, the ones the appraiser managed to assess in his two-day visit to West Wind, are kept in a room in the archives of the O'Leary Library at UMass. It's pretty isolated, but at least it's dry, warm, and rodent-free. I visit them often, under fluorescent lights. Occasionally I take my students. It is not exactly Houghton Library: There are no watchful librarians or even proper tables, just shelves and books. My students don't seem to mind. In fact, they seem to like the cramped and understated intimacy of packing themselves between the shelves. At one point I made them wear gloves, but eventually I decided that any book that survived at West Wind could probably be handled with bare hands. I just tell them to be careful, and they are. I still think of the books at West Wind as I first found them—priceless but vulnerable, a bit like life itself.

•

If you enter Sever Gate on the east side of Harvard Yard and walk toward Holden Chapel, you'll notice a boxy building to your left, which houses the philosophy department. This is Emerson Hall, named after that sage of Concord. On the second floor you'll find the department office and Robbins Library. Reginald Robbins was a student of James and Royce. At the back of Robbins Library is a broom closet that doubles as a little-used storage space. In the midst of finding West Wind, I'd found this broom closet. It was filled with cleaning supplies, no small amount of dust, and the single most moving piece of writing I've ever read. At one point someone had been similarly moved, and had decided to frame it, but in subsequent years the frame had been wedged between the waste bin and the file cabinet. I'd pried it out far enough to see the words written on the bottom of the now-yellowing piece of paper inside the frame:

"Last written words of Josiah Royce . . ."

I pulled the frame out of its hiding place, and I couldn't help thinking how ironic it was that Royce's dying words ended up in a janitor's closet and Hocking's had been buried at West Wind, both signs that philosophy had taken an unfortunate turn away from the existential problems that these philosophers had found so compelling: how to live a creative, meaningful life in the face of our inevitable demise. As I read the scribbled writing inside the picture frame, I wasn't surprised to see Royce attempting to cope with the tragic one last time in his final hours. Royce's penmanship declined in his later life, and by his final year, 1916, it was almost illegible. But this note was surprisingly clear and deliberate:

> Among the motives that have made the religious life of humanity intense, endlessly disposed to renew its youth despite all its disillusionments and unfailingly precious despite all of its changes and disappointments is the motive expressed in one of the oldest and newest of cults—the cult of the dead . . .

This rivals my first encounter with West Wind as the most haunting moment I've ever had as a philosopher. But it's also one of the most profound. I knew what Royce was talking about, at least intellectually. The "cult of the dead" was a reference to a very old institution that sought to memorialize and counteract the tragedy of human finitude. It's sometimes referred to as the "ancestor cult," in which members spend their lives working to keep the dead alive, at least in memory. The ancient Celts had one, the Egyptians too. Royce hoped that such a cult could survive the forward-looking tendencies of modernity. Hocking had created a monument to this cult at West Wind.

If the ultimate tragedy of life can be summed up in Ecclesiastes's suggestion that "all is vanity," it was the job of the cult of the dead to respectfully, enduringly disagree. The cult commemorated the dead and spoke for them long after they were gone. It affirmed what most of us wish someone would say about us when we die: that we are still relevant, that we still matter.

On that afternoon in the broom closet, I wiped off the dust obscuring the rest of Royce's words:

> This cult has survived countless changes of opinion. It will survive countless transformations of belief such as the future may have in store for us. Its spirit will grow . . . So long as love and memory and record and monument keep the thought of our dead near to our lives and hearts, so long as . . . the spirit of brotherhood enables us to prize what we owe to those who have lived and died for us, the cult of the dead will be an unfailing source to us of new and genuinely religious life.

As I sat on the floor of the closet, cleaning the rest of the frame and thinking about the library at West Wind, it could have been easy to think that Royce had been dead wrong. We die, and despite the heroism of our final words, our remains end up at West Wind or in some hidden closet, wedged between a trash can and a file cabinet. All of this is true, but I now have some sense of how sacred these last remains can be.

West Wind taught me many things. About longevity in the face of destruction, about dealing with loss, about love and freedom, but also about the discipline of philosophy. Philosophy, and the humanities more generally, once served as an effective cult of the dead—documenting, explaining, and revitalizing the meaning and value of human pursuits. It tried to figure out how to preserve what is noble and most worthy about us. At its best, philosophy tried to explain why our lives, so fragile and ephemeral, might have lasting significance. In Hocking's words in *The Meaning of Immortality*, we must learn to "treat the present moment as if it were engaged in business allotted to it by that total life which stretches indefinitely beyond." Royce's son Stephen had written an inscription at the bottom of his father's note: "Last written words of Josiah Royce found on his desk after his death never completed." Never completed. At least that is the hope—when it comes to both the cult of the dead and philosophy's dying words.

•

In 1850 John Hayward published a collection of sketches from his time at Harvard entitled *College Scenes*. One of these scenes is of a darkly lit room filled with skeletons and a couple of young pranksters with lanterns. One student holds the light while the other tries to make love to a corpse. At the bottom of the sketch, a shaky hand had scrawled, "A Midnight Foray into the Medical Room at Holden Chapel."

When William James addressed his audience at Holden in 1895 to wrestle with the question "Is Life Worth Living?" he was undoubtedly aware of the macabre "forays" that had transpired beneath his feet (pictures from the 1890s show what look like human ribs stolen from anatomy labs and hung from the mantels of student dormitory rooms). Holden was renovated a century later, at which point the construction crew unearthed a dry well filled with human remains—after the college students were finished with their necrophilic pranks, the bones had been pitched down the hole and forgotten.

When I spent time at Holden in 2008, I was obsessed with the bones—how easily, abruptly, meaninglessly life could end. James was not blind to this possibility. However, he wasn't resigned to it either. To the question of life's worth in the face of its abiding difficulties, James responds: Maybe. Maybe life is a hollow waste, but maybe it could, even in the face of inevitable destruction, be something more. James suggests that we stake our lives on that chance. "For such a half-wild, half-saved universe," James contends, "our nature is adapted."

Anatomy classes are no longer held at Holden. Today it houses the Harvard Glee Club. In the fall, as the ground grows cold and the days short, the choir begins to practice the "Gloria" from William Byrd's *Mass for Three Voices*. The small building practically quivers with the sound.

In the medieval era it was not uncommon to bury the bones of the dead in buildings—for example, in the floors and walls of chapels across the British Isles. It is believed that these remains not only served as safeguards against demons but also had a more practical function: They were good for the acoustics. The songs of the living, reverberating through these dead remains, could escape the earthen walls and begin their ascent. These chapels would ring with the strange mix of the tragic and the spiritual—with the perfect pitch of a *maybe*.

SELECTED BIBLIOGRAPHY
AND SUGGESTED READING

Addams, J. *Newer Ideals of Peace*. New York: Macmillan, 1911.

———. *Twenty Years at Hull-House*. Chicago: University of Illinois Press, 1990.

———. *Democracy and Social Ethics*. Edited by C. H. Seigfried. Urbana: University of Illinois Press, 2002.

Alexander, T. M. *John Dewey's Theory of Art, Experience, and Nature: The Horizons of Feeling*. Albany: State University of New York Press, 1987.

Anderson, D. R. *Creativity and the Philosophy of C. S. Peirce*. Boston: Kluwer Academic, 1987.

———. *Philosophy Americana: Making Philosophy at Home in American Culture*. New York: Fordham University Press, 2006.

Anderson, D. R., and C. R. Hausman. *Conversations on Peirce: Reals and Ideals*. New York: Fordham University Press, 2012.

Anderson, D. R., and C. S. Peirce. *Strands of System: The Philosophy of Charles Peirce*. West Lafayette, IN: Purdue University Press, 1995.

Barzun, J. *A Stroll with William James*. New York: Harper & Row, 1983.

Bernstein, R. J. *John Dewey*. New York: Washington Square Press, 1966.

———. *Praxis and Action*. London: Duckworth, 1971.

Boisvert, R. D. *Dewey's Metaphysics*. New York: Fordham University Press, 1988.

Boydston, J. *John Dewey: The Middle Works, 1899–1924*. Carbondale: Southern Illinois University Press, 1976–83.

Buck, P. S. *The Good Earth*. New York: Washington Square Press, 1931.

———. *East Wind: West Wind: The Saga of a Chinese Family*. New York: Open Road Media, 2012.

————. *The Goddess Abides: A Novel*. New York: Open Road Media, 2013.

Carus, P. *Buddhism and Its Christian Critics*. Chicago: The Open Court, 1897.

Cavell, S. *Cities of Words: Pedagogical Letters on a Register of the Moral Life*. Cambridge, MA: Belknap Press, 2005.

————. *Philosophy the Day After Tomorrow*. Cambridge, MA: Belknap Press, 2006.

Child, L. M. *The History of the Condition of Women in Various Ages and Nations*. London: Simpkin, Marshall, 1835.

————. *The American Frugal Housewife*. Mineola, NY: Dover, 1844/1999.

————. *Letters of Lydia Maria Child: With a Biographical Introduction by J. G. Whittier and Appendix by W. Phillips*. Boston: Houghton Mifflin, 1882.

Clendenning, J. *The Life and Thought of Josiah Royce*. 2nd ed. Nashville, TN: Vanderbilt University Press, 1999.

Colapietro, V. M. *Peirce's Approach to the Self: A Semiotic Perspective on Human Subjectivity*. Albany: State University of New York Press, 1989.

Coleridge, S. T. *Aids to Reflection*. Burlington, MA: Chauncey Goodrich, 1840.

Cudworth, R. *The True Intellectual System of the Universe*. Port Chester, NY: Adegi Graphics, 1820/2001.

————. *Collected Works of Ralph Cudworth*. New York: G. Olms, 1979.

Dewey, J. *John Dewey on Experience, Nature, and Freedom. Representative Selections*. Edited, with an Introduction, by Richard J. Bernstein. New York: Liberal Arts Press, 1960.

————. *The Essential Dewey: Volume 1*. Edited by L. A. Hickman and T. M. Alexander. Bloomington: Indiana University Press, 1998.

————. *The Correspondence of John Dewey, 1871–1952*, three volumes. Edited by Larry Hickman. Electronic Edition. Charlottesville, VA: InteLex Corporation, 2005.

Edel, L. *Henry James: The Middle Years, 1882–1895*. London: Hart Davis, 1963.

Emerson, R. W. *Collected Works of Ralph Waldo Emerson*, ten volumes. Cambridge, MA: Belknap Press of Harvard University Press, 2010.

Esposito, J. L. *Evolutionary Metaphysics: The Development of Peirce's Theory of Categories*. Athens: Ohio University Press, 1980.

Foust, M. A. *Loyalty to Loyalty: Josiah Royce and the Genuine Moral Life*. New York: Fordham University Press, 2012.

Frost, R. *A Boy's Will*. New York: Henry Holt, 1915.

Fuller, M. *Woman in the Nineteenth Century: And Kindred Papers Relating to the Sphere, Condition and Duties, of Woman*. Boston: J. P. Jewett, 1860.

Gale, R. M. *The Divided Self of William James*. Cambridge: Cambridge University Press, 1999.

Gavin, W. J. *William James and the Reinstatement of the Vague*. Philadelphia: Temple University Press, 1992.

Gilman, C. P. *The Yellow Wallpaper*. Boston: Small, Maynard, 1899.

Good, J. A. *A Search for Unity in Diversity: The "Permanent Hegelian Deposit" in the Philosophy of John Dewey*. Lanham, MD: Lexington Books, 2006.

Haack, S. *Deviant Logic, Fuzzy Logic: Beyond the Formalism*. Chicago: University of Chicago Press, 1974/1996.

Hickman, L. A. *John Dewey's Pragmatic Technology*. Bloomington: Indiana University Press, 1992.

Hobbes, T. *The English Works of Thomas Hobbes of Malmesbury*, collected and edited by W. Molesworth. London: John Bohn, 1840.

Hocking, W. E. *The Meaning of God in Human Experience: A Philosophic Study of Religion*. New Haven, CT: Yale University Press, 1912.

———. *Re-Thinking Missions: A Laymen's Inquiry After One Hundred Years*. New York: Harper & Brothers, 1932.

———. *Living Religions and a World Faith*. New York: Macmillan, 1940.

———. *The Coming of World Civilization*. New York: Harper, 1956.

Hookway, C. *Peirce*. London: Routledge & Kegan Paul, 1985.

Huxley, T. H. *Evidence as to Man's Place in Nature*. New York: D. Appleton, 1863.

———. *Darwiniana: Essays by Thomas H. Huxley*. New York: D. Appleton, 1896.

James, H., and W. James. *The Literary Remains of Henry James*. Boston: Houghton Mifflin, 1885.

James, W. "The Sentiment of Rationality." *Mind* 4:317–46, 1879.

———. *Are We Automata?* Gloucester, UK: Dodo Press, 1879/2008.

———. *The Principles of Psychology*. New York: Henry Holt, 1890.

———. *Psychology: Briefer Course*. New York: Henry Holt, 1892.

———. *The Will to Believe, and Other Essays in Popular Philosophy*. New York: Longmans, Green, 1897.

———. *Human Immortality: Two Supposed Objections to the Doctrine*. Boston: Houghton Mifflin, 1898.

———. *Talks to Teachers on Psychology: And to Students on Some of Life's Ideals*. New York: Henry Holt, 1899.

———. *The Varieties of Religious Experience: A Study in Human Nature*. New York: Longmans, Green, 1902.

———. *Pragmatism: A New Name for Some Old Ways of Thinking*. Cambridge, MA: Harvard University Press, 1907/1975.

———. *A Pluralistic Universe*. New York: Longmans, Green, 1909.

———. *The Meaning of Truth*. Rockville, MD: Arc Manor, 1909/2008.

Kant, I. *The Critique of Judgement*. Radford, VA: Wilder, 2008.

———. *Groundwork of the Metaphysics of Morals*. New York: Start Publishing, 2012.

Karcher, C. *The First Woman in the Republic: A Cultural Biography of Lydia Maria Child*. Durham: Duke University Press, 1994.

Kestenbaum, V. *The Phenomenological Sense of John Dewey: Habit and Meaning*. Atlantic Highlands, NJ: Humanities Press, 1977.

Knight, L. W. *Citizen: Jane Addams and the Struggle for Democracy*. Chicago: University of Chicago Press, 2005.

Koopman, C. *Pragmatism as Transition: Historicity and Hope in James, Dewey, and Rorty*. New York: Columbia University Press, 2009.

Krieg, J. P. *Whitman and the Irish*. Iowa City: University of Iowa Press, 2000.

Leopold, A. *A Sand County Almanac, and Sketches Here and There*. New York: Oxford University Press, 1949.

Locke, J. *Two Treatises of Government*. London: Whitmore and Fenn, C. Brown, 1821.

Lowell, J. R., and C. E. Norton. *The Complete Writings of James Russell Lowell*. Boston: Houghton Mifflin, 1904.

Lysaker, J. T. *Emerson and Self-Culture*. Bloomington: Indiana University Press, 2008.

Marcel, G. *The Mystery of Being*. Chicago: Henry Regnery, 1964.

———. *Homo Viator: Introduction to the Metaphysic of Hope*. South Bend, IN: St. Augustine's Press, 2010.

McDermott, J. *The Drama of Possibility: Experience as Philosophy in Culture*. Edited by D. Anderson. New York: Fordham University Press, 2007.

Mill, J. S. *On Liberty*. Boston: Ticknor & Fields, 1863.

Muller, F. M. *The Sacred Books of the East in 50 Volumes*. Richmond, UK: Curzon Press, 1895/2001.

Oppenheim, F. M. *Royce's Voyage Down Under: A Journey of the Mind*. Lexington: University Press of Kentucky, 1980.

O'Reilly, J. B. *Selected Poems of John Boyle O'Reilly*. Boston: H. M. Caldwell, 1904.

Palmer, G. H. *The English Works of George Herbert*. Boston: Houghton Mifflin, 1905.

Pappas, G. F. *John Dewey's Ethics: Democracy as Experience*. Bloomington: Indiana University Press, 2008.

Parnell, F. *The Hovels of Ireland*. Charleston, SC: BiblioBazaar, 1880/2010.

Peirce, C. S. *Collected Papers of Charles Sanders Peirce*. Edited by C. Hartshorne, P. Weiss, and A. W. Burks. Cambridge, MA: Belknap Press of Harvard University Press, 1931–58.

Putnam, H. *Mind, Language, and Reality*. Cambridge, UK: Cambridge University Press, 1975.

Raposa, M. L. *Peirce's Philosophy of Religion*. Bloomington: Indiana University Press, 1989.

Richardson, R. D. *Emerson: The Mind on Fire*. Berkeley: University of California Press, 1995.

Rorty, R. *The Linguistic Turn: Recent Essays in Philosophical Method*. Chicago: University of Chicago Press, 1967.

Rosenbaum, S. E. *Pragmatism and the Reflective Life*. Lanham, MD: Lexington Books, 2009.

Royce, J. *The Basic Writings of Josiah Royce*. Edited by J. J. McDermott. Chicago: University of Chicago Press, 1969.

Sarton, M. *I Knew a Phoenix*. New York: W. W. Norton, 1954.

———. *Journal of a Solitude*. New York: W. W. Norton, 1973.

Sartwell, C. *The Six Names of Beauty*. New York: Routledge, 2004.

Schelling, F.W.J. *Philosophical Investigations into the Essence of Human Freedom*. Albany: State University of New York Press, 2006.

Schneider, H. W. *A History of American Philosophy*. New York: Columbia University Press, 1946.

Schopenhauer, A. *The Works of Arthur Schopenhauer: The Wisdom of Life and Other Essays*. New York: Walter J. Black, 1935.

Shelley, P. B. *Poems Selected from Percy Bysshe Shelley, with Preface by R. Garnett*. London: C. Kegan Paul, 1880.

Simon, L. *Genuine Reality: A Life of William James*. New York: Harcourt Brace, 1998.

Smith, J. E. *Royce's Social Infinite: The Community of Interpretation*. New York: Liberal Arts Press, 1950.

Smyth, R. A. *Reading Peirce Reading*. Lanham, MD: Rowman & Littlefield, 1997.

Spencer, H. *First Principles of a New System of Philosophy*. New York: D. Appleton, 1898.

Stuhr, J. J., ed. *100 Years of Pragmatism: William James's Revolutionary Philosophy*. Bloomington: Indiana University Press, 2010.

Talisse, R. B., and S. F. Aikin, eds. *The Pragmatism Reader: From Peirce Through the Present*. Princeton, NJ: Princeton University Press, 2011.

Thoreau, H. D. *The Selected Works of Thoreau*. Edited by W. Harding. Boston: Houghton Mifflin, 1975.

Traubel, H. *With Walt Whitman in Camden: March 28–July 14, 1888*. Lanham, MD: Rowman & Littlefield, 1961.

Tunstall, D. A. *Yes, but Not Quite: Encountering Josiah Royce's Ethico-religious Insight*. New York: Fordham University Press, 2009.

Tuttle, H., and J. M. Peebles. *The Year Book of Spiritualism for 1871*. Boston: William White, 1871.

Warren, H. C. *Buddhism in Translation: Passages Selected from the Buddhist Sacred Books*. Whitefish, MT: Kessinger, 1915/2003.

West, C. *Prophetic Thought on Postmodern Times.* Monroe, ME: Common Courage Press, 1993.

Whately, R. *The Elements of Logic.* 2nd ed. London: W. Clowes, 1827.

Whitehead, A. N. *Science and the Modern World.* New York: Macmillan, 1925.

————. *Process and Reality.* New York: Harper & Row, 1960.

Whitehead, A. N., and B. Russell. *Principia Mathematica.* Cambridge, UK: Cambridge University Press, 1912.

Whitman, W. *Walt Whitman's Leaves of Grass.* New York: Oxford University Press, 2005.

Wilshire, B. *Fashionable Nihilism: A Critique of Analytic Philosophy.* New York: State University of New York Press, 2002.

ACKNOWLEDGMENTS

I wish to thank my editor, Ileene Smith. Much of what is beautiful or right about this book can be attributed to the guidance that she and her team at FSG provided; many of the places that remain rough or stilted represent moments when I chose to ignore her advice. I cannot thank Ileene, her colleague John Knight, and my agent, Markus Hoffmann, enough for believing in the project, for seeing it through to completion.

I would like to thank Douglas Anderson. I met Doug when I was seventeen, in my first term at college. Over the next decade, he exposed me to the meaning and spirit of American philosophy—its openness, its diversity, its hidden origins, and its existential depth. He had visited Ernest Hocking at West Wind in the 1980s and had passed on the knowledge of the library many years before I discovered it for myself. He was my closest friend as I went through my early months at West Wind. There are many moments of experience that should have made it into the book, but didn't—building a fire with Doug on the upper fields above the Hocking library is one of them. We talked through the night, about Holden Chapel and Pauline Goldmark and all the other things that "good philosophers" are meant to outgrow. Mark Johnson, John J. McDermott, Scott Pratt, Erin McKenna, Victor

Kestenbaum, Marilyn Fischer, David Leary, Claire Katz, Dan Conway, and Michael Raposa joined Doug as my trusted teachers and mentors in the American philosophical tradition. I thank each of them for reading early drafts of this manuscript and providing invaluable feedback.

The transition from academic scholarship to writing for a general audience is not an easy one. If you are trained as a professional philosopher (and expected to master the jargon that often comes with it), it is especially difficult. At least it was for me. I would like to thank a number of individuals who made this transition easier: Jean Tamarin, Alex Kafka, Peter Catapano, Simon Critchley, Emily Stokes, Joe Kloc, Phil and Gordon Marino, Rebecca Attwood, Jill Lepore, Andre Dubus III, and Evan Goldstein. My time at the American Academy of Arts and Sciences as a Visiting Scholar in 2008 gave me the chance to think through James's lesson from Holden Chapel, and I want to thank Patricia Meyer Spacks and David Sehat for the encouragement they offered during this difficult time. David particularly pushed me to integrate philosophical speculation with the pointedly personal and psychological challenge of daily life. I would also like to thank the administration and my colleagues at the University of Massachusetts Lowell for their continued support. Clancy Martin—one of the few philosophers I know who successfully bridges the divide between philosophical and creative writing—has been a consummate mentor in the drafting of *American Philosophy: A Love Story*.

I feel very fortunate to count Clancy as a friend, and so many others: Peter Aldinger, Jose Mendoza, Amelia Wirts, Jen McWeeny, Steven Miller, Romel Sharma, Nick Pupik, Susanne Sreedhar, Heidi and Mac Furey, David Livingstone-Smith, Brian Hay and the rest of the Hay Draude Watters clan, Whit Kaufman, Marianna Alessandri (who read draft after draft of the book), Sara Clemence (who meticulously edited the manuscript), Becca Greeves, Tess and Ken Pope, Alice Frye, and Luis Falcon. Special thanks to the Hocking family: Jennifer, Penny, Jill, Katie, Joanna, and the rest. A percent of the royalties from this book will be donated to the Hocking estate for the preservation of the rest of the books and the maintenance of the grounds.

When I was a little boy, I often wanted to grow up faster than humanly possible. But one of the troubles of growing up, as I saw it when I was seven, was that it entailed owing your parents more and more for the life you lived. And if your life went well—all the worse, at least when it came to indebtedness and gratitude. Now that I have children of my own, I understand how horribly misguided this idea is. I am the most fortunate of men: to have a mother and brother like mine is to be deeply blessed. They love in a way that requires no recompense. I don't deserve such love, because it is not, by its very nature, something that is meant to be paid back.

In a lecture entitled "What Makes Life Significant?" William James suggests that the meaning of human existence turns on a strange little word: zest. Zest, the particular, peculiar thrill of experience, is the ultimate source of existential value. For a long time I thought this was complete rubbish. But after meeting Carol, I knew, in the pit of my stomach, that James was once again right. Yes, duty and relationships and community and loyalty and work and marriage all have their place, but without zest—that certain something that makes these things pointedly "mine"—life would mean painfully little. I thank Carol and our daughter, Becca Briony Kaag-Hay, for the zest: for making life worth living.

INDEX